THE PRACTICE OF CRITICISM

D. H. RAWLINSON

Lecturer in English
University of Singapore

CAMBRIDGE
AT THE UNIVERSITY PRESS
1968

Published by the Syndics of the Cambridge University Press
Bentley House, 200 Euston Road, London, N.W.1
American Branch: 32 East 57th Street, New York, N.Y. 10022

Library of Congress Catalogue Card Number: 68–8948

Standard Book Numbers:
521 06045 1 Clothbound
521 09540 9 Paperback

Printed in Great Britain
at the University Printing House, Cambridge
(Brooke Crutchley, University Printer)

Contents

Contents

Acknowledgements

I should like to acknowledge Professor D. J. Enright's most generous help in reading my manuscript and making many helpful suggestions. I am also indebted to my colleagues and students in Singapore with whom I have discussed the exercises included in this book, and I should like to thank Mrs Magdalene Chang of the English Department for her services as typist.

Thanks are due to the following for permission to reproduce copyright material for this book: Allen and Unwin Ltd for ex. 40, from *A History of Western Philosophy*, by Bertrand Russell.—Edward Arnold Ltd and Harcourt, Brace and World, Inc. for ex. 33 B, from *Two Cheers for Democracy*, by E. M. Forster.—Jonathan Cape Ltd and Holt, Rinehart and Winston, Inc. for ex. 13 A, 'The Road not Taken', from *The Complete Poems of Robert Frost*. Copyright 1916 by Holt, Rinehart and Winston, Inc. Copyright 1944 by Robert Frost.—Chatto and Windus Ltd for ex. 35 B, from *Revaluation* by F. R. Leavis; Chatto and Windus Ltd and the author's Literary Estate for ex. 41 C, from *Queen Victoria*, by Lytton Strachey.—Constable and Co. Ltd and Charles Scribner's Sons for ex. 43 B, from *The Life of Reason*, by G. Santayana. Copyright 1955 by Charles Scribner's Sons.—J. M. Dent and Sons Ltd, and the Trustees of the Joseph Conrad Estate for exx. 30 B and 38 B, from *The Shadow-Line and Two Other Tales*, by Joseph Conrad. Also for ex. 38 A, from *Youth, Heart of Darkness, The End of the Tether*, by Joseph Conrad.—Eyre and Spottiswoode Ltd for ex. 26 A, 'Piazza Piece', from *Selected Poems* by John Crowe Ransom.—Faber and Faber Ltd for ex. 28 A, 'Mr Nixon', from *Selected Poems* by Ezra Pound; Faber and Faber Ltd, and Harcourt, Brace and World, Inc. for ex. 28 B, 'Mr Apollinax', from *Collected Poems* 1909–1935 by T. S. Eliot; for ex. 46 B, from *Selected Essays* by T. S. Eliot; Faber and Faber Ltd and Miss Myfany Thomas for ex. 13 B, 'The Sign Post', from *Collected Poems*, by Edward Thomas.—A. M. Heath and Co.,

Acknowledgements

Secker and Warburg Ltd and Harcourt, Brace and World, Inc., for ex. 39 B, from *The Road to Wigan Pier* by George Orwell.—Richard Hoggart and *The Critical Quarterly* for exx. 44 A, B and C, from 'A Question of Tone', *The Critical Quarterly*, vol. v, no. 1, (Spring, 1963).—Miss Olwyn Hughes for ex. 18 A, 'Tutorial' by Ted Hughes.—MacGibbon and Kee Ltd and Mr M. D. MacCarthy for ex. 35 A, from *Humanities* by Desmond MacCarthy.—Macmillan and Co. Ltd, Mrs George Bambridge, Methuen and Co. Ltd and Doubleday and Company, Inc. for ex. 29, 'Epitaphs of the War' from *The Years Between* by Rudyard Kipling; Macmillan and Co. Ltd, the Trustees of the Hardy Estate and the Macmillan Company, New York for ex. 12 A, 'The Shadow on the Stone' and 12 B 'The Voice', from *Collected Poems* by Thomas Hardy. Copyright by the Macmillan Company 1952. Macmillan and Co. Ltd and Mr M. B. Yeats for ex. 18 B 'The Scholars', from *The Collected Poems of W. B. Yeats*.—Houghton Mifflin Co. for ex. 33 A, from *American Criticism; a study in literary theory from Poe to the present*, by N. Foerster.—Oxford University Press for ex. 25, 'Elegy for Alfred Hubbard' from *With Love Somehow* by Tony Connor.—Laurence Pollinger Ltd, the Estate of the late Mrs Frieda Lawrence and The Viking Press, Inc. for ex. 23 A, 'Shadows' by D. H. Lawrence from *The Complete Poems of D. H. Lawrence*, volume II, edited by F. Warren Roberts and Vivian de Solar Pinto. Copyright 1933 by Frieda Lawrence. *All rights reserved*. Also for ex. 32 B, 'The White Stocking' by D. H. Lawrence, from *The Complete Short Stories of D. H. Lawrence*, volume I. *All rights reserved*. Also for exx. 34 A and B, 'Benjamin Franklin' by D. H. Lawrence from *Studies in Classic American Literature* by D. H. Lawrence. Copyright 1923, 1951 by Frieda Lawrence. *All rights reserved*.—The Society of Authors, as the literary representative of the Estate of the late John Middleton Murray for ex. 43 A, from *John Clare and Other Studies*, by John Middleton Murray.—C. P. Snow, for ex. 39 A, 'The Two Cultures', published in *Encounter*, nos. 69 and 70.

DAVID H. RAWLINSON

Preface

I think it certain, that most men are naturally not only capable of being pleased with that which raises agreeable pictures in the fancy but willing also to own it. But then there are many who, by false applications of some rules ill understood, or out of deference to men whose opinions they value, have formed to themselves certain schemes and systems of satisfaction, and will not be pleased out of their own way. These are not critics themselves, but readers of critics, who, without the labour of perusing authors, are able to give their characters in general; and know just as much of the several species of poetry, as those who read books of geography do of the genius of this or that people or nation.　　POPE

The main cause that led to the writing of this book is the tendency of university courses in literature to turn into courses in literary criticism. This is a problem partly created by having literature as a university subject in the first place. Most great literature was not written to be studied in universities, and there is something artificial in the idea of a literature course— though, however much we may deplore it, literature will have to be read in universities if it is to be read widely and seriously in our time. To substitute criticism for literature as the main focus of interest, to replace the thing itself with ideas about the thing, is always a danger in academic departments, which are congenitally happier when moving in a world of their own creation than when trying to engage with the actual world. And for the student, criticism can provide a short cut to neat, coherent writing which avoids all the struggle of real contact with literature, all the effort to discover what one's own feelings really are and to find language to express them, which ought to be at the centre of a literary education. Modern criticism on the whole is complex but ordered. It lends itself to study under academic conditions so much more readily than literature does. Not surprisingly, most students, under the pressure of a university curriculum, find it easier to handle the more ordered reproductions of the great writers which they can find in criticism than to approach the writers themselves, since that is a more uneconomical, unpredictable business altogether. In the feeble, inferior student this is usually nothing more than the clumsy device of a person who will not profit from a literature course however the subject is tackled. And there is always the born journalist, the man with the lucky verbal facility who can pass his examinations, gain his qualifications and be apparently educated on the strength of a thorough assimilation of modern criticism (or parts of it), while reading the literature itself perfunctorily and developing little personal feeling for it. He is, I believe, a universal phenomenon, and very hard to deal with fairly when he is met with. But, probably because present-day education as a whole tends to foster such processes, the more genuinely intelligent students, the ones we hope will become real readers and critics, frequently become suggestible to criticism before they develop a sensitiveness to literature. An interest in the one precedes an interest in the other, which is surely wrong. It is quite common to find students who can manipulate critical language and ideas with remarkable confidence and ease at a time when they are still faltering and diffident when it comes to deciding what the impact of a particular poem is like. Unless the tendency is checked—and the check will have to come, initially, from the teacher—they are only too likely to remain at this stage, saturated in critics but not in authors, fluent in views and ideas but with only an illusion of having read literature. For some of the brighter students, much criticism will seem to offer a recognisable intellectual challenge in itself. But I suspect that the best students, those whose talents naturally fit them for the study of literature, will by this time have sensed that there is an illusion somewhere, and be reading another subject.

Users of this book will recognise in the above paragraph a familiar enough charge against university English Literature. The danger is felt, acutely or vaguely, by almost everyone who teaches the subject. But this is so much more genuine a problem than some of the 'problems' that are often canvassed nowadays as the besetting difficulties of teaching English Literature (particularly teaching English Literature outside English-speaking countries) that I offer no apology for making it my starting point. The tendency to study ideas about literature, rather than literature itself, is a far more insidious difficulty than unfamiliarity of allusion, difference of 'background' (of which more later) or even hardness of language. A more exacting effort of the intelligence is required to master it, for this is not a question of providing information or simply expounding correct principles, but (to put the contrast as strongly as I can) of providing the right *atmosphere*, of encouraging the right responsiveness in people to whom literature may have previously meant little or nothing. Looking at the tepid, derivative writing that students produce so much of, one sees how hard it is to make people respond to literature at that personal, intimate level at which they are truly themselves, where their real sympathies and antipathies come into play, and where their thoughts and feelings are completely their own, whatever they might owe to the critics they have read. Literature is difficult to teach because it can only partially be taught; it does not appeal to a series of ideas and opinions that can be readily 'learned', but to a more timid inwardness which it it never easy to be articulate about in any circumstances, and which it is only too easy to lose in the circumstances of a university course. A critic, however competent he may be, can never do the essential work of responding for us. He can suggest, persuade, put things in a fresh light, but it is always left to us to try to listen to the voice of true judgment within—to make an act of self-exploration often needing the most delicate and developed self-discipline. This is what always happens, at least, with the great literary critics. Johnson is precise, definite, trenchant but never dictatorial, and we know from his tone and attitude that the definiteness is not there to intimidate us, but to help us to be absolutely clear about our views, and to know exactly where we differ from him. Arnold, by his choice of language, forces us to make a creative effort of response our-

selves, and discourages us from assimilating his views passively
and automatically. It is certainly true that people who have no
talent for introspection will not get very far with literature.
And, if the creative work of responding is not done, the
teacher and critic become arid dictators to be tamely followed
and imitated. The truth of this is perhaps easy enough to admit
in the abstract, but to act on this truth, and in the spirit of it,
is another matter. We can gather some idea of how rarely we
succeed if we ask how many students, particularly those not
connected with education professionally, ever look again at
the literature they once read as pupils after they have left the
university.

So much seems to stand in the way of our making the study
of literature the personal and intimate thing it ought to be: the
huge numbers that have to be taught, the little inclination there
generally is to make efforts in the right direction, the strong
inclination, sometimes, to make efforts in the wrong direction,
and perhaps even the high professional prestige of published
criticism in the academic world. A good deal of the material
now being put out to help students, in the form of exhaustive
analyses of different works, seems to me only likely to make the
right kind of effort more difficult. Implicitly offering to tell
him all he needs to know about a poem, play or novel, these
commentaries invite him to assimilate criticism in a way we
should be anxious to avoid. Criticism is a thing which, as
teachers and students, we need, but which we need less of than
we usually think. There is probably as much as we require at
our disposal at the moment—or more than enough. What the
teaching of English Literature needs is teachers who can use
the best criticism judiciously and effectively.

Among the readers this book may find in Britain, some will
be familiar with the exercise known as 'practical criticism' in
one form or another, and some may know it and have reser-
vations about it. But in my experience it is much less widely
known and used elsewhere; and it is there, where the student is
usually rather less confident of himself in starting to read a
literature course than his British or American counterpart, and

particularly prone to getting literature and criticism in their wrong places, that practical criticism seems to me especially important. In schools and universities which teach English Literature outside the English-speaking countries it is not used nearly enough at present. Practical criticism is no *panacea*, but it offers one of the best chances we have of making literature something personal instead of a set of teachings embodied in a series of admired authorities. In discussions and analysis of 'unseen'[1] pieces of prose and verse we can, given the limitations involved when we use extracts, reasonably hope for first-hand reactions, and here, if anywhere, the students can gain the vital training in perceiving the shades of tone and meaning, the subtleties of language, which are the great writer's means of communicating with us. Like any method of teaching, it will fail if used badly, and recent attacks on practical criticism as the central discipline in university English appear to me to condemn the abuse of the idea rather than the idea itself. Pursued in a mechanical, relentless way, detailed comparison and analysis of poetry or prose can lead rapidly to that listless routine which is the death of literature. It can lead to an artificial narrowing of sympathies, and can teach students to like some kinds of poetry (the kinds which lend themselves, or apparently lend themselves, most readily to close analysis) at the expense of other kinds. It can provide students with a narrow, lifeless, semi-technical vocabulary, and, especially where novels are concerned, train what Pope called a 'microscope of wit' which can only see small details of a work at a time. Most of all, it can give the impression—and the total impression is always so important in teaching, and hard to correct once it is made—that there are two kinds of poetry, the good and the bad (or, as these terms so often become in practice, the 'in' and the 'out') and so produce a dictatorial

[1] There is, of course, no special reason to put a premium on *speed* in reading, and exercises of the kind suggested in this book can always be given out in advance, though in my experience most people can say what they have to say about a short poem or extract inside an hour, and a certain freshness and spontaneity is gained if everyone in the class is coming to a poem for the first time. Anonymity seems to me usually an important advantage.

habit of judgment. Such a habit excludes any real feeling for literature. I believe it is even possible to teach a cunning substitute for judgment which tells the student to prefer the poem he guesses he is expected to prefer. These dangers we can only guard against. There are no fool-proof remedies in teaching literature; any means of teaching can be turned into a meaningless routine if used unimaginatively. But what practical criticism does offer, and offer superbly if it is taught well, is a chance to ask in the simplest, most direct and practical way (and later in increasingly complex ways) what reading a poem involves, and what it is like to make personal decisions about poetry. In this, of course, it is not really to be distinguished from the work we do in other courses, but practical criticism affords an opportunity to concentrate on the question of how to read literature which the student, at the start of his university education, or late in his secondary education, urgently needs.

The phrase 'practical criticism' is nowadays threadbare and stale, and it is tempting to look for another phrase to do the same work. Rather than do this, however, I would like to quote, from a critic who wrote before the phrase became current, a passage which seems to me as good a description of the *raison d'être* of practical criticism as can be found. Arnold, in his *Last Words On Translating Homer*, says of the criticism of poetry that

> To press to the sense of the thing itself with which one is dealing, not to go off on some collateral issue about the thing, is the hardest matter in the world...The critic of poetry should have the finest tact, the nicest moderation, the most free, flexible and elastic spirit imaginable...The less he can deal with his object simply and freely, the more things he has to take into account in dealing with it, the more, in short, he has to encumber himself, so much the greater force of spirit he needs to retain his elasticity. But one cannot exactly have this greater force by wishing for it; so, for the force of spirit he has, the load put upon it is often heavier than it will bear...

What the beginning student of literature needs, above all, is to be able to deal with his object simply and freely. If what Arnold says of the literary critic and his 'force of spirit' is true then it is far more true of the student. In practical criticism, which is not tied to chronology like most literary courses, the student can be given literature he can deal with simply and freely; he can be less 'encumbered', in Arnold's phrase, with works of criticism or literary history, with 'background' or other secondary considerations. In practical criticism, where the stress is less on erudition and more insistently on personal response, he is most likely to begin to develop his capacity to read. And it is under these conditions, if the class is well guided, that he is most likely to begin to find literature attractive.

One of the aims of this book is to provide as wide a variety of examples as possible in the available space, and to insist in this way that practical criticism doesn't necessarily involve one 'method' of reading or lead to a narrowing of sympathies. I have tried, in other words, to make a strategic selection; no one can cover all the varieties of poetry, still less of prose, in one short book (even if the intention were well advised, and I don't think it would be). Knowing that it is *sometimes* possible for students to go wrong with a poem because of a lack of 'background' information (though I think the danger is usually exaggerated) I have chosen poems in which there seems least likelihood of this happening. I have tried to avoid poems involving difficult literary conventions which the student cannot be expected to grasp at first sight; in the earlier stages I aim to trouble the student as little as possible with questions of the differences of convention and kind in literature. But the course I shall try to describe needs to be given in conjunction with other courses, and related to them. As we progress to more difficult exercises, we shall have to rely increasingly on the growing literary sophistication which the students should be acquiring in their university course as a whole. Practical criticism should never be thought of as something isolated from and inconsistent with the work done in other courses. I must add that I am not trying to offer a representative survey of English poetry and prose. My main aim is to provide a useful start.

Since this book is intended for use in schools and universities in Commonwealth countries as well as in the United Kingdom and U.S.A., I should like to say something here about the non-English-speaking student and his problems—as they are, and as they are sometimes imagined to be. There is a widespread impression, not confined to Britain alone, that teaching English literature outside Britain is a specialised job, hampered by special difficulties. The literature has to be put across to people of entirely different background who have never seen, say, a colliery town, a London fog or a daffodil. A novel about nineteenth-century English industrial development must seem ineradicably alien to a Singapore Chinese or a West African, whose worlds are so different from the Englishman's and from each other. And, so this impression runs, anyone who is teaching English Literature in Africa or Singapore must do a lot of preliminary spadework in order to make its foreign frame of reference comprehensible. The students have to be put in possession of an English 'background' artificially, as their own experience by itself will not enable them to read competently and respond relevantly.

It should, of course, be possible to argue convincingly, given the space, that the worlds of the educated African, Englishman, American and Singaporean are not all that different in any case, and are becoming less so. They are certainly far less different than the modern Englishman's or American's world is from the Elizabethan world of Shakespeare's first audience. But the worst error underlying the 'background' misconception is that it underestimates literature's power to communicate itself. Johnson, trying to sum up as briefly as possible what it was that, for him, made Shakespeare the supreme English author, wrote that 'Shakespeare approximates the remote and familiarises the wonderful'; he has, as inferior authors have not, the power of making whatever he writes of vividly and movingly close to us. Difficulties do sometimes arise because of a reader's unfamiliarity with certain allusions or conventions—though the modern Englishman seems to me at no very special natural advantage here—but these problems are temporary and incidental. They are far less striking in practice than the communicating, creative force of literature which Johnson felt so strongly in Shakespeare and described so memorably. Great literature surely *is* great partly because its appeal is not limited to one time or place. I believe that, generally speaking, the greater a work of literature is—that is, the stronger its appeal to a common humanity—the less help it will need to make its impact. And a work which seems to need elaborate 'background' assistance will probably never make an impact at all.[1] English Literature is not as provincial as the 'background' misconception makes it look. In my experience there is nothing essentially different about teaching it in places as remote from its country of origin as Singapore (if any large centre of population nowadays is remote). The reasons why students sometimes make so little of literature are much the same in both places. If the 'overseas' student is at a disadvantage, it will not be because of some foreign, unassimilable quality in the literature. More likely his disadvantage will lie in a cramped education in overcrowded schools, with poor conditions and opportunities for study. English may be the language of his education and his first language in ordinary use, but his education may not have given him a really firm hold of it (though one wonders, after teaching in England and the United States, if the overseas student has always something to envy here). A teacher of literature will have to go slower, at least initially, than he might like, and he must take special care that the literature he chooses doesn't put any avoidable difficulties in his students' way. Archaic language, for instance, and certain kinds of eccentricity in a writer are avoidable difficulties, and some poems which are in themselves elusive must clearly be left alone for a while. But in this, the teacher's own feeling for literature plus his common sense will be his best guides, and these are the guides I shall try to follow in this book.

[1] Arnold once wrote that 'the way to get a great writer understood is not to raise as much discussion about his meaning as possible, but as little as possible'. This sentence seems even more true today when, as has often been pointed out, extensive 'background' research on Shakespeare has had the effect not of bringing him nearer to our age, but of making him seem more distant.

CHAPTER I

Practical Criticism and 'Method'

The commonest expectation of students starting a practical criticism course is that they will be given a method of criticism, with its own terminology, categories and correct procedures which, if consistently applied, will allow them to deal competently with any poem or prose passage. Unfamiliarity with literature, and a sense of helplessness, especially when dealing with poetry, often show themselves in this notion of a *mystique* of practical criticism—as though there was a secret process which would, when mastered, make understanding literature easy. But a good reader of literature is not one who has a series of categories to fit poems (or prose) into, or a special vocabulary to describe them. He does not carry an apparatus of terminology and method around in his head. He is a good reader partly because he can respond to the unfamiliar, for which there can be no previously worked-out critical account. There is no knowing beforehand with literature just how we shall be expected to respond, and the demand for an all-competent systematic procedure is one that practical criticism can never properly meet. One of I. A. Richards's best remarks in his book *Practical Criticism* is that rules of metre and scansion are popular with students because they are, or appear to be, capable of external application: they *look* as though one can use them without the trouble of entering imaginatively into a poem. Terms like imagery, metaphor, alliteration and so on have a seductive air of being the clues to poetry, but excogitating meanings for these words and fitting them into a theory of poetry or a method of reading will not make us better readers. Strict definitions are only likely to get in the way.

To clear the air of the misleading suggestions of the word 'method' and to remind ourselves of how little, in reading a poem or novel, we are applying a rehearsed procedure, there is no better place to go than the opening paragraph of

D. H. Lawrence's essay on Galsworthy. This may remind us, too, of how a single short passage, written by a great mind in contact with literature, can often awaken more interest in literature, and help us to read better, than any amount of extended, developed argument.

Literary criticism can be no more than a reasoned account of the effect produced upon the critic by the book he is criticising. Criticism can never be a science: it is, in the first place, much too personal, and in the second, it is concerned with values that science ignores. The touchstone is emotion, not reason. We judge a work of art by its effect on our sincere and vital emotion, and nothing else. All the critical twiddle-twaddle about style and form, all this pseudo-scientific classifying and analysing of books in an imitation-botanical fashion, is mere impertinence and mostly dull jargon...A critic must be able to *feel* the impact of a work of art in all its complexity and force. To do so, he must be a man of force and complexity himself, which few critics are. A man with a paltry, impudent nature will never write anything but paltry, impudent criticism. And a man who is emotionally educated is rare as a phoenix. The more scholastically educated a man is, generally, the more he is an emotional bore.

In the bewildering mass of published criticism, this passage is worth remembering because it puts literature and criticism in a true light. Generalised though it is, the spirit and the wording of it are so exactly right that to have it at the back of one's mind is to have an insurance against half-hearted, inattentive reading. It is impossible not to feel a call to be quick and generous in response—as, we sense in reading the passage, Lawrence is himself.

Lawrence is probably justified in implying that a lot of the more elaborate critical analysis we read is the work of critics who are more interested in their own ideas, in their own expertise, than in what they feel about a novel or poem. But there can still be a kind of critical analysis of literature in which the emotional impact does not get lost in clever (or solemn) technical talk—a detailed, extended, argued discussion in which 'method' or procedure does not take control of the interest and in which the mind of the critic remains completely subservient to the experience of reading the work he is talking about. This sort of discussion, vitally important to the teacher and student of literature, has been very convincingly described by F. R. Leavis in *Education and the University:*

> Analysis...is the process by which we seek to attain a complete reading of a poem—a reading that approaches as nearly as possible to the perfect reading. There is about it nothing in the nature of 'murdering to dissect', and suggestions that it can be anything in the nature of laboratory-method misrepresent it entirely. We can have the poem only by an inner kind of possession; it is 'there' for analysis only in so far as we are responding appropriately to the words on the page. In pointing to them (and there is nothing else to point to) what we are doing is to bring into sharp focus in turn, this, that and the other detail, juncture or relation in our total response; or (since 'sharp focus' may be a misleading account of the kind of attention sometimes required), what we are doing is to dwell with a deliberate, considering responsiveness on this, that or the other node or focal point in the complete organisation that the poem is, in so far as we have it. Analysis is not a dissection of something that is already and passively there. What we call analysis is, of course, a constructive or creative process. It is a more deliberate following-through of that process of creation in response to the poet's words which reading is. It is a re-creation in which, by a considering attentiveness, we ensure a more than ordinary faithfulness and completeness.

Though Leavis's manner and idiom are different from Lawrence's, the critical analysis described here is not alien to Lawrence's 'We judge a work of art by its effect on our sincere and vital emotion and nothing else'. A little reflection will show, I think, that there is no inconsistency between the passages, and that a concern for detailed analysis of a poem need not necessarily mean losing emotional contact with it.

The essential questions which a reader must put to a work of literature, and from which criticism must begin, are roughly along these lines (there is no need to define them precisely, as I am only indicating a general line of thought): Is this poem— and prose is analogous here—about something which in some sense I can understand and which seems important? Can I respond to the poem in the way the poet wants me to respond? Can I in a way identify myself with the spirit in which it was written? In practice the implications of these questions are infinitely various—we cannot tell beforehand just how we will have to respond, there can be no adequate previously learned formula to tell us, and we may have to do any number of things to find the answers. But at some point these general questions must turn into more particular questions, like: What is gained by this effect? Does this detail seem successful? Does it relate meaningfully to a general effect? What, precisely, is the intention here, how are we to take this? In other words, to discover where our real preferences lie often involves a searching, exacting appraisal of everything that makes up the total effect of the poem, and Leavis's description of critical analysis suggests very well the alert, questioning attention that poetry usually needs. An inexperienced reader, when first asked to say what he thinks of a poem, will, if he has read it cursorily, usually fall into mere assertion—I like this, this appeals to me, and so on. But we haven't really read a poem until we know what we like about it more fully than this. Reflecting on a poem, deciding just where we stand in relation to it, and finding the right language to express ourselves about it, are essential parts of reading the poem. We recognise this, in a way, when we say that a poem has 'come home' to us some time after we have read it. What we mean is that we have responded newly to it, realising just what it is that we like about it, and that a vivid and accurate description of what we like has come to us as part of this realisation. If we are genuinly moved by literature we shall be able to find a sharper, more strongly felt description than 'I like this', and until we have found a description that satisfies, we know instinctively that we haven't fully grasped it. This is not to say that a half-recognised response is not *there*— but it is not fully there until it is clearly recognised. A liking for literature has to be an understanding, discerning liking, a liking in detail as well as for the whole. It is so common to find students who are perfectly confident when talking about literature in general terms—the cosmic order in Shakespeare's plays, the unifying power of metaphysical wit—but who have nothing striking or interesting to say when it comes to describing the effect of a particular poem. What Leavis defines in fact is something that, if we read well, we do naturally for ourselves; it is part of the process by which we make a poem fully *ours*.

Analysis, if it is to be more than a 'pseudo-scientific classifying and analysing of books in an imitation-botanical fashion', must be a sort of running commentary on what happens when we read a poem. Practical criticism, at the early stages at any rate, must aim to take students through this commentary slowly, arguing in greater detail than would normally be necessary with experienced readers—with beginners, analysis must be unusually full and explicit. Laboriousness is always a danger. But it is worth risking some overscrupulousness in showing how detailed questions can be put to a poem and answered, how detailed questions can relate to general questions, and, most of all, in showing that it is the poem itself which ultimately tells us how it is to be taken, not the prescriptions of a previously worked-out method. In doing this, we should be discovering a general truth about critical discussion which is vitally important to our whole undertaking. In discussion (the word tends to carry inappropriate suggestions) what we are doing is to test our own response against another person's in a co-operative interchange. We try out one another's comments to see if they answer to the poem, as far as we are concerned. Critical discussion is not often a matter of driving someone else from an untenable position by irrefutable logic, though this may be involved in an ancillary way. Rather, we are trying to discover our deepest response which the conscious, articulate mind, preoccupied with a more superficial view, has been suppressing or ignoring. To make a real change of view is to feel an inner, answering assurance, an acknowledgement that this is what we genuinely feel to be right. If we reach agreement, we shall not have proved a hard, incontestable fact so much as established an understanding, a full and vital kind of sympathy. This is, of course, what the literary critic seeks to do with his readers, and this aim should always decide the tone of his writing. It is certainly true that when we are writing about a poem, we shall write most effectively if we address an imaginary reader, not yet convinced about the poem but ready to listen to our comments and test them out for himself.

With classes the size they are today it is whimsical to talk about 'intimate class atmosphere'. Most of the readers likely to use this book will be in classes so large that discussion of any kind will be hard to manage at all. This doesn't mean, however, that the kind of work recommended here is impracticable. Written work can, to some extent, take the place of discussion, and is anyway an essential part of the training, for the discipline of ordering and articulating our thoughts on paper is invaluable if we are to gain the wider vocabulary, the livelier awareness of the meanings of words, which we must have if we are to get very much from the study of literature. My own method as teacher has been to hand out exercises, collect the answers and consider the more interesting and illuminating comments—strictly anonymously—at the next lecture. This was, of course, the method used by I. A. Richards, and it seems to me the only way of handling a large class. It is far from ideal; but the discussion of the answers is usually listened to with lively attention, and, even if class discussion is impossible, the students are in an important sense still taking part. Ideally, practical criticism should be done with groups of up to ten people, but this is an ideal few will be able to realise.

An important point to stress from the outset is that the clearly mistaken comments and judgments which most students, when they begin at least, are bound to make, are not necessarily regrettable; they do not represent dead loss. Some errors are worth making. To make a comment, see what is wrong with it and change one's mind is a far more valuable piece of education than a lucky guess (and far more valuable than to *reproduce* a correct view from a recognised critic—a process which really represents dead loss). Perhaps even more important, if the class atmosphere is to be the right one, is to avoid the impression that critical judgments are cut and dried, absolute and obvious—and in my experience this is the impression that most beginning classes are only too anxious to get. Inexperienced readers who feel uncertain of themselves are always ready to look for an assurance that the rights and wrongs of the subject are clear-cut. Correcting this view is not a question of receiving a simple direction (it rarely is in practical criticism), but of receiving corrective experience in actual reading, suitably guided and enforced by discussion. I believe that in the early stages there is some value in discussing fairly obvious cases, using comparisons (where we make use of them) which are as far as possible decisive and not likely to be controversial. The first thing to learn is that there is such a thing as critical judgment, and that critical judgments are important. But before long it must be made clear, through examples, that as readers of literature we are not always, or even often, making 'knock down' judgments. The less obvious judgments, the ones requiring great tact and delicacy in balancing different qualities against each other, are frequently the most important ones. Matthew Arnold once said that '...the critical perception of poetic truth is of all things the most volatile, elusive and evanescent; by pressing too impetuously after it, one runs the risk of losing it'. The practical criticism course which presses too impetuously after critical perception will certainly run the risk of losing it. 'Loaded' exercises, and the misleading impression which students draw from them, are something to be avoided. They provide poor training for the critical sense. I have selected some exercises mainly because they involve no clear-cut preference, and have included a number in which no comparison is called for. But in these matters this book, like any other of its kind, will have to rely on the sympathy and understanding of the teacher who uses it.

Practical criticism, of course, can never be learned from a book alone. The presence of a teacher is essential to guide discussion, to consider and comment on individual impression and opinions, to ensure that a co-operative interchange of views really does take place. No two discussions should ever follow quite the same course, even if they reach the same conclusions; no two classes should seem exactly alike. For what makes literature a marvellous thing to teach—though it may make it difficult to regulate on academic lines—is that no discussion of a good poem can be inclusively final. Reading is a process of individual creative discovery, and the individual,

CHAPTER 2

Rhythm, Tone and the Dangers of
Eye-reading

*It all depends on the pause—the natural pause, the
natural lingering of the voice according to the feeling—
it is the hidden emotional pattern that makes poetry,
not the obvious form...It is the lapse of feeling, something as indefinite as expression in the voice carrying
emotion...The ebbing and lifting emotion should be
master, and the ear the transmitter.*

D. H. LAWRENCE on metre

'I can't tell you', Lawrence wrote in the letter to Edward
Marsh from which the above quotation is taken, 'what *pattern*
I see in any poetry, save one complete thing.' This sums up the
difficulty of talking effectively about the criticism of poetry
(and prose, as so often, can largely be included in the generalisation). We can divide up a poem for the purposes of analysis
into imagery, rhythm, diction, stanza-(or verse-) form, but
the poem itself is not the sum total of all these things: it is all of
them at once. And if one of these elements is isolated from the
others, it almost always presents a misleading appearance. To
discuss imagery without being aware of rhythm is inevitably
to get the wrong impression of the imagery; to try to discuss
rhythm by itself is to end up with something almost meaningless, poetic 'music' or rhythm as a mere adjunct to poetry,
which is the error Lawrence discusses so illuminatingly in the
quotation. Yet inexperienced readers are usually only too ready
to seize on these different 'elements', forgetting that they are
simply provisional, imprecise terms which the critic invents
for his own convenience, and attempting to see them one at a
time as distinct ingredients—in the belief, perhaps, that the
difficulties of poetry can be lessened if the different parts of a
poem are mastered severally. But to try to take things one at a
time is to attempt something which, with poetry, we can never

really do: we must try to respond to 'the one complete thing', not to parts of it, and any part or detail we consider must be considered in the context of the whole. How can we best see the one complete thing, and not simply look for a series of components?

The real answer to these problems, of course, is to provide the corrective experience that the students lack; to show in actual demonstration how various poems make their impact and how imagery, metaphor, rhythm, diction, verse-structure are all inseparably part of the impact. This, it is hoped, is what the exercises provided in this book will do, or will at least go some way towards doing. But it is, I believe, worth considering the inexperienced reader and his tendencies more fully at this point, so that the stress can be laid in the most effective ways in our opening discussions.

The cause of many failures with poetry (and prose) is what I have chosen to call 'eye-reading'. Most inexperienced readers never seriously try to *hear* a poem. They read with the eye alone, in the casual, inattentive manner bred by the modern world's usual acquaintance with the printed word. The student, having decided, probably, what the subject-matter of the poem is, and having made a rough mental paraphrase, runs his eye down the poem looking for details of imagery, metaphor—for these are the things he can most easily be told to look for —and does not feel the movement of the verse. This process of picking things out of the poem for inspection without hearing the poem is fatal, and causes more trouble than perhaps any other error. The tone, the emotional atmosphere of a poem will never be caught properly in this kind of a reading, which can lead to the most unbelievable misconceptions of the poet's intention; and I think that no one who reads in this fashion was ever strongly moved by what he read. How little beginning students hear what they read is well suggested by the fact that many errors of interpretation can be corrected simply by reading out the poem or hearing it read—a method which may prove far quicker and more convincing than any amount of extended argument. Reading aloud is, of course, difficult, and few people can manage it well (though the stumbling, painful efforts many students make when they try to read poetry aloud give some idea of how unaccustomed they are to paying attention to tone and movement in their ordinary reading). But everyone has a voice in the imagination, with which they can mime the physical voice reading, and this imaginary re-enactment is always far more sensitive to shades of tone than any rendering of the poem we could give aloud. It is by means of this inner ear that we largely form our idea of the distinctive sound of a poet's voice, that individual timbre by which, if he is a great poet, we can always recognise him. This inner ear must be trained if we are to read at all competently.

Some examples of the sort of error caused by eye-reading will perhaps make my meaning clearer. The following comparison of Wordsworth's well-known 'A slumber did my spirit seal' with Hartley Coleridge's pastiche has produced so many errors of this kind that it seems an obvious choice for illustration (though teachers are recommended to use the Autumn Ode comparison (Exercise 1) as the first exercise with their class). The point of the comparison is that it depends so much on the reader's sensitiveness to tone and movement. Both poems follow regular stanza-forms, and some readers are inclined to pronounce both 'mere doggerel' at first sight. For them, the *sight*, not the sound, of a regular stanza-form is enough. Such readers need to be told that to catch the movement of poetry is not always the matter of a moment's scrutiny. In the present case, what will look at first sight like only slight differences between the poems will gradually, as we begin to discover the Wordsworth, come to seem very important. It is typical of Wordsworth that apparently slight characteristics on the surface should mean a great deal underneath, and we can contrast his sensitive and expressive control of tone and movement with Hartley Coleridge's real doggerel.

A   A slumber did my spirit seal,
      I had no human fears;
    She seem'd a thing that could not feel
      The touch of earthly years.

No motion has she now, no force,
    She neither hears nor sees,
Roll'd round in earth's diurnal course
    With rocks and stones and trees.

B

She pass'd away like morning dew
    Before the sun was high;
So brief her time, she scarcely knew
    The meaning of a sigh.

As round the rose its sweet perfume
    Sweet love around her floated;
Admired she grew—while mortal doom
    Crept on, unfear'd, unnoted.

Love was her guardian angel here,
    But Love to Death resign'd her;
Though Love was kind, why should we fear
    But holy Death is kinder?

    Neither poem contains any 'avoidable' difficulty—there are no abstruse ideas, no obscure allusions, and the vocabulary in each case is simple. But on all the occasions on which I have used the exercise, explanations of the meaning of the Wordsworth poem have differed widely, as have the descriptions of its emotional atmosphere. It has been found 'surprisingly heartless about the death of the girl, unlike poem B which is tender', and generally 'cold, remote, detached'. The closing lines always gave trouble. It is typical of the inexperienced reader to go wrong in a place like this, and to put something of his own there, which he vaguely feels is probable, instead of trying to find what it is that the poet is offering. Several of my readers had to find elaborate meanings and introduce ideas which, plainly, are not in the poet's mind at all. Is the girl in heaven? Does the poem mean that she is in a happier state, and the poem is therefore a comforting poem? Or does he mean, as some readers imagined, that she is dead, there's no point in worrying, and we all ought to accept death with no nonsense anyway? These rather bemused ponderings could only be possible to people who read with the eye alone—who had extracted phrases from the poem and, not feeling the emotional atmosphere, did not know what to do with them. They failed to respond to the emotional atmosphere, I suggest, because they never tried to feel or hear the expressive tones of the poet's voice. Anyone who has done so will, I think, reject all of these comments as more or less distorted. Revealingly, several of the readers who made these comments were unable to read the first stanza correctly, believing that the slumber itself is death and even quoting the first line as 'a slumber did *her* spirit seal', an example of slackness of attention of a quite fatal sort. One reader was driven to the conclusion that the poet himself is looking at his/her own body. The poem is perfectly clear: 'A slumber *did* my spirit seal', 'No motion *has* she now . . .' The first stanza recalls a time before her death, and the slumber cannot possibly mean death. These are, I know, obvious errors, but I mention them because the mental process behind them is familiar and representative—a hasty assessment of the subject-matter, and a loose conjecture as to the poem that the reader feels may probably be there.

How do we hear the tone of a poem? Nothing obscure or unusual is involved. After all, it is partly by the tone or accent of a person's voice that we judge his attitude towards us, or his feelings towards what he is talking about, and to some extent we form our idea of what sort of a person he is from the tone he uses. In life we do this instinctively, and usually the more acute we are as judges of people the sharper will be our 'ear' for shades and inflections in a voice. Most readers, once they have overcome their eye-reading prejudice about the printed word, and realised that poetry is real speech (the poet is 'a man speaking to men'), should become as sensitive to the tones of voice in poetry as they are to the tones of real voices in life. We don't need a recording of the poet reading the poem himself in order to know what the tone is like, or to hear his individual accents as a poet—recordings, in practice, are liable to disappoint and get in the way. These things are best perceived in the poem itself. The most useful as well as the most obvious direction that can be given is to read the poem through several times, trying to let the movement establish itself naturally and not jumping to conclusions like the readers who thought that the regular stanza-form inevitably meant doggerel. Eye-reading is responsible for a comment like 'the rhythm is jerky'; and the comment on rhythm which is thrown in as an afterthought should always be distrusted, for it is a clear sign that the reader has not made the effort of recreation in response which poetry demands. If we listen carefully, the shades and inflections of tone in the poet's voice will gradually emerge, even in a poem as apparently bare and simple in verse-structure as poem A. In the first line of the poem, the tone is unmistakably withdrawn, reminiscing, self-communing—the voice comes to rest on the unexpected word 'seal', giving the line its gentle but perceptible physical impact. The sense of living an intense inner life, cut off from the ordinary routine of existence, is given us chiefly by this word, which so obviously hasn't been put there just for the sake of an easy alliteration. A heightened, trance-like feeling is being recalled, a time when the poet was so intently absorbed in his own emotions that he was 'sealed off' from the ordinary world. This suggestion is reinforced by 'human' in the next line, a word with a telling effect not easy to sum up. The pre-occupied poet has forgotten the ordinary conditions of life, particularly mortality, and 'human' makes the exaltation seem further from commonplace normality, more rarefied, but not less intense for being rarefied. It is characteristic of Wordsworth to be able to recreate heightened, intensely withdrawn and private states of feeling apparently almost without effort ('moods' would almost fit, if the word didn't hint at something too trivial). The phrase 'human fears' stays in the mind with that sharp distinctness we associate with poetry that has moved us strongly, but there is nothing of conscious contrivance about it, and nothing could be further from the *mot juste* (the elegant, witty word) or from the phrase one remembers simply because it's an unusual coinage. The word 'thing' in the next line has this same, almost deceptively simple quality. It worried several of my student readers who didn't know what to do with it—it seemed to them banal, ineptly flat. But when we are closer to the poem we can see that this word is perfectly 'right', expressing a particular shade of feeling which is crucially important in the development of the poem as a whole. For there has been something impersonal as well as personal in Wordsworth's feeling for the woman, an element of idealising, detached wonder that such a woman could exist, which is very different from the disrespect that some of my students believed they found there (a classic example of what may happen when a word is examined out of its context).

This impersonal element in Wordsworth's feeling must be recognised if we are to understand and fully respond to the second stanza. We must, that is, realise just how unusual a love poem this is—if indeed it can be called a love poem in the conventional sense (and a number of my students went wrong because, seeing the poem was about a woman and about death, they expected to be asked to respond in a conventional way). There is the contrast with the first stanza: the woman has no motion, no force, no positive independent will of her own, and the poet has been awakened from his slumber. But there is more in the poem than simply the feeling of dereliction, of utter loss. In the remarkable evocation of the vast, impersonal forces of nature in this stanza there is the sense that the woman has passed into a larger, non-human existence. The cosmic, 'astronomical' touch in the last two lines, the suggestion of a greater, universal life in which the girl is carried with 'rocks and stones and trees' is beautifully and effortlessly done. The change of perspective, from the rapt wonder with which he had regarded her in life to the rapt wonder with which he thinks of her now as merged into the great processes of nature, could only have been managed successfully by a major poet. The last line, especially, manages to *create* what it is talking about. The reader's imagination is brought into active life in a way that would have been impossible had Wordsworth used stale, second-hand phrasing, had the movement been less marvellously expressive. It is an austere vision, which makes no concessions to conventional, sentimental comfort. The poet is left contemplating with awe those powers which now possess the thing he loves; the relationship, we might say, is now wholly 'impersonal', a development of the special kind of feeling he had for her in life (and we now understand how essential the work of defining this feeling done in the first stanza is). It would be difficult to imagine a better example of the truth of Lawrence's remark at the beginning of this section, that rhythm is not a matter of metrical feet but of 'the lapse of feeling, something as indefinite as expression in the voice carrying emotion'; or of the general truth that rhythm, movement (the word 'rhythm' has an unfortunate connotation of a regular beat, and 'movement' seems to me the better term) cannot be thought of (or perceived) as something separate from the total meaning of the poem.

There is no need to add, surely, that Wordsworth is not being 'tough' in this poem. There is no implication whatever that it is weak or futile to grieve over death. And the notion that the girl is now in heaven and 'better off' is a confused and largely irrelevant guess. To import the idea of heaven into the poem means certain failure to respond: this is the record of the feelings of a man who, at this moment, did not envisage a heaven in the traditional sense, and had Wordsworth done so, he would have written a different poem. Some of my readers obviously wanted to find explicit protest or comment in the poem, or, in other words, they wanted to be *told* by the poet what to feel. But had Wordsworth added explicit comment of this sort (and as a rule he is certainly given to doing this) he would have weakened the effect. The poem is complete as it stands, an experience vividly and movingly recorded.

I believe most readers who prefer the Hartley Coleridge do so because they feel more confident that they have understood it. The Wordsworth is not an unusually difficult poem, but 'understanding' it involves responding to it; the two processes are inseparable, and if we don't read responsively we are not likely to interpret it faithfully. The Hartley Coleridge, on the other hand, doesn't seriously ask us to respond. The emotional pointers are all there, crudely offered us, and the reader is expected to respond appropriately along conventional lines. As the poem depends on a 'ready-made' effect, no real effort is involved. There is no 'hidden emotional pattern'. The language is pretty-precious and the sentiment saccharine, and the movement is obvious, insensitive and undistinguished (notice how often the poet has had to strain to find rhymes). There is no need to feel triumphant contempt for the author of the poem, or to adopt the severely reprehending tone of self-righteous indignation that students are liable to pick up if they are allowed to. The poet hasn't revealed any really despicable kind of hollowness; he has merely thrown off a very trivial piece of poetasting. Vaguely similar at first sight, the poems are, on closer reading, very different in quality.

CHAPTER 3

Imagery, Metaphor and Visualisation

A useful tip for sensing the tone of a poem—not an infallible rule—is to ask if it could conceivably be read aloud to a small group of people, of friends perhaps, without embarrassment or awkwardness. This is a rough test for detecting oratorical inflation, eloquent pretentiousness and various kinds of affectation. To read a poem aloud means temporarily to commit oneself to it, and I doubt if most of us could read the Hartley Coleridge poem, for instance, to a group of people who knew us well in ordinary life. We would be uncomfortably aware of adopting some kind of pose, which our hearers would easily see through. In making the comparison of the translations from Seneca (Chapter 11 below), the test is useful in showing up the crudely oratorical quality of the Cowley version, which would be hard to read with conviction whatever the circumstances, and whatever strained or unnatural tone of voice we were able to adopt. The Wyatt version, in contrast, can be read out to a friendly but sceptical group without the least embarrassment. The Keats sonnet (Exercise 15) needs particularly careful discrimination. Most readers will find the opening lines extremely effective, the mood being perfectly captured in the touches of cool exaltation. But the contrasting warmth of the sestet is less well handled. There seems to be a lapse with 'pillow'd upon my fair love's ripening breast', and convincing reading becomes difficult at this point. It is not a question of affectation so much as gauche sentimentality. But the tip can be illustrated from any number of poems. It is useful as long as we remember it is only a tip, a hint for recalling us from a possible wayward indulgence to real life, and something (or the equivalent of something) which is done instinctively by the experienced reader.

Movement and tone; this is certainly where a special stress must be laid right from the start. Movement is almost always far more neglected by the beginning reader than imagery, largely because it is much less readily apparent to him. Metaphorical language is usually recognisable as such, but movement is more elusive. It is as 'indefinite as expression in the voice carrying emotion', and is usually much less easy to perceive and describe than imagery at any rate *appears* to be to the inexperienced. But in this lies something of its importance. Nothing is more easily started than an image-search; the temptation to pick out metaphors for individual inspection is a strong one: ingenuity is usually easier to exercise than sensitiveness. But, once the irrelevant theory of metrics[1] is disposed of, it is very much harder for the reader to look for movement in a mechanical way. To describe the movement (and hence, inevitably, the tone) we must ask ourselves what it feels like; we must try to enter into it, to respond. By laying special stress here, a teacher can I think positively encourage his students to make a creative effort in reading; he may induce them to listen actively for the ebbing and flowing emotion, and abandon the cold, detached process of eye-reading. This is not to deny that movement and tone are sometimes tricky things to handle. What is being suggested here is not a short and easy way of producing good readers of poetry; it is what seems to me a productive emphasis that ought to be made when introducing students to poetry for the first time. The inner ear, which is critical awareness of movement in language, is a thing few students are likely to possess in any developed, conscious way, before they begin. The sooner we can start to bring this faculty to active life, the better.

No discussion of imagery will get very close to a poem unless it keeps the liveliest consciousness of the movement. The two cannot be separated as different elements on expression, at least in a successful poem. The way in which movement

---

[1] I have not thought it worth while discussing this theory, which was foisted on to English poetry by scholars of Greek and Latin, and which is surely now thoroughly dead.

reinforces metaphor needs to be seen in a wide range of examples if we are to avoid some of the misapprehensions about imagery that often dog practical criticism. One is the notion that criticism of poetry must be an image-search. Another, related misconception is the tiresome supposition that 'imagery' necessarily involves something visual, and that every poem is a series of little pictures. Visual effects are, of course, common in poetry, and many images are partly visual (to an extent that probably varies sometimes with individual readers). But the belief that 'imagery' *necessarily* implies something visualised and nothing else is a naivity which makes intelligent reading impossible, and it must be disposed of firmly. At this point a discussion of a poem particularly rich in metaphor may help in showing how little, in practice, imagery can be separated from movement and tone, and how little imagery needs to depend on purely visual effects. Keats's *Ode to Autumn* (Exercise I) suits this purpose so well that I make no apologies for using a very familiar poem to illustrate these points. The Ode has all those qualities which make it a good poem to use at the start of a practical criticism course. There is no difficulty in deciding what the subject is, and in giving an account of it, and the intention is basically so simple that one might almost say this is a poem not easy to go wrong on. Yet it is full of strikingly successful effects of language, all contributing to a powerful total impact. Most people take to the poem very readily, and liking for it increases as it is considered in detail. I shall discuss only the opening stanza here, comparing it to stanzas from Hood's pastiche, a useful contrast. The complete poems can, however, be found in the Exercises.

I

A   Season of mists and mellow fruitfulness!
    Close bosom-friend of the maturing sun;
Conspiring with him how to load and bless
    With fruit the vines that round the thatch-eves run;
To bend with apples the moss'd cottage trees,
    And fill all fruit with ripeness to the core;

> To swell the gourd, and plump the hazel-shells
> With a sweet kernel; to set budding more
> And still more later flowers for the bees,
> Until they think warm days will never cease
> For summer has o'er brimmed their clammy cells.

B

> I saw old Autumn in the misty morn
> Stand shadowless like Silence, listening
> To Silence, for no lonely bird would sing
> Into his hollow ear from woods forlorn,
> Nor lowly hedge nor solitary thorn:—
> Shaking his languid locks all dewy bright
> With tangled gossamer that fell by night,
> Pearling his coronet of golden corn.

. . . .

> The squirrel gloats on his accomplish'd hoard,
> The ants have brimm'd their garners with ripe grain,
> And honey bees have stor'd
> The sweets of summer in their luscious cells;
> The swallows all have wing'd across the main;
> But here the Autumn melancholy dwells,
> And sighs her tearful spells
> Among the sunless shadows of the plain.

There should be no great difficulty in realising that the notion of imagery as pictures ('the poet paints a picture in the next line of...') is entirely inadequate when we are reading the Keats. A whole range of other sensations besides sight is wonderfully caught in the language. We notice first the rich satisfaction of the tone, which has a touch of awe in it nevertheless. At every point in the poem the control of movement is sensitive and precise; we know with unusual exactness just which inflection is intended by the poet. In the first line, for instance, the voice is made to linger on the words 'mellow fruitfulness' with just the right degree of appreciating content. The line is saved from any feeling of excessive lushness by the contrast of 'mists' and 'mellow,' and the unobtrusive way the alliterative *m*s point this contrast and direct the voice is masterly, whether the device was conscious or not. In the next line we can notice how effectively the personification of Autumn as 'bosom-friend' of the sun is handled. There is not the least clumsiness in the use of this device, which in the hands of lesser poets often seems such an obvious contrivance. It enables Keats to concentrate suggestions in 'conspiring'. The ripeness is the work of Autumn and his bosom-friend the 'maturing sun', and these great natural forces seem to share a mysterious secret of life between them. The slight retarding of the movement on 'thatch-eves' which seems, in its supple way, to lengthen the line, suggests to me the slight pause as the poet's eye travels along the eves, marvelling at the heavy fullness of the vines which grow in every cranny. We certainly visualise something as we read this, but in the following lines, while we still visualise the apple trees, the different fruits and the cells of the bees, we are more and more aware of the wonderfully varied and distinct physical sensations. The impact of 'bend' in 'To bend with apples' is only in part a matter of visualising—we sense the loaded fullness more directly, and this physical sense of loaded richness is taken up in different ways throughout the stanza, as the poet notices the various ripening fruits. Here it gives way to the deeply relished satisfaction of 'ripeness to the core' (it would take a very insensitive reader not to feel the movement here, and to understand that the phrase conveys far more than the tired cliché which we usually utter when we use these words). The effect becomes unmistakably tactual in

> To swell the gourd and plump the hazel shells.

In the imagination we sense the poet's hand feeling the roundness of the ripened gourd, and weighing the hazel-nuts to judge the increased size of the 'sweet kernel' with anticipated pleasure. The stanza closes on the extraordinary 'clammy cells', a success of a sort possible only to an original poet. The 'clammy cells', o'er brimmed after the dreamy luxuriance of summer days, are not conventionally 'pretty'; there is a sharp distinctness of observation here that is rare in nature poetry, and captures, I think, the unexpectedness and strangeness of some details of nature when we examine them really closely. This last line, of course, is in balanced contrast to the different sensations that have gone before, and it brings the stanza to a close superbly.

Since we have been praising the poem for its sensuous richness, its vivid rendering of physical sensation, it is worth asking why and how the poem seems so much more than a mere orgy of the senses. Why is it not just an indulgence of a straightforward kind, such as can be had from many sources, and which (I have had this response from students who can think independently) doesn't seem material enough for great poetry? First of all, perhaps, as our analysis has shown (or ought to have shown) the way in which sensuous pleasure is rendered is far too distinct to suggest an easily achieved gratification. Keats does not 'lose distinction in his joys'—there is nothing in the poem to suggest heady indulgence, nothing cloying. We might compare some of his earlier poems, in which pleasure is much more of an end in itself, and a good deal of splather results. Here, there is no need to contrast sensation and thought. But surely the main answer to the objection must lie in that touch of wonder which in various ways pervades the whole poem. The satisfactions Keats writes of are something more than the mere satisfaction of the appetite. Love and appreciation of Nature in poetry are now so familiar to us—familiar in the deadliest possible way—that one is inclined to dismiss Nature poetry as old hat. Why bother? But this poem has a power to awaken us to a new sense of natural things, refreshing and sustaining. We don't switch off part of ourselves in reading it.

Finally, we need to make it clear that while we can pick out this or that effect, produced by this or that device of language, the poem itself leaves us with no sense of conscious contrivance. The language is so spontaneous we seem to share the poet's experiences without being aware of a conscious medium of expression between us. There is no self-regarding 'beauty', no conventionality of diction. The theme and intentions are limited, but the intentions are perfectly carried out. In contrast, the Hood is, of course, a pastiche, or something near it (in fairness to Hood it might be an idea to read one of his humorous poems), but it is useful because it echoes Keats so closely, even trying to reproduce some of his effects:

> The squirrel gloats on his accomplish'd hoard,
> The ants have filled their garners with ripe grain
> And honey bees have stor'd
> The sweets of summer in their luscious cells...

This language, compared to Keats's, is not creative; it altogether lacks the sensuous vividness of the *Ode to Autumn* stanza. 'His accomplish'd hoard' is weak, the unexpressive adjective getting a stress which it cannot properly stand ('completed' would do the same work equally well). Besides, 'gloats' seems rather forced—it is plainly *not* a description of a wild creature, but a clumsy over-explicit hyperbole. Compare 'plump the hazel-shells' in which we are not merely *told* that nature is rich, but something actual—a piece of real observation—is presented to us. The same is true of 'ripe grain', 'stor'd the sweets of summer', 'luscious cells'. This is weakly adjectival writing—compare the feebly explicit 'luscious cells' with 'clammy cells'. The movement of the Hood is insipid too, not surprisingly, in view of the poverty of content and the dim, second-hand way the poet feels about what he writes of. The movement in B is merely regular, mechanical. In the lines preceding those quoted above, Hood appears to be interested in poetic melancholy, that most ready-made ingredient of poetry, in echoing, hollow sounds and mournfulness. 'Stand shadowless like Silence' is an obvious, contrived use of alliteration which makes good comparison with the Keats (cf. 'mists and mellow fruitfulness'). 'Silence listening to Silence' seems to me meaningless. There is something awkward and unwanted in the personification of Autumn as a somewhat dreary old man—again we can compare Keats's more tactful use of this device—and when in the second stanza in extract B, Autumn becomes 'Autumn melancholy', the distinction seems pointless, and the change of sex ludicrous. With 'woods forlorn' and 'tearful spells', we are at the level of poetic diction in its worst fatuity. There is surely no need to insist any further on the entirely artificial character of the inspiration. The value of the comparison is in throwing the Keats into relief. Elsewhere in the poem, other Romantic poets form the subject of the pastiche, and detecting Hood's sources is a useful exercise. The other two stanzas of the Keats must, of course, be looked at, particularly the contrasting last stanza.

CHAPTER 4

Early and Late Shakespearean Verse

As I have already pointed out, an impression I am very anxious to avoid giving in this commentary is that there are a certain number of readily definable ways of using language shared between the great writers, and that these can be illustrated one after the other in well-chosen examples. The impression is easily given. To write a book on practical criticism seems almost to commit one to this view, so strongly do a course, and a guiding textbook, seem to imply a systematic programme of study. Certainly, if literature were susceptible to this systematic, categorising treatment, a practical criticism course would be a lot easier to plan than it actually is. But literature is not. It would be more true (if still not completely true) to say that every writer who matters has his own distinctive way of using language, which is representative of himself and no one else; and plainly, no book can hope to exemplify all the possible ways. But a practical criticism course does not have to be thought of as a necessarily inadequate attempt to cover varied and complex material with rough, simplifying generalisations; we only have to think of it in this way if we fall victim to the 'method' misconception of criticism, which lies behind so many notions of what practical criticism ought to be. Practical criticism is better thought of as trying to bring into motion a sensibility which will largely be able to develop of its own accord, given the right stimulus. As we read, our capacity to respond increases; we grow more flexible, not less—assuming we have the capacity to respond in the first place. There is no need to think that if we have discussed one poet we have gained 'critical equipment' for reading just that one kind of poetry, or that one poet. We are, basically, only trying to start and develop an interest in literature which we might naturally acquire for ourselves; we are not acquiring a mechanism which we couldn't have acquired without help. To train (if that is the right word) a reader to respond to Shakespeare is to train him to respond to Keats, different as he is, to Pope, different as he is, and to Wordsworth, different as he is. To be really moved by one poem is to learn much more than that one poem—which is why students with a talent for literature, given the right encouragement, can learn so quickly. For instance, I think it is quite possible to recognise conventionality in poetry even when we are not familiar with the particular clichés of a period. Once we have responded to the living in literature, and felt its presence, we develop a sense for the stale, the commonplace. We don't need to know, for example, exactly which are the favourite tropes of Elizabethan poetry in order to recognise that

O she is fallen into a pit of ink

is a bad line, and to feel the stale odour of conventionality about it. The crucial thing is to have made living contact with literature *somewhere*. Once this is done, subsequent development will partly follow naturally, though it can be encouraged by intelligent guidance or hindered by bad guidance. We are not, in the strict sense, starting 'at the beginning' of our practical criticism course—we are simply starting in what seems to be a promising place. Thereafter, the course cannot be a neatly ordered progression so much as a series of examples to mobilise sensibility. The more varied they can be, the more they will suggest the flexibility we need as readers of literature. To a certain extent only can they be graded in difficulty.

Shakespeare must, however, come near the beginning of the course, and hold an important place throughout. As he has used language to express experience of greater range and depth than any other writer in English, this is inevitable; and, besides, he provides particularly good opportunities for training the critical sense in practical criticism as his development throughout his career is constantly reflected in his increasing power over language. As the bright, adept young writer turns into the great tragic dramatist, the development is, of course, in every direction; we can only appreciate it in part by comparing extracts from early and late plays in close analysis. Yet any intelligent comparison of this sort will lead naturally to other considerations; there need be no distorting emphasis on verbal analysis, especially if, as I have suggested before, our practical criticism course is properly related to other courses in literature. The aim of this kind of exercise must be to heighten our sense of what Shakespeare's maturity means as a whole. Its greatest disadvantage, of course, is that in each case we are only looking at a brief extract from a long work, and this disadvantage can be only partly overcome. Pope was quite right in including in *The Dunciad* the critics who are so taken up with close analysis that they fail to see the whole of a work of art:[1] anyone who teaches or follows a practical criticism course should have his words by heart. To some extent we can make up for the lack of context by a brief description. But, as so often with practical criticism, being aware of the dangers is our main means of avoiding them and their consequences. Tactful choice of passages, and tactful handling of discussion, is the real answer; there is no easier solution.

Exercise **2** is intended for use in the introductory discussion which must familiarise the class with this sort of exercise. It contrasts two speeches on justice and mercy, one written at a comparatively early period in Shakespeare's career, the other written in his maturity. The aim of the exercise is to show what can be shown of Shakespeare's development in detailed analysis of particular passages.

2

A   The quality of mercy is not strained,
                It droppeth as the gentle rain from heaven
                Upon the place beneath: it is twice blessed,
                It blesseth him that gives, and him that takes,

[1] The critic eye, that microscope of wit,
    Sees hairs and pores, examines bit by bit.
    How parts relate to parts, and they to whole,
    The body's harmony, the beaming soul,
    Are things which Kuster, Burman, Wasse shall see
    When man's whole frame is obvious to a flea.

'Tis mightiest in the mightiest, it becomes
The throned monarch better than his crown.
His sceptre shows the force of temporal power,
The attribute to awe and majesty,
Wherein doth sit the dread and fear of kings:
But mercy is above this sceptred sway,
It is enthroned in the hearts of kings,
It is an attribute of God himself;
And earthly power doth then show likest God's
When mercy seasons justice. . .

B   Well, believe this,
No ceremony that to great ones 'longs,
Not the king's crown, not the deputed sword,
The marshall's truncheon, nor the judge's robe,
Become them with one half so good a grace
As mercy does.
If he had been as you, and you as he,
You would have slipped like him—but he, like you,
Would not have been so stern.

If the class is not familiar with either play, the teacher must do what he can to remedy the lack of context with a brief description. This is not always easy. The description must be careful not to say anything tendentious, and loose wording almost inevitably leads to misunderstandings. Whatever is said will, of course, have to be makeshift in any case. The points to be made clear here are that speech A is made in court by the heroine, disguised as a lawyer, on behalf of a man technically condemned by the law through a trick though morally innocent, and that speech B is by a young woman pleading for mercy for her brother who is condemned to death under a severe chastity law. Both appeal directly to the person responsible for setting the law in motion. More description could be given, but this seems sufficient (in written work descriptions must be as brief and simple as possible). The nature of the 'slip' in B must be known, of course, as the students might suppose another crime and misconstrue the whole speech.

Speech A, from *The Merchant of Venice*, is probably better known, yet we are in a different world when we read the second speech. A is a very competent piece of writing, but the comparison makes it look stiff. It has, generally, the effect of a set-speech, a piece of recitation, an effect which no amount of allowance for the fact that it is a court-speech can quite do away with. The verse-paragraph is carefully built up for the maximum eloquence; the phrases balance one against the other, and the ending is carefully turned. This is the art of the orator, and it is not an art which is interested in vividly evoking real speech and the actual situations of life. The passage is essentially undramatic; the action stops for a while and declamation takes over, a frequent occurrence in the early Shakespeare, in which eloquence is often there to be enjoyed for its own sake. And the writing has a related sententious quality, it moves in terms of maxims and clichés (' 'Tis mightiest in the mightiest' is typical). I think we can fairly say that it is memorable mainly because it is neatly turned, not for any great urgency in what is conveyed. The movement is fluent and smooth, and there are no *meaningful* changes of pace or modulations of tone (as the description 'eloquent' implies). There are, in fact, no effects of any kind to hold us up with a distinct impression, or make us pause to assimilate something new and illuminating. The frequent tautologies ('the dread and fear of kings', 'throned monarch', etc.) are the clearest possible indication that there is no precise meaning to be conveyed, and the famous simile,

> It droppeth as the gentle rain from heaven
> Upon the place beneath,

is a pretty, tasteful conceit not beyond a number of Shakespeare's contemporaries.

In the passage from *Measure for Measure* the quality of the language is quite different; this is so obviously real speech. The tone and, almost, the gesture of the speaker are convincingly caught, as she bursts out in passionate indignation. Unmistakably, she turns upon the hearer, Angelo, with 'Well, believe this'—a colloquial directness a long way from the studied speech of A—and, with increasing fervour, she goes through the symbols of office (a list which is genuinely emotionally charged, and quite different from the sententious listing of 'sceptre', etc., in A), until the climax is reached on 'one half so good a grace', an effect utterly alien to the more contrived art of passage A. Then follow the personal accusations—we can notice how convincingly Shakespeare has followed the movement of Isabella's mind, which naturally turns from a general truth to a direct frontal attack on Angelo. The way 'like' is taken up is particularly effective in suggesting the way the speaker is galvanised into acuteness by the situation; we can imagine the flushed and angry resentment with which Isabella goes for Angelo. It would be impossible to remember this speech as a series of platitudes about mercy. We cannot think of it without recalling the impression of a roused, passionate woman—and, if we remember the context of the speech in the actual play, without recalling the unparalleled psychological insight of the scene, in which Isabella, whom we have thought of as a severely pure novice (and who thinks of herself in this light) suddenly shows herself capable of passion—the feminine warmth which Angelo finds irresistibly provocative. The scene, with its characteristic fullness of understanding, would have been unthinkable without the control of the expressive resources of language which we have noticed in our extract. There is no danger of Isabella being a cardboard figure; she is, like Angelo, fully and convincingly a human being.

But a longer example needs to be looked at if we are to have a proper, representative glimpse of the range and power of Shakespeare's mature verse. In Exercise 3 I shall take two speeches by important characters in soliloquy—two studies of a mind communing with itself. The first is from *Richard III*. On the night before the battle of Bosworth Field, the king is troubled by a nightmare in which the ghosts of his victims haunt him. The soliloquy begins as he starts from sleep:

3

A   Give me another horse! Bind up my wounds!
    Have mercy, Jesu!—Soft, I did but dream.
    O coward conscience, how thou didst afflict me!

The lights burn blue. It is now dead midnight.
Cold fearful drops stand on my trembling flesh.
What do I fear? myself? there's none else by.
Richard loves Richard; that is, I am I.
Is there a murderer here? No—yes, I am:
Then fly. What, from myself? Great reason why—
Lest I revenge. Myself upon myself?
Alack, I love myself. For any good
That I myself have done unto myself?
O, no! Alas, I rather hate myself
For hateful deeds committed by myself!
I am a villain: yet I lie, I am not.
Fool, of thyself speak well: fool, do not flatter.
My conscience hath a thousand several tongues,
And every tongue brings in a several tale,
And every tale condemns me for a villain.
Perjury, perjury, in the high'st degree;
Murder, stern murder, in the dir'st degree;
All several sins, all used in each degree,
Throng to the bar, crying all 'Guilty, guilty!'.
I shall despair. There is no creature loves me;
And if I die, no soul will pity me:
Nay, wherefore should they, since that I myself
Find in myself no pity to myself?
Methought the souls of all that I have murdered
Came to my tent, and every one did threat
To-morrow's vengeance on the head of Richard.

The second is Macbeth's soliloquy from Act I, Scene vii, in which he is trying to steel himself to commit the murder:

B   If it were done when 'tis done, then 'twere well
It were done quickly: if th'assassination
Could trammel up the consequence, and catch
With his surcease success; that but this blow
Might be the be-all and the end-all—here,
But here, upon this bank and shoal of time,
We'd jump the life to come.—But in these cases
We still have judgment here; that we but teach
Bloody instructions, which, being taught, return
To plague th'inventor: this even-handed Justice
Commends th'ingredience of our poison'd chalice
To our own lips. He's here in double trust:
First, as I am his kinsman and his subject,

> Strong both against the deed; then, as his host,
> Who should against his murtherer shut the door,
> Nor bear the knife myself. Besides, this Duncan
> Hath borne his faculties so meek, hath been
> So clear in his great office, that his virtues
> Will plead like angels, trumpet-tongu'd, against
> The deep damnation of his taking-off;
> And pity, like a naked, new-born babe,
> Striding the blast, or heaven's Cherubims, hors'd
> Upon the sightless couriers of the air,
> Shall blow the horrid deed in every eye,
> That tears shall drown the wind.—I have no spur
> To prick the sides of my intent, but only
> Vaulting ambition, which o'er leaps itself
> And falls on the other [side].

Perhaps we can add a third passage with advantage, from Webster's *The Duchess of Malfi*, in which Bosola, who has murdered the Duchess, repents as she finally expires:

c
> Oh, she's gone again! there the cords of life broke.
> O sacred innocence, that sweetly sleeps
> On turtle's feathers, whilst a guilty conscience
> Is a black register, wherein is writ
> All our good deeds and bad, a perspective
> That shows us hell! That we cannot be suffer'd
> To do good when we have a mind to it!
> This is manly sorrow;
> These tears, I am very certain, never grew
> In my mother's milk; my estate is sunk
> Below the degree of fear: where were
> These penitent fountains while she was living?
> Oh, they were frozen up! Here is a sight
> As direful to my soul as is the sword
> Unto a wretch hath slain his father. Come,
> I'll bear thee hence...

The situations of the three speakers are not parallel, but the grounds for comparison are clear enough. They each contemplate the murder or murders they have committed or are about to commit; and they are each troubled by remorse or conscience, though in the case of Macbeth he doesn't properly recognise that it *is* conscience. It is often helpful to formulate

the critical issues in a question, and in this case the question we
need to put to the passages must clearly be: in which passage
are we vividly presented with a convincingly real human being,
fully understood in all his sufferings, his moral blindness or
insight, his temptations, his delusions? And, conversely, in
which passage is the situation being exploited for some cheaper
effect, the dramatist being interested in something more trivial
than sensitive, accurate presentation and understanding?

For the present writer, passage C is the one most obviously
interested in exploiting the external possibilities of the situation
for sensational purposes. It is not, certainly, a good piece of
Webster, though anyone familiar with the play will recognise
something of his characteristically corrosive sense of futility in
the lines:

> That we cannot be suffer'd
> To do good when we have a mind to it!

Bosola is, however, largely an unconvincing piece of stage-
convention, and 'external' seems a fair word to use of the
rather ready-to-hand imagery with its cheaply heightened
contrasts:

> O sacred innocence that sweetly sleeps
> On turtle's feathers, whilst a guilty conscience
> Is a black register...
>   ...where were
> These penitent fountains while she was living?
> O they were frozen up!

The final figure seems feebly obvious and unilluminating:

> Here is a sight
> As direful to my wretched soul as is the sword
> Unto a wretch hath slain his father...

The intensities are all too explicit. The language is loosely
selected, adjectival, and vehement only because it uses superlatives. Bosola does not begin to seem real.

The speech from *Richard III* is one of the most memorable
in the play. This is the only moment at which Richard suffers
from the 'compunctious visitings of nature' and Shakespeare
is clearly trying to exploit the opportunity. If we compare the

speech to the Webster, Shakespeare's resources at this point of his career seem comparatively unsophisticated, particularly in movement; Webster writes at a later date in the development of the drama, when dramatic blank verse is much more flexible in rhythm and altogether closer to actual speech. As has often been pointed out, this sophistication, associated with such poverty of content, is a sign of decadence in Webster, and one might well prefer *Richard III* as a less ambivalent piece of writing which uses the resources it has with simple conviction. To compare it to the *Macbeth* soliloquy, however, is to realise how far Shakespeare has developed between the plays, both in insight and the power to convey insight. For of the three speeches it is only B which presents us with a mind that is convincingly real in its sufferings, weaknesses and delusions, and only in B does the poetry owe nothing to conventional, preconceived theatrical effects.

The movement in A is, as I have already suggested, not flexible; it is stereotyped, following the customary lines of the fairly routine dramatic blank verse of Shakespeare's early period.

> O coward conscience, how thou did'st afflict me!
> The lights burn blue. It is now dead midnight.
> Cold fearful drops stand on my trembling flesh...

There are no effects here which ask for a precise response. The language altogether lacks that distinctive sharpness which makes us read creatively, and we move easily over the surface, as Shakespeare is doing himself. The cold fearful drops seem a very easily found touch, and 'trembling flesh' has equally found its way into the poetry without much effort. But perhaps a more important point to note is that while the speech is mainly taken up with an inner debate, as Richard gradually realises that he *has* a conscience, and that his conscience terrifies him, the poetry as a whole fails to suggest the spontaneous movement of a mind. The construction of the speech is mechanical, not natural—in this sense the passage is 'external'. As Richard begins his inner debate, it becomes clear that Shakespeare is too interested in purely verbal parallels and antitheses, in making neat phrases (the likeness in this respect to the passage from *The Merchant of Venice* may be noted). For instance, the structure of the lines

> My conscience hath a thousand several tongues,
> And every tongue brings in a several tale,
> And every tale condemns me for a villain,

does not follow the natural contours of speech carrying emotion, but rather fits a pattern; the stylisation seems an arbitrary device to get a preconceived effect of eloquence culminating with the word 'villain'. The speech is full of such patterns, and ultimately their effect is to weaken the impact of the poetry rather than strengthen it; they have nothing to do with any precise detail of response that we must make, and any impression we may have of a correspondence between Richard's tortured self-questionings and the balanced reiteration of the phrasing rapidly gives way before the much stronger impression that Shakespeare is using these word-patterns for their own sake. They are part of his stock of eloquent effects.

> Perjury, perjury in the high'st degree;
> Murder, stern murder, in the dir'st degree...

There is little sense of intimacy in these lines, of a poignant moment of self-revelation; the means of expression are too close to theatrical declamation. The figurative language throughout is drawn from the Elizabethan poet's stock of tropes ('My conscience hath a thousand several tongues', Richard's sins 'Throng to the bar, crying all "Guilty, guilty"'), and there should be no difficulty in picking these out for comment in class discussion. What still remains to be said about the passage, I think, is that it has generally the effect of a *tour de force*—it clearly asks to be played up to the hilt, uninhibitedly. An actor who is not prepared to do this and looks for subtleties will certainly not manage to make a success of the speech, which, of course, applies to the whole play. *Richard III* is most successful in the theatre if the characters are allowed to retain a stylised quality, not fully human (this was, I think, admirably done in the film starring Laurence Olivier). In this vision of unmitigated Macchiavellian evil, the blood and horror are stage blood and horror, quite different from the blood and horror in *Macbeth*. The *tour de force* quality is recognisable in this speech in the uncomplicated extremes of feeling envisaged (one can hardly say 'presented'), in the way the fairly simple devices are liberally turned on. This is tragedy done with youthful exuberance, and, read in the right spirit, it can be enjoyed for what it is.

But in the speech from *Macbeth* the poetry follows the inner movements of a mind which is intimately understood, at a moment of real personal crisis. The feeling, the 'atmosphere' of the exact moment is wonderfully caught as Macbeth, lacking the determination of his wife and inwardly uncertain of himself, tries to work out the probable consequences of murdering Duncan.

> If it were done when 'tis done, then 'twere well
> It were done quickly...

This is the rapid, tense speech of someone under almost unbearable stress (the way the speech-movement is played off against the blank verse structure to get this effect is as far as possible from the 'patterns' of the *Richard III* speech). Macbeth is incomparably more alive than Bosola, with his rather stilted exclamations, or Richard, with his measured rhetoric. Macbeth is telling himself that he is going to weigh up the consequences of murdering Duncan as a cool, calculating criminal, to think purely in terms of material cause and effect. He is prepared to forget about ('jump') the life to come, and ignore moral and religious scruples: is it going to be worth his while to kill Duncan in terms of the benefits he can expect from the crime in this life? But, at this stage of the play, he is not yet 'supp'd full with horrors'. He cannot think of the crime without the most anguished apprehension, and in the speech we can sense his rapid pulse-beat, his instinctive physical horror of the impending crisis. Whatever he tells himself, he still *feels* morally. What he would like to commit, he says, would be a crime in which the consequences are somehow averted:

> if th'assassination
> Could trammel up the consequence, and catch
> With his surcease, success...

but what he expresses here is an overpowering conviction that the consequences can only be averted by a miracle. 'Trammel', a word typical of the mature Shakespeare in its marvellously appropriate suggestiveness, means 'tangle up' as in weaving. If the consequences could somehow be tangled up, out of this confusion might come success. But the effect of the language is to make us realise how little Macbeth is able to visualise a neatly worked-out, deftly executed and unpunished crime: if the consequences could be tangled up, out of this confusion, by a desperate, lucky effort, he might 'catch' success (the expressive placing of the word suggests the desperateness of the chancy effort, and this physical movement is tellingly contrasted with the different physical movement of trammelling). The effect of 'surcease, success', a characteristic, daring use of language, is to force the reader (or actor) to pronounce the word 'success' with just the right longing triumph. If only

> this blow
> Might be the be-all and the end-all,—here,
> But here, upon this bank and shoal of time,
> We'd jump the life to come...

Pathetically (if the word is applicable) Macbeth wants to get everything over quickly, and live in peace and contentment—in this life, at any rate. But 'this bank and shoal of time' is a disquieting phrase from someone who is prepared to 'jump the life to come', and, as Macbeth goes on to consider the inexpediency of killing Duncan, his language belongs less and less to his pretended character of the cool, calculating criminal. 'Even-handed Justice' seems too loaded with moral feeling to stand as a detached description of cause and effect, and, as Macbeth reflects that killing a good king is likely to make his future course all the more difficult, his instinctive horror of the crime and his overpowering sense of guilt take hold of him. He imagines the public outcry ('Pity') at the murder, something bound to trouble Duncan's successor, but what he sees, in Dr Leavis's words, is 'a vision, dread and inescapable, of an outraged moral order vindicated by supernatural sanctions':

> his virtues
> Will plead like angels, trumpet-tongu'd, against
> The deep damnation of his taking-off;
> And pity, like a naked new-born babe,
> Striding the blast, or heaven's cherubims, hors'd
> Upon the sightless couriers of the air,
> Shall blow the horrid deed in every eye,
> That tears shall drown the wind.

Macbeth's 'conscience-tormented imagination, quick with the terror of the supernatural' transforms the meek Duncan's virtues and the general pity at his brutal murder into gigantic and appalling avengers of justice. Pity, which we normally think of as gentle and passive in its operation ('a naked new-born babe') suddenly becomes a titanic figure, 'striding the blast' (one feels Macbeth's mounting terror with this phrase), and he sees a host of angels and a cataclysmic flood of tears. The gathering conviction behind the speech ('the deep damnation of his taking-off') is irresistible. Macbeth is drawn on by a power far stronger than his rationalising mind, his sense of guilt, and it is a measure of the speech's effect on us that the revelation it contains has nothing about it that we can dismiss as 'superstition'. The element of fantasy in the vision does nothing to weaken its impact, or make us—as certainly would have been the result with a lesser poet—take the revelation less seriously. Macbeth's profoundest being revolts against the murder. It is a remarkable art which can make us aware of profoundest being in any case, and perhaps when we reflect how Shakespeare has shown us a Macbeth confused, misinterpreting his fear and unconscious of the real nature of his feelings, the speech, in its psychological and moral insight, seems more remarkable still. In the way it follows the movements of a mind, its delusions and involuntary inner promptings at a crucial moment, it could hardly form a greater contrast to the speech from *Richard III* with its external rhetorical structure. With the last words quoted above, Macbeth is closer to real insight into his situation than at any other time, and he begins to see his own ambition ('vaulting ambition') in its true proportions. It is like a spur which he has to apply to himself in order to galvanise himself into action; it is uncertain to hit his target, he may grasp nothing. This is the point at which Lady Macbeth enters to 'chastise him with the valour' of her tongue. After analysing the speech, the class should certainly be taken, however briefly, through the Macbeths' following debate, in which Macbeth feebly tries to temporise with his wife, and finally, responding to a trivial taunt, suppresses as far as he can his inner horror of the murder—a horror which is all the stronger for not being clearly recognised and understood.[1]

[1] In connection with this speech, it is useful to look at Lady Macbeth's very acute summing-up of her husband's character in Act I, Scene v, lines 16–25.

CHAPTER 5

Two Epitaphs by Ben Jonson

On page xvii I remarked that, as students *sometimes* err in criticism because of lack of 'background' knowledge, the teacher of practical criticism should be careful to choose exercises in which there seems least likelihood of this happening. Another obvious desideratum of practical criticism exercises at the beginning stage is that, where comparisons are involved, the student should be as little encumbered as possible with questions of differences of convention and kind in poetry. At a later stage we will be in a position to make comparisons between poems of very different sorts, and ask what, in their different idioms and manners, the poets have been able to achieve. But at present, comparisons which involve similar poems, where differences in quality can be considered most directly and simply, will suit us best. I have chosen the Ben Jonson poems (Exercise 4) because of this—they go so naturally together—and also because, unlike the Wordsworth/ Hartley Coleridge and Keats/Hood examples we have been looking at, no absolutely clear-cut judgment in favour of one poem is called for. Our final judgment will be more delicately balanced, and we shall find a good deal that we like in the 'inferior' poem.

The tone of these poems is distinctively personal, especially the second. The first might conceivably have been written by someone else, but I think that even in this poem we feel a strongly marked personality behind the writing. George Orwell said in his essay on Dickens that 'when one reads any strongly individual piece of writing, one has the impression of seeing a face somewhere behind the page', and the same is true of Jonson's best poems. Consider, for example, how the poet has made the Biblical allusion completely and naturally his own in 'Child of my right hand and joy'. The line glances at the Bible, and this ought to be explained, as Benjamin was

Jacob's favourite son and Benjamin is clearly the name of Jonson's son. But, even if we didn't know this, we would still know from the line that there was a very special relationship between the poet and this son. There is no strained sense of something having been imported from outside. Only a strongly individual poet can use an allusion, or, if you like, borrow a thought, in this way.

The personal tone is, as I have said, less strongly marked in the first poem. The right words to describe *On My First Daughter* seem to be 'gentle', 'tactful'. The child has hardly been alive; she had no time to grow into a distinct person, and the sense of loss is not concentrated by any developed relationship between the child and the poet. The father finds comfort in the religious reflection that all heaven's gifts are heaven's due—indeed she has been like a gift, offered and taken away again, not something the father has had time to make his own. The recognition that the mother's sufferings are greater seems not in the least clumsy, and not at all—as some readers of the poem are apt to say—a hard-boiled admission by the poet that he 'doesn't care'. The child is, at this age, closer to the mother; she has borne the pain and felt the joy of childbirth so recently, and she, more than the father, needs comforting. There seems to me no difficulty in accepting this as a relevant fact when reading the poem. Just the right amount of feeling is expressed. The idea of the child's innocence produces the charming fancy of the virgin-train, and 'the daughter of their youth' strikes just the right note of intimacy: the death is especially poignant as this child has been the child of their youthful love. Perhaps because the poem expresses a tempered grief, some of the students who did the comparison for me were inclined to write it off as 'cold', 'insensitive'. It is not as immediate as the second poem (the ending is rather conventional) but it is not empty of emotion. *On My First Daughter* is a sensitively tactful rendering of a certain kind of sadness which we should have no difficulty in recognising as sadness.

But the second poem was clearly written in much greater

distress. It is far more strongly felt, and for many readers besides myself it must be one of Jonson's most moving poems. If I had to defend Jonson against the charge of being the ideal laureate, decent, responsible, but rather conscious of formal dignity, rather needing to have every fold of his garment in place before speaking on any subject, I would not choose *On My First Daughter* as my starting point. I would certainly choose *On His First Son*. The idea of fate, which plays an important part in this poem, is a dangerous one in poems about death—especially intimate ones. It often leads to something false, distorting or feeble, and we tend to suspect the poet who mentions fate when he is speaking of the death of someone close to him. But we can tell, even from the first four lines which introduce the thought, that there is going to be no let-down. The deliberate, moving, submissive tone is caught too well for us to expect a failure, and, as Jonson contrasts his own feelings with the disaster he knows he must learn to live with, his touch does not falter for an instant. He reviews the thoughts which ought to help him reconcile himself to his loss, and comfort and strengthen him. He could reason away grief, he says, if only he could lose his fatherly feelings (the sense of 'O could I lose all father now', which careless readers are liable to misconstrue). The child has escaped the certain miseries of adult life. But when he is trying to comfort himself by thinking of the miseries his son will never suffer ('world's and flesh's rage', and, inescapably, age) we realise not how fortunate the child is now, but how important the child's innocence has been to Jonson, and how little he can afford to do without it. The lines

> To have so soon 'scaped world's and flesh's rage,
> And if no other misery, yet age...

are moving not because of their logical value as argument, but because of the tenderness they express for childish innocence. They are full of Jonson's characteristic pessimistic sense of life—adult life, that is—and we know from them why the child was so precious to him. He makes no attempt to answer

CHAPTER 6

An Early Draft of Blake's 'London'

A very good opening for close analysis is always provided when there exists an early draft (or drafts) of a great poem. Few things can deepen our understanding more than to consider the revisions the poet has made, changing words, rearranging stanzas, altering effects, modifying rhythms. It is almost as though we were being given a demonstration of practical criticism by the poet himself. We can learn how he weighs the meanings and effects of words, as he searches for language which will have precisely the impact he wants. We can see how much difference, sometimes, is made by the changing of a single word (compare the change Hardy made in *The Voice*, to be discussed later, Chapter 13 and Exercise 12 B).

A large number of early versions of Blake's poems is extant, and because his poetry is unusually concentrated he lends himself to our purposes particularly well. Blake has, of course, a reputation for obscurity, and perhaps some reservation should be made about this last statement. In the well-known case of *The Tyger*, which underwent many revisions, it seems clear that Blake gave up the struggle to write a completely coherent poem that satisfied him in every respect. The results are obscure, in the sense that we cannot discover the poem's meaning from the poem as it stands. They are impressive, because an important meaning is obviously there somewhere, but the uncertainties are too great for us to respond securely. But this reservation still leaves us with a number of poems which are entirely free from these difficulties, poems in which Blake's disturbing, penetrating insights are unequivocally expressed. *London* is one of these (Exercise 5). It seems to me perfectly accessible to students at the stage presumed in the exercises in this book, and undoubtedly the poem to send people to who are reading Blake for the first time.[1] True, the

---

[1] There are more early drafts of *London* than the one I discuss here.

poem is a 'vision', and supernatural or visionary things take place, notably in the third stanza. But the word 'vision' tends to intimidate us unnecessarily. It suggests something remote, abstruse, arbitrary and eccentric, and none of these descriptions fits *London*. We can almost do without the word altogether, for in the opening stanza Blake is describing an actual walk through the streets of London, and the visionary or metaphorical part of the poem grows so naturally out of this beginning that there are no difficult transitions into another kind or level of expression. This is typical of Blake's most successful poems—compare *A Poison Tree*, in which the tree seems to 'grow' irresistibly out of the first stanza. *London* is convincingly a nightmare. It is close enough to actuality to have the terrifying reality of a nightmare, and the element of unreal heightening allows Blake all the concentrating suggestiveness of metaphor which he uses with unforgettable power in phrases like 'the mind-forg'd manacles', 'runs in blood down palace walls'.

The second stanza remains unchanged in the final version. The word 'dirty' becomes 'charter'd' in the first stanza, there is an alteration in the third stanza, and considerable rearrangement in the last stanza. These alterations are not uncertain attempts to hit a target (as the alterations appear to be in the case of *The Tyger*). Blake was, I think, very clear about his intentions by the time he wrote version A, and his revisions here are part of an assured attempt to find exactly the right language to produce the effects he knows he wants. In the first two stanzas, there is a good deal of reiteration and some beginning students, determined eye-readers, have pronounced this a sign of weakness in the poem—a mere patterning for the sake of external effects, to make it poetry rather than prose. But the effect is not external. The reiteration is one of Blake's means of achieving tone—the intensely depressed tone with a compassionate edge to its indignation which no one who has really responded to the poem will forget. In the first stanza, Blake originally reiterated 'dirty', but his revision seems to me superior. 'Dirty' is more commonplace and 'charter'd' (students often misread this as 'charted') has a sardonic bitterness which makes a far more telling introduction to the poem. The word means 'privileged', 'licensed'; this, Blake is saying, is the city which has all the benefits, the privileges, of our marvellous, advanced civilisation, but it fills me with revulsion. The feeling is intensified, not weakened, by the repetition, as the poet wanders dejectedly through streets which have nothing attractive or refreshing in them. This depression is not in the least wilful or self-regarding; it is the depression of heightened awareness, and in the next two lines we seem to sense, in the repeated 'mark', the keen glance of the poet as he picks out the essential traits in the faces of passers-by. In the second stanza, the reiteration is used to produce the remarkable build-up to the climactic phrase, 'mind-forg'd manacles'; the effect of the movement is to get the very most out of this phrase which, in its vivid, passionate perceptiveness, is one that only Blake could have found. The first three lines tell us that this is a general blight (the reiteration helps, I think, to suggest that the realisation is forced onto the poet: the misery crowds in upon him) and the last sums up the nature of the blight in this astonishingly concentrated description. The manacles are forged by the mind; they are not material, not easily recognised, and they are elusive. But they are forged, as solidly real and constricting as iron chains. One of the things this phrase does, I think, is to make us realise, in a way we never knew before, just how entirely the 'mind' can hold life in bondage. There is a shock of recognition as we read the line; there is nothing second-hand, nothing ready-made in this perception. Even the placing of 'hear' adds something. The word is obviously working, not just inertly filling out the sense, and to me it suggests an important fact about the forged manacles. They are something we hear or sense beneath the ordinary surface of life, something deeply rooted which the sufferers, in their helpless misery, are only partially aware of.

In the third stanza, where the imagery becomes more explicitly visionary or nightmarish, there is an important change. In the first version, the main effect is there: the chimney-sweeper's cry metaphorically blackens the churches, but the power of the line resides mostly, I think, in the fantastic vision of the chimney-sweepers exhaling over the city the soot that has filled their lungs, and the force of the line increases when we recall how smoke-blackened the churches of modern cities really are. This is, then, not just an arbitrary flight of the imagination; it is a metaphor which keeps in touch with the actual world, and the effect would be largely lost if we weren't reminded of an actual impression, the dismal dirty ugliness of these buildings. Blake tells us that this ugliness has been created at the expense—the savage expense—of human life. But he must have felt that the two line-endings on 'walls' in the same stanza were unfortunate, and that the alteration would have to be made in the second line. 'Palace walls' is necessary because the soldiers normally stand guard outside the palaces, the blood is running *down*, and the walls are the imposing exterior which the palaces present to the populace; whereas the church walls can be dispensed with. The alteration he made is in every way an improvement. 'Blackening' still keeps the suggestion originally made in 'blackens o'er' that the chimney-sweepers' breath is blackening the churches, but it strengthens the non-literal, moral connotation as well. The most important change, however, is the addition of 'appalls', a word which the reader instinctively feels is 'right', though its effectiveness is not easy to explain. The line might mean that the 'church', that is the priest and congregation as well as the building, are appalled, i.e. horrified, by the sufferings of the chimney-sweepers, though they are really partly responsible for them. But, in view of the general drift or tenor of the poem, it is rather hard to accept this explanation. It is much easier to believe that the clergy and congregation are indifferent, whatever pious clichés they may utter about charity, and that it is an ideal church which is being referred to. The grimy exterior is an accusation which metaphorically horrifies the ideal church, not the actual church: the actual church is made appalling, in fact, rather than 'appalled'.

Whether Blake also intended us to find another meaning here, a pall of smoke covering the churches, is probably up to the reader to decide. There are no linguistic grounds for taking the word in this sense—in fact, 'appall' means to make pale—but Blake didn't always write according to the rules, and was I believe quite capable of suiting himself on an occasion like this; in which case the word would be a kind of pun. It is, at any rate, tempting to feel that the pall of smoke over the city was in Blake's mind when he found this word. This is a case in which there is genuinely some latitude for interpretation, and such cases are by no means rare in poetry. It can sometimes be a delicate matter to decide just how far we ought to carry conjecture. The most important thing is for the critic to be alert enough to recognise when he has reached such a point, and to know when he is passing beyond what ought to be immediately evident to every reader; and he must make it clear that his preferences are individual, and that there is more than one possibility. I will return to this question later. Suffice it to say at present that no criticism will be correctly tempered unless it is alive to possible differences in interpretation; and, conversely, unless it is alive to the fact that each reader must make a decision, one way or the other. In the present case, there is not perhaps a great deal of difference involved. Whichever way we read this detail, the lines are horrific in the best possible sense. They are shocking, and the shock goes home.

The last stanza contains the most extensive alterations.

> But most the midnight harlot's curse
> Through every dismal street I hear,
> Weaves around the marriage hearse
> And blasts the new born infant's tear

becomes

> But most thro' midnight streets I hear
> How the youthful harlot's curse
> Blasts the new born infant's tear,
> And blights with plagues the marriage hearse.

I don't think it is simply my familiarity with the final version that makes the earlier version sound less effectively modulated.

The more definite syntax of the final version, even, helps to carry greater conviction and impetus—the first version at first reading already seems comparatively nerveless: it is so evidently provisional. And when we look at the changes in more detail, we can see what a transformation Blake has worked on his first draft. 'And blasts the new born infant's tear' is a very strong and characteristic line, but how much more tellingly its power is used in the final version, where it balances the last line in a culminating indictment (notice, too, how much Blake has gained by the placing of 'blasts' in the final version). In the first version some of this power is lost because the line is less effectively led up to. 'Weaves around the marriage hearse' seems to me the weakest line in the first draft. 'Weaves around' is a comparatively forced metaphor (perhaps it owes something to the conventional 'weaving a spell') and it fails to suggest vividly enough a sinister, blighting, corrupting process. It is far feebler than 'blights with plagues', and the line altogether fails to balance the final line in impact, which it must do if the stanza is to close convincingly. In the first two lines, Blake has dropped the rather ordinary 'every dismal street' (after all, we have had this before in the first stanza), and substituted 'midnight streets', which has the semi-secretive, sinister overtones he wants. And 'midnight harlot' has become 'youthful harlot', both more poignant and more full of the burning indignation which lies behind the poem. This last example illustrates very well how a poet can 'realise' his intentions in revision. The fact that the harlot is a midnight harlot doesn't matter nearly as much as the fact that she is *youthful*. It is the appalling callous waste of human life which horrifies Blake. The harlot is no longer a conventional tart walking the dismal streets; she is touchingly young, her innocence only recently lost in misery and cynicism.

There has, of course, been a great deal of poetry written on this theme. Dislike of life in large modern cities has been one of the commonest themes in the poetry of this century. But I know of no comparable modern poem which has the emotional force of Blake's poem. At a later time, when students are more familiar with modern poetry, they can be asked to ponder the difference between *London* and the comparable parts of T. S. Eliot's *The Waste Land*. Eliot can give us the boredom, the ugliness of a modern city, the repulsion it inspires; how different this life is, in its meaningless tedium, from the life civilised men ought to lead. But Blake's repulsion has a different quality; it is more direct and passionate. He is not bored, he is outraged, and his anger is of the kind that can only spring from the strongest compassion and love. His sources of inspiration are deeper than Eliot's and he, more than Eliot, can shake us out of ordinary, everyday protective complacencies. To read this poem is to have our own capacity for compassion increased.

But what matters most for our present purposes is that Blake's *London* does not have to be read against a background of other poetry to be fully understood. We do not need to compare other poems in order to see its full greatness. Our own experience should be enough for this. It is hard to think of poetry which is more universal in its appeal, and more timeless. For almost every reader will feel this is, in spite of its date, a distinctively 'modern' poem; not 'modern' in the sense that it contains modern symbols, or modern ambiguities, but modern in the sense that it is so obviously contemporary, so obviously an insight into something we know and can recognise. As I have picked out T. S. Eliot's *The Waste Land* for unfavourable (or partly unfavourable) comparison with Blake—and it is not a very original thing to find fault with *The Waste Land* these days—I will finish by quoting Eliot's description of this timeless quality in Blake, a description which it would be difficult to improve upon: Blake has

...a peculiar honesty, which, in a world too frightened to be honest, is peculiarly terrifying. It is an honesty against which the whole world conspires, because it is unpleasant. Blake's poetry has the unpleasantness of great poetry. Nothing that can be called morbid or abnormal or perverse, none of the things which exemplify the sickness of an epoch or a fashion, has this quality; only those things which, by some extraordinary labour of simplification, exhibit the essential sickness or strength of the human soul.

CHAPTER 7

Relevance and Irrelevance in Response: Another Blake Poem

On page 19 I touched briefly on the dangers of irrelevant ingenuity in the interpretation of a poem, and I should like to say rather more about the problem in this chapter. Every poem we read is in a sense a test of relevance for us, and relevance in response and reading ability are so nearly synonymous that there may seem, at first sight, not much point in singling out the topic for separate discussion. Relevance is another word for what we have been concerned with all along. But it does seem to me necessary at some point to make relevance explicitly an issue in practical criticism; that is, as opposed to irrelevant ingenuity and speculation. The temptation to irrelevance of this sort is a strong one, and while some poetry doesn't give much scope for it, there is certainly a good deal which does. Most of us start with some awe of the complexity of poetry, and some people have a *penchant* for irrelevant cleverness—metaphors and symbols are for them an appetite. This misdirected intelligence (and often, enthusiasm) needs to be guided, and this is, like so much in practical criticism, a matter for constant alertness. An example, though it won't 'solve' the problem, can fix a warning in the mind (in the way examples can if they are properly handled) and help to create this alertness. There are, it needs to be added, difficult cases of genuine uncertainty in poetry, where more than one interpretation is possible; and a competent reader must have experience in these cases, and know how to recognise them.

How do we decide when our interpretation of a poem is beginning to leave the poem and turn into something of our own? How do we sense the point at which our own mind is no longer engaging with the poet's mind? This is a point which even great literary critics have sometimes failed to recognise, and

T. S. Eliot has described this failure in Coleridge: the passage is important enough to us to deserve quoting at some length:

Coleridge, again, whose natural abilities, and some of whose performances, are probably more remarkable than those of any other modern critic, cannot be estimated as an intelligence completely free. The nature of the restraint in his case is quite different from that which limited the seventeenth-century critics, and is much more personal. Coleridge's metaphysical interest was quite genuine, and was, like most metaphysical interest, an affair of his emotions. But a literary critic should have no emotions except those immediately provoked by a work of art... Coleridge is apt to take leave of the data of criticism, and arouse the suspicion that he has been diverted into a metaphysical hare and hounds. His end does not always appear to be to return to the work of art with improved perceptions and intensified, because more conscious, enjoyment; his centre of interest changes, his feelings are impure...

While we do not expect to be liable to the particular kind of irrelevance which led Coleridge away from the literature he was reading, the last sentence especially is worth remembering in a practical criticism class. The only real test for relevance is the inward one. Does this suggestion really fit the poem? Does it seem to illuminate the poem, to be genuinely sympathetic to the feeling in that place? It is only by self-questioning along these lines that we can settle our doubts; the more practised we are in putting these questions to ourselves, the more relevant and assured our reading will be. I have found Blake's *The Human Abstract* (Exercise **6**) helpful in making students aware of certain dangers of irrelevance—the effects caused by inexperience with metaphor, such as irrelevant ingenuity and speculation. The poem follows effectively after *London*; it has a similar kind of inspiration, and embodies a similar protest (the original ending, which we will look at, makes this very plain, apart from the poem itself), but it is very different in its way of conveying meaning. It is altogether more abstract (as the title suggests), more entirely metaphorical. As far as I am concerned, the poem is, perhaps for this reason, slightly less powerful than *London*. But this doesn't mean that it is in any sense weak or lacking in immediacy of its own kind, and it contains effects which Blake could only have achieved in this mode. And, if it is more 'symbolic' than *London*, it is still entirely comprehensible as it stands—there is no problem in interpretation which should be insurmountable. Less directly than *London*, perhaps, it still appeals to our sense of what life is like, and asks us to use this sense in understanding its statements.

When asked to comment on the success of the poem, a good many readers always express bewilderment. 'Only the cognoscenti could understand this poem'; 'There is a maze of images and symbols'. It is common for readers to believe that any explanation of the meaning of the poem has *got* to be complicated, 'difficult' and remote, and behind most of the perplexity there lies, I believe, the feeling that understanding the poem involves some kind of abstruse process, some obscure trick which ordinary intelligence, in possession of ordinary resources, cannot really be expected to perform. The readers who produced complicated cat's-cradles-like discussions of the significance of brains and trees, or those who ingeniously begged the question by saying that the poet is trying to reproduce a perplexed, confused state of mind in the poem, clearly believed they were being asked to read some kind of cipher. There is, on the other hand, an opposite tendency to turn the poem confidently into a recognisable commonplace—'The evils of the world grow out of our own hearts, and the poet tells us to understand ourselves and eliminate that evil'—but as statements of this sort are, in my experience, never related very closely to the poem, and fairly obviously reveal no detailed understanding of it, I take it that this is simply the same kind of bewilderment I have just noted, under a disguise. Besides, no poem which is going to hold our attention for very long can be satisfactorily described in terms of a cliché. To reach the good poems needs a determined stringency which will make us continually sift our language, reject worn, tired, second-hand phrasing and work till we have found exactly the right phrase, which is always a new, a fresh one.

One of the more encouraging reactions I have noticed to the poem is that most readers recognise, at least, that it is free from poetic commonplace. More intelligent readers have no difficulty in seeing that there is something too distinctive about the poem for it to be dismissed as waywardly eccentric. But reading the poem has nothing in common with reading a cipher. We don't have to attribute arbitrary significance to things, and by using our normal sense of the meanings of words, and by careful reading, we can respond to the language of the poem as the author wants us to respond. This means, of course, an avoidance of the temptation to jump to arbitrary conclusions, a readiness to see individual details in the light of the whole poem, and a realisation that sensitive reading is a much surer guide than juggling with patterns. As I have been at pains to explain in chapter 3, movement, tone give as much guidance as to how to 'take' the details as systematic relation between the images: we must try to sense the mood, the atmosphere, at the same time as we are trying to decide the intention, and not separate the processes. Reading a poem is a delicate exploration, not a relentless process of ferreting out patterns and schemes of meaning.

The first stanza is not difficult, though it may be taken in two ways. It can be a simple though sardonic statement of fact by the poet, the 'we' including the poet and the comfortable, secure reader. Or it can be thought of as a statement by one of the capitalists, one of the exploiters (or whatever word we care to use) who feature in the poem. In this case, there could be inverted commas round the first stanza. This is, I think, a minor difference in interpretation. In the second case the reader is less explicitly involved, though, later, he can hardly escape being implicated in the last line of the poem; the human brain, with its capabilities, is what we all possess. In either case, the first stanza is *not* composed of smart paradoxes, as readers who saw the stanza by itself tended to believe (nothing could be further from this poem, or from its author, than conscious cleverness). The second stanza begins Blake's commentary on the situation revealed in the first stanza, and his analysis (if that is the right word) of what this kind of thinking and this kind of attitude must inevitably lead to. Beneath the surface of security and respectability, with its watchwords 'Pity', 'Mercy', this is what is really happening. 'And mutual fear brings peace'; there is no doubt at all that Blake means a phoney peace produced by an underlying rottenness, something Blake hates and despises. It is only the peace of mutual fear, and naturally in these conditions the selfishness which has caused the fear and peace is bound to increase. A process is set in motion. The law, which keeps vigilance over the social order, becomes cruel, and the metaphor in which Blake tells us this has all his characteristic insight:

> ...Cruelty knits a snare,
> And spreads his baits with care...

The potency of these lines lies, I think, in the way they suggest stealth. Cruelty is not necessarily a thing which bursts upon us and shocks and surprises us. It is always on the watch, and it can move subtly and deceptively under various moral disguises; cruelty, the lines make us realise, is most dangerous when it deludes. The metaphor could only have been found by a man who had made the most profound and intent observation of human behaviour. The next lines clearly describe the persecuting spirit.

> He sits down with holy fears
> And waters the ground with tears...

The establishment, the social system, which is, Blake says, some people's means of protecting their property and position, has found a pseudo-moral, pseudo-religious justification for protecting itself. 'Holy' is a sarcasm. The context makes this abundantly clear, and 'waters the ground with tears' beautifully parodies the false piety, the exaggerated emotional hypocrisy of persecution. In the next two lines, 'Humility' takes root underneath his foot, and this is *false* humility. 'Underneath his foot' suggests that humility begins humbly, by abasing itself, but it also suggests that this humility is really morally 'low', really contemptible; it is an evil growth which springs from beneath cruelty's foot.

But already the main metaphor of the poem—the tree—is

beginning to appear. Like the poison tree in the poem of that name, it seems to have suggested itself, rather than to have been deliberately put there by Blake. There is nothing arbitrary or external about it. It allows Blake to concentrate a variety of suggestions he needs in the poem, most of all the suggestion of growth, of a sinister, irresistible process taking place. The tree grows out of the imagery of the third stanza, and it carries its meaning effortlessly.

In the next stanza the 'dismal shade' of Mystery spreads over Cruelty's head. I do not think Blake was making unreasonable demands of his readers in expecting them to understand that 'Mystery' is false, abstract doctrine supporting false morality, not sincerely felt or believed in. We have been prepared for this already by 'holy fears', and know that the poem is about moral and religious hypocrisy. Besides, the tenor of the phrase 'dismal shade / Of Mystery' is unmistakable, as is the sarcastic play in 'Mystery' (the holy mystery and the falsely mysterious which cannot bear examination and is probably non-existent). There follow the creatures which flourish in the shade of the poison tree. The sinister note, which has been quietly but perceptibly present in the poem so far, is more explicitly accentuated here. The caterpillar, the fly and the raven have given trouble to a number of my student readers, but this again I believe to be the result of inappropriate (and unimaginitive) expectations. There is no need to try to relate these creatures to specific things or people, as the too literal-minded are apt to do; no need, in other words, to try to revisualise them as something else. They are, as the increasingly metaphorical nature of the poem helps us to realise, directly evocative. They stand for corruption and explain themselves. Blake is comparing the process of corruption in society with the process of corruption in nature, and the imagery, with its concentrated atmosphere of moral depravity, will lose its evocative power if we look for specific equivalents. No strained or unnatural act of the imagination is necessary to see this. Imagine, for instance, how the poetry would be spoiled if foot-notes were supplied giving exact explanations. The fruit of Deceit is near to a familiar proverbial phrase and should give trouble to no one, though we can notice how effectively Blake has taken up this phrase and filled it with new, forceful meaning (it is 'ruddy and sweet to eat', a vivid rendering of corrosive, self-indulgent luxury). The Raven, as in much other poetry, stands for some ultimate evil. 'Its thickest shade' wonderfully hints at the hidden viciousness that is at the centre of the hypocrisy and high-minded selfishness that rule the social establishment. The phrase is a culminating last touch to this penetrating vision of the motives and desires that often underlie the respectable and dignified surface of law and order.

Finally, the Gods of the earth and sea search for the tree and fail to find it, for it grows in the human brain. The gods, we gather (and there should be no problem here), are natural deities whose duty it is to see that everything is running properly, and we accept them for the purposes of the poem. Nature—as opposed to man—is outraged at the existence of this man-made corruption. It is interesting to compare the ending as Blake originally wrote it, in which the gods discover the tree and give an account of their findings. What happens in the original version, it seems to me, is that the poem changes its character; the last seven lines are more in the vein of *London*, a direct comment on society. While the last stanza is very fine in its own right (the stark bitterness of the last line especially) Blake must have felt that an unwanted transition took place. There is no need to explain the 'mystery' (when the word occurs for the second time, in the original version, it seems to refer more to the general paradoxical confusion of the whole situation). The poem certainly gains in tautness in the final version. More, the change which Blake made gives the line

> There grows one in the human brain

a new and striking prominence. There is now—as there wasn't in the first version—a shock of realisation for the reader. The perspective is suddenly and disquietingly changed. So far, the processes described in the poem, even if we include ourselves in the 'we' in the first stanza, are ones which we can, without much difficulty, think of as affecting society but taking place outside ourselves. We can almost make ourselves detached observers and critics. But the last line dramatically changes our involvement. This is something which happens within, something to which we are liable, and the disease is more terrible, less easily escaped or cured, than we may have imagined. It is worth reflecting how very much inferior the line would have been if Blake had written (considerations of rhyme aside for the moment) 'the human heart'—which is to realise how idiosyncratic, how searching the actual phrase is. There are few poets who can 'find us' so unerringly as Blake. The last line, as it stands in the final version, is one of the chief features which give the poem its timelessness. There is no escape for the reader in the thought that Blake is writing of his own times, and a situation which has now passed. The human brain is not so easily changed; and the persecuting images of false Humility and Cruelty, with his 'holy fears' (the fact that the holy fears of today may not take a religious form doesn't lessen the relevance of the phrase to our times) are as real as when Blake wrote of them. The poem is about something which can happen in any age, and in any organised society.

The words 'moral' and 'psychological' often give trouble in the criticism of poetry—that is, if we don't use them with understanding and discretion. If difficulties over these words have arisen in loose descriptions and formulations, this poem gives a class a good opportunity of discovering how inadequate such ready-made descriptions can be in criticism. Blake's interests in this poem are both moral and psychological—either word by itself will not do. *The Human Abstract* is certainly 'moral', for it makes judgments of moral value; but it has a knowledge of the workings of the human mind which equally deserves to be called 'psychological'. What readers of poetry must be made to realise (it is a long process involving much experience of literature) is that words like 'moral' and 'psychological' tend to have a limiting effect on the person who uses them; whoever uses them unthinkingly will be applying a description to a poem which may not properly fit. A literary critic must be able to use language for his own purposes, getting exactly the sense he wants by using, if necessary, descriptive phrases instead of single words; he must not *be used by* easy, ready-to-hand phrases. But unless difficulties of this sort over these words have arisen, I think a teacher would be better advised not to bring up the topic deliberately. This sort of question is best handled in relation to actual practice—to a loose description made by someone and corrected by a complete analysis of the poem. More abstract, generalised discussion of topics like 'Is poetry moral?' or 'Is poetry psychologically true?' seems to me, especially when they are raised *in vacuo* for their own sake, to give only an illusion of profit and progress.

As Blake will not be appearing in these pages again, I should like to mention that his manuscript poem, *Auguries of Innocence*, taken by itself, forms a very good piece of practical criticism for class discussion. The poem is really a series of gnomic sayings, some of them rather commonplace, but some of them highly individual and striking. Compare:

> The game-cock, clipped and armed for fight,
> Does the rising sun affright...

> Each outcry of the hunted hare
> A fibre from the brain does tear...

> The wild deer, wandering here and there,
> Keep the human soul from care...

The last example seems rather conventional and unilluminating. It doesn't do very much with the familiar idea that it is pleasant and refreshing to see wild animals in their natural freedom. But the other examples, particularly the second, have Blake's power unmistakably. The cruel outrage of cock-fighting is seen in a startlingly new—but right—perspective in the first couplet, and in the second all the inhumanity of the hunt, and the unbearable agony of the sensitive onlooker (whose brain doesn't merely respond to, but is actually damaged by, the hare's cries), are captured in the briefest possible space. There is nothing of English sentimentality about animals in these lines. Poetry like this can make us more sympathetic and more imaginative, and in discussing it we have to discuss our own sympathies and our own opinions. It would be very hard to use Blake as an occasion for turning practical criticism into a sterile exercise in technical method.

CHAPTER 8

Lyrical Grace and Warmth: Two Seventeenth-Century Lyrics

There are plenty of current phrases to describe the seventeenth-century lyric, and they are usually honoured in student essays on the poetry of the period. 'Lyric grace'—'urbane poise'—these are familiar parts of the critical vocabulary. But I believe that a real liking for cavalier love poetry is comparatively rare, and that for many students there lingers a feeling of artificiality about this poetry, whether it be admitted or not. Donne's and Herbert's religious poetry is found more accessible, more easily comprehensible; a man is trying to solve his personal problems, and it is not difficult to sympathise with him. But cavalier verse, with its closer relation to music, its limited material, its more self-conscious manner, seems stilted—a cultivated pleasure for the *literati*, perhaps, but rather remote from real life as we know it. After all, most real life has not much elegance and hardly any poise. Tributes to the seventeenth century lyric tend, in my experience, to sound rather frigid. Of course these objections hold good for a great deal of this poetry—anyone who reads it will from time to time remember Johnson's remarks about 'the makers of little stanzas':

Of these petty compositions [Waller's love poems] neither the beauties not the faults deserve much attention. The amorous verses have this to recommend them, that they are less hyperbolical than those of some other poets. Waller is not always at the last gasp; he does not die of a frown, nor live upon a smile. There is, however, too much love, and too many trifles. Little things are made too important; and the Empire of Beauty is represented as exerting its influence further than can be allowed by the multiplicity of human passions, and the variety of human wants. Such books, therefore, may be considered as showing the world under a false appearance, and, so far as they obtain credit from the young and inexperienced, as misleading expectation, and misguiding practice.

It would be difficult to imagine a more trenchant and better-taken criticism; this prose shows the realistic strength of Johnson's literary taste in every phrase. And, where a good many seventeenth-century lyrics are concerned, I can only echo Johnson and say that they are very slight indeed; they cannot relate very closely or importantly to anything which really matters to us. But there are a number of these poems of which this is not true—poems which we can like without relishing a special taste, and which we need no special frame of mind to enjoy. I have included Exercise 7 in order to try to bring out the qualities of two of these poems and to convince my readers of the truth of my last sentence. The poems also give an opportunity of re-enforcing and enlarging upon some of the points I have been developing in the previous exercises.

The grounds for comparison are strong, since one poem was suggested by the other. The subject at once hints at triviality —the poets are telling us what they like in women's dress. But one of these poems, at least, is something more than an exercise in literary elegance. Most of my students, I find, prefer the second poem to the first. B is sometimes a target for irrelevant objections:

A advocates simplicity, which is quite reasonable, but B likes 'A sweet disorder in the dress' and prefers carelessness to preciseness, which is a bit too much. Surely in dressing up one has to be precise! One should be simple, not affected, as A advocates, but if we are to be careless, it will not do.

B is quite right about this [i.e. his view about disorder] but quite often a careless way of dressing just shows the carelessness of one's character...

Both these comments were written by people who hadn't made any effort to attend to the poem. They have merely taken a prescription from the poem out of its context and commented on what they thought the prescription might mean (both remarks seem to me at about the level of a woman's fashion magazine); they never bothered to discover what the poet meant. In fact, anyone who looks at B closely will understand at once that the poet is *not* asking for slovenliness—he is asking, rather archly, for a pleasing spontaneity and freshness as opposed to studied 'art'. But most readers are able to feel the success of poem B. Notice how cleverly a certain kind of surface titillation or excitement is suggested in words like 'kindles', 'distraction', 'enthrals', tempestuous', 'bewitched'. The poet shows a fastidious skill in his choice of language. He relishes this light, provocative excitement with a touch of good-humoured naughtiness which justifies the poem. But many of my students who liked poem B saw very little in poem A—it seemed, in comparison, empty of content. 'Where is the poetry?' was the main objection:

The poet [in A] expresses his attitude towards feminine beauty in simple language with no comparisons made in the form of similes and metaphors and images of any kind. Thus we do not have a clear picture of what he means when he expresses his feeling that beauty is beauty in simplicity.

No profound meaning can be read between the lines. There is no appeal to the imagination. The meaning is explicit, and the poem is cold.

These comments seem to me instructive, especially in the way they link the supposed coldness and lack of content in the poem with the lack of imagery. B is not exactly rich in metaphor, but some of its success depends on the use of metaphorical language, and perhaps the writers of the comments believed that poetry and metaphor are one and the same thing—a very good example of how a 'tip' for reading (in this case the tip to look for metaphor) can be taken and applied mechanically and unintelligently as a rule, an all-embracing truth. The view, certainly, is not uncommon, and when it crops up it needs to be corrected. Expressiveness in poetry is not always a question of metaphor. What we have here, in fact, is a fairly clear case of eye-reading; the commentators know nothing of the feeling that is conveyed by tone, by movement (notice the betraying phrase 'we do not have a clear picture of what he means' in the first comment). A is anything but empty of feeling. It is, in fact, a far warmer, more vivid poem than B, which, when we look back at it, begins to seem a bit thin and trivial by comparison.

Comments like 'The regular rhythm is catching and

delightful' or, worse, 'The many stops give the poem a jerky effect', 'The ponderous repetitions...and heavy emphasis...' all show a complete deficiency of ear, a complete deafness to the poetry. Even the comment 'The movement is too neat to convey the idea of sweet neglect', which looks in a way more promising, is only a rather mechanical piece of ingenuity. The poet is not trying to *mime* the impression of what he is talking about, to give us a tactual impression of 'sweet neglect' (I suspect this comment originated in a recollection of an earlier analysis of another poem; again, an example of a precedent being mechanically, ritually applied). His expressiveness is not of a tactual sort. It is true that the stanza form is very regular, that lines are balanced in antithesis; but there is no feeling of constraint in the movement. The tones of the voice, on the contrary, are sensitively handled. In lines 1 and 3, the reiterated 'still' (meaning 'always') has a mildly incredulous, reproving emphasis; 'As you were going to a feast'—what an absurd kind of excess! There is no 'heavy moralising emphasis', as one reader found; the poet is precise and controlled in manner, though of course he is being cutting. Those who think the stanza-form is mechanical should look at the slight change of movement in line 3 in contrast to line 1, one of those minor surface details which, in Ben Jonson's poetry, are often so effective. It is this change which gives the lines their naturalness of gesture, as the poet comes to the point in the fourth line. 'Presum'd', the word on which the stanza turns, has just the right, insinuating edge. You may hide your motives cleverly enough, but we can still *feel* that something is wrong. The insinuation is there, too, in the last line, not just in the sense of the words, but in the way in which they are let fall (Jonson is not simply forming a neat pattern with his language).

There is almost a Swiftian suggestion that under a careful, clean façade lies something offensive and unpleasant—the pock-marks, the pimples and perspiration beneath the thick layer of make-up. But Jonson doesn't linger on this suggestion, as Swift might have done. In the next stanza, in refreshing

CHAPTER 9

Emotion and Emotionality:
Herbert's 'Life' and E. B. Browning's
'Irreparableness'

In the nature of things there must always be a temptation for a poet to heighten or magnify his feelings for the sake of effect; to write as though he feels more than he does feel. Few writers probably do this knowingly, and fewer still can consciously keep it up for long. But to heighten one's feelings and be an unconscious party to the operation, to see oneself in a heroic or sympathetic light, is one of the subtlest forms of self-deception, in literature as in life (where surely only the superhuman or the hard-boiled have never practised it at some time), and anyone who reads very much poetry must soon become aware of it, in one way or another. We tend to think of this trait as being a typically nineteenth-century one, though perhaps the nineteenth century only indulged it in its more obvious forms. Few poets have understood the late Romantic variation of this trait as thoroughly as W. B. Yeats, whose early verse is saturated in the late nineteenth-century tradition of the soulful, the beautiful, and whose development necessitated an escape from 'the poetic'. Some of his own remarks on his early poems give a vivid idea of the sort of effort he had to make and how difficult and concentrated it had to be:

...I tried from then on to write of my emotions exactly as they came to me in life, not changing them to make them more beautiful. 'If I can be sincere and make my language natural, and without becoming discursive, like a novelist, and so indiscreet and prosaic,' I said to myself, 'I shall, if good luck or bad luck make my life interesting, be a great poet; for it will be no longer a matter of literature at all.' Yet when I re-read those early poems which gave me so much trouble, I find little but romantic convention, unconscious drama. It is so many years before one can believe enough in what one feels even to know what the feeling is.

The difference between the actual and the dramatised, between emotion and emotionality, is one that must concern a practical criticism class, and it is closely related to a poet's way of using language. The difference will concern us incidentally in many forms, but it should, I think, be made the subject of at least a few exercises. Exercise 8 is, I hope, fairly representative (it also asks us to consider how a conventional figure may be used or abused). The choice of poems may seem rather 'loaded', but as we are at the beginning of our course I believe there is a need for some fairly obvious cases. The students need to know that there is such a thing as a definite critical opinion, and a comparatively simple case may help to give them confidence.

The poems are commonplace in theme: the withering of flowers reminds the poet of the transience of life. This, however dispiriting it sounds, need not kill our interest at the start, for a poet can, by sensitive and tactful handling, make a conventional theme, a poetic commonplace, fresh and individual (if this were not true, a lot of great poetry could never have been written). He may make the commonplace his own; though he may, of course, simply produce another threadbare poem, using the commonplace unimaginatively, clumsily or sententiously. A number of my readers found poem A superior, in that it is 'simple, direct and strongly felt; in B the feelings are less powerful, and the poet is fanciful. Revealingly, there is no fear of death in B, which seems unnatural, and the poet has none of A's richer experience of sadness. B lacks intensity'. There is no difficulty in seeing how these judgments have been arrived at. But, instead of contrasting strong, heartfelt emotion with 'fancy' and whim, I would rather contrast emotion and emotionality: writing which has the modesty, delicacy and humour of a sensitive man who knows the relative worth of what he is saying, and writing in which feeling is simulated or worked up for the occasion. To use Dr Leavis's useful distinction, I should like to contrast poetry in which the content is 'actually presented' with poetry in which the content is merely 'talked about'.

The theme allows a good deal of possible scope for the

tragic, the pathetic and the heroic, especially when the common-place is represented as an incident happening to the poet, and all the evidence is that in A these opportunities have been seized on without any kind of restraint. The tragic and the pathetic are explicitly insisted on; the pang is relished to the full. And everywhere there is evidence too that the supposed situation and events of the poem have not been imaginatively entered into at all—they never even promise to be convincing. The 'incident' of the poem is a feebly sustained fantasy with nothing in it to hold our interest for long. Reading the first four lines, we notice the rather irritatingly pseudo-'dramatic' device, 'that you see' (we don't), and the facile rhymes. 'Singing within myself as bird or bee' is commonplace of the wrong sort (it is certainly not free from the ludicrous), as is 'morn of May' ('fieldwork' is merely clumsy). These stilted phrases are plainly part of a routine ritual; they are part of the rigmarole of poetry, letting us know that we are in the presence of 'the poetic', the nobly uplifting, to which we are expected to defer. But the language is quite incapable of rendering anything with precision; there can be no question of an experience fully en-tered into and completely understood, that is, completely *known*, at every point. We are being invited to share the pang—to take up the posture which we must take up if we are going to respond to the poem (again, conceive of the problems of reading this out to a small, sceptical group of people we are familiar with).

'Decay' (another word put there by exigencies of rhyme?) has met the flowers because they were 'more warmly clasped'. This, in its vague hint that the more we love beauty the quicker it will die, seems to me tear-jerking, and

> sobs are free
> To come instead of songs,

in the sheer awkwardness of its attempt to convey strong emotion, is mawkish. 'Sweet councillors, dear friends'—we are wallowing here, or, inevitably, being rather ridiculous. The plangency is always tinged with eloquence:

> Another, sooth, may do it, but not I

with its tiresomely affected and useless 'sooth', gives way to the pseudo-simplicity of

> My heart is very tired, my strength is low,

typical of the poem in its hint at vast resources of tragic experience just out of sight below the surface. The ending too is characteristic. Perhaps the flowers (though we don't really know) stand for vanished beauty, vanished joys, but the metaphor of the poetess clutching the flowers until her death is pretty unfortunate.

There is, naturally, a good deal that is pleasing and re-assuring in the feeling that one is world-wearied, a noble, sympathetic sufferer in a tragic world. Perhaps Elizabeth Barrett Browning had more excuse than most of us for seeing herself in this way at the time she wrote the poem. But so little is actually presented in the poem to justify the extremes of emotion suggested, and the details are so unreal, that only a reader who was very determined to get from the poem the kind of satisfaction it offers would be able to accept its invitation.[1]

The empty expansiveness of A can be compared with the perfect proportion between feeling and object in B. That is, instead of a dead-set at emotion, the situation and details of the poem are beautifully matched to the feeling the poet wants to arouse. The poem, in contrast to the sprawling emotionality of A, holds itself so well; we might almost say, so sensibly. Nothing is blown up to tragic proportions. The incident is handled lightly, sensitively, even humorously, and the language is fresh and natural.

The opening analogy between the poet's life and the flowers is recognised to be a piece of fancy, and it is treated gently and unpretentiously:

> I made a posie while the day ran by

suggests that the poet is indulging in a pleasant daydream (he forgets that time is running by). He will 'smell' his remnant out and tie his life within this band. This is whimsy, the

---

[1] Other poets have, of course, given a similar sort of invitation more seductively—the early Yeats being one.

fanciful indulgence of a man entranced by the attractiveness of the flowers (and we notice, here and later in the poem, that these are real flowers, as well as being 'emblems'). But he is taken by surprise; the dream leads him where he doesn't expect to go. 'But time did beckon to the flowers'—the euphemism is felicitously judged and exactly befits this incident, in which grave things are gently, prettily acted out. '. . . they / Most cunningly did steal away': the tone is rueful, with a touch of self-critical humour in it, and in the next stanza the poet takes in the significance of the withering of the flowers.

> My hand was next to them, and then my heart:

the analogy comes to him naturally and effortlessly. There is a pang, but it is not crudely forced or insisted on. This is a 'gentle admonition' (admirably chosen phrase), which the poet can take 'in good part'. He knows this is a hint of death, and he senses ('smells') the meaning, but the suspicion is 'sugared': the reminder is not a violent or horrifying one, and the whole incident has a tender poignance which seems to belong to it by its own right, not to have been deliberately injected by the poet. The flowers are delicate in their beauty, and their passing away is too tranquil to inspire soul-rending shudders. The final verse is a pleasing tribute to them. They have a real, independent existence, unlike the flowers in A:

> Farewell, deare flowers, sweetly your time ye spent,
> Fit, while ye liv'd, for smell or ornament,
> And after death for cures...

This, in its sensible, realistic appreciation of the flowers, is so unlike the pseudo-agonies of 'Sweet councillors, dear friends', and the poet can say, without the least sense of strain, that if his own life could have as pleasant an odour then, however brief, he could end it happily. The metaphorical meaning of 'odour' here is completely unforced: this is the spontaneity and natural beauty which the poet envies. He would like to be touched with the same freshness and composure as the flowers. I see no reason to complain that 'there is no fear of death'. Rather, the ending shows a moral insight which is the reverse of escapist: the quality of life, not its length, is what really matters, and this is not a mere platitude here because the poem itself has told us, creatively, something about this quality:

> Embalmed flowers are not flowers, immortelles are not flowers;
> Flowers are just a motion, a swift motion, a coloured gesture;
> That is their loveliness...

as Lawrence puts it in one of his poems. So Herbert, writing a 'slight', unpretentious poem, can be, in a modest way, genuinely profound. We can compare this profundity, which is closely bound up with the success of every detail of the poem, with the pseudo-profundities and inflated manner of A.

CHAPTER 10

Meaning Stated and Meaning Created: Two More Herbert Poems

I have already pointed out that the course outlined in this book is intended to be given in conjunction with other courses in literature, and one of the poems in this comparison (Exercise 9) is bound to occur in any poetry course which includes the seventeenth century. As I believe opportunities of relating what we are doing in this course to what is being done in other courses should be made the most of, rather than avoided, I have not hesitated about including it, though naturally anyone using the exercise will have to be careful about timing. This comparison follows the previous one in that it asks us to consider the difference between creation and pseudo-creation, between meaning 'actually presented' and meaning 'talked about', in another way—perhaps a simpler way. Herbert was not, of course, open to the dangers of self-idealising rhetoric in the Elizabeth Barrett Browning strain, but, as he tended to write many times on the same theme (his poetry has very few themes) and as he inevitably wrote at lower pressure on some occasions than on others, most of his good poems can be compared with similar but inferior poems in which there is a failure of creative power. The failure, put simply, is usually that Herbert has not entered fully into the poem, which remains an external conception, coherent but too neatly put together, his store of metaphors and 'little allegories' (as Grierson aptly calls them) easily sustaining a respectable level of interest but no more. In these poems, too, there appears (a sure sign of perfunctory involvement) a heaviness or clumsiness in the poet's touch which is not disguised by the neatness of plan or pattern. His best insights not fully brought to life, Herbert loses his spiritual fineness and becomes platitudinous.

The poems in this comparison are about rebellion against

God, that is, about the difficulty of living the religious life and about the sense of frustration and failure which sometimes besets the man who dedicates himself to this rigorous calling. This is probably the poet's greatest theme, the one which called forth his best poetry, but nevertheless behind poem A there seems to me no very strong compulsion to write. The rebellion is ostensibly violent, but Herbert does nothing to make us feel this violence, and we can only conclude from this that he didn't really feel it himself. He merely uses superlatives:

> Full of rebellion, I would die...

We have only the poet's word for it. There is nothing in the language—in the movement, in the effects of imagery—to give the rebellion a created existence of its own. It is not dramatically alive; it is merely 'talked about'. The line is hard to read with much conviction (a sure sign that it probably wasn't written with much conviction). The movement of the first three lines, in fact, is perfunctory, and the easily found extremes ('Full of rebellion', 'die', etc.) seem much too cheaply thrown off. The short lines in the stanza-form, which Herbert elsewhere can use so effectively, are not used to any definite purpose here; the stanza-form is fluently handled, as always with this poet, but it seems more a decoration than a means of achieving precise, important effects. The 'venom' in stanza 2 is a stereotyped ingredient (and, in view of the general lack of tension, a little melodramatic) and 'fume' and 'work' follow much as we might expect. In a good Herbert poem, we would have felt the sinister quality of this venom, and the subtlety and danger of the working suggestions. The idea of the soul turning to bubbles and vanishing into the wind is routine—there is nothing in the way Herbert uses the idea to make it vivid or illuminating—and, in the last stanza, there follows more undistinguished, commonplace imagery. 'Smooth my rugged heart'—surely a number of seventeenth-century religious poets could have written this without much difficulty. 'Engrave they law' and 'sapless' and 'stone', as they are used here, are pretty overworked items from the seventeenth-century poet's stock of images.[1] The 'turn' which ends the poem is not a sudden illumination. We wonder instead if Herbert is moving from stock-image to stock-image, making a neat pattern. He certainly isn't working out an experience, an intuition, in all its detail. The things he talks about simply are not present to him; he is 'talking about' his theme, in the pallid language of second-hand reporting. Despite its explicit claim to intensity the poem as a whole seems rather tame, and, in its predictable and somewhat heavily taken distinctions, rather obvious.

The rebellion in B, on the other hand, is real. The suggestions actually do 'fume and work', and there is no doubting for an instant that Herbert is writing about a real personal crisis which doesn't need to be tepidly recollected. The angry tones of the speaker are wonderfully caught in the verse movement. The sudden flash of anger as the poet strikes the board (the altar)

> I struck the board and cried, No more...

is matched by the shrill, overemphatic speech of the outburst which follows. This is the language of a man who is working himself into a passion; he doesn't simply lapse into anger, but works himself into it in stages. He has the angry trait of fixing the rhythm of a phrase and repeating the pattern in different words, a trick which in another mood belongs to the orator but which we sometimes unconsciously slip into in angry speech, the chief characteristic of which is its intemperate overemphasis—

> No flowers, no garlands gay? all blasted?
> All wasted?

The trait is captured in the verse with complete dramatic authenticity. The pattern changes slightly with 'Sure, there was wine', as Herbert reaches another 'stage' of anger, and again when the answers come, 'Not so, my heart', as though Herbert had, up to this point, been goading himself into this

---

[1] Some of the results I have had with this exercise in class bear out my re-mark on p. 27, that the staleness of some tropes can be felt by readers who have no previous knowledge of the clichés of a particular period.

outburst. The speaker is, of course, jeering at himself, at his own ideals and everything he has tried to do with his life. His anger has the lacerating quality of self-contempt. This is no ordinary rebellion of high spirits, a youthful desire to 'break loose', but the bitter resentment of a man who has deeply invested himself in a rigorous calling and feels he has achieved pitifully little. He turns on his own 'record', telling himself he had better give up the unequal struggle for which he was never fitted. He ridicules his own efforts as, in this mood of exacerbated impatience, perhaps most of our efforts to achieve high and difficult ideals can be ridiculed ('Cold dispute', 'rope of sands', etc.). He tells himself his life is being wasted, and he wants to grasp what still remains while there is still time. But—and this is typical of his mood—he doesn't have any real plan of action, and he doesn't really know what it is that he wants to enjoy:

> . . . free as the road,
> Loose as the wind, as large as store. . .

These expressions are vivid not because they suggest anything precise in themselves, directly, but because of their vagueness. What is actually conveyed is the speaker's petulant sense that he has been deprived of something he feels is his by a natural right, though he doesn't quite know what. The note of petulant—but dangerous—egotism is sounded. These things ought to have been mine, my life ought to have been a series of pleasures and satisfactions, not blighted by hard, unattractive effort: worthwhile work should bring its satisfactions readily. But, reading the poem, we realise that no one is 'free as the road, loose as the wind, as large as store'. The speaker, in a moment of revolt against an exacting, dedicated calling, feels that all other ways of life must be intoxicatingly attractive. 'Deserves his load' is the last angry self-accusation: the thought that goads him most of all is the thought that he has brought all this upon himself of his own free will.

Few of us have dedicated ourselves to anything as stringent and exacting as the religious life that Herbert embraced, but this does not mean that the poem loses its significance for us, or that only those who have lived the religious life can feel its force. As we get closer to the poem, we realise that this a crisis we know and can recognise. There is a fundamental human problem here, though Herbert, with far deeper involvement than we have, and with far greater capacity for passionate feeling, can show us this crisis with a clarity and power that we could never have attained merely by reflecting on our own experience. The anger directed against a chosen calling, which is really anger against the self; the glamorous light in which all alternatives appear, as long as we don't look at them too closely; in all this Herbert has revealed the distortion, the delusion that surrounds this sort of rebellious crisis. 'As I grew more fierce and wild'; the deflating words near the end of the poem are decisive and apt, especially 'At every word', which hints at the self-induced nature of the anger. The poet is recalled to himself, and sees his rebellion for what it is, though of course Herbert, in writing the poem, has all along understood, with a perceptiveness which he can command only when there is real pressure behind his poetry. The contrast with *Nature* is revealing. *The Collar* was certainly not written by 'holy George', and reading this poem we cannot doubt (as we sometimes doubt elsewhere) that Herbert was a warm and passionate man.

CHAPTER II

Translations of a Latin Poem

The inclusion of poem A in this exercise (Exercise **10**) needs some explanation in view of my earlier remarks about the need, in choosing practical criticism exercises, to avoid the difficulties created by archaic language. Poem A contains words which some students may not know, but if these are explained and the poem read out, the difficulties will not seem very great; in my experience the poem's appeal is quite strong enough to overcome them. The unusual words will be 'list', 'trace' and 'crop' (none of these are very obscure) and possibly 'estate', though any class reading Shakespeare should have no trouble here; and the archaic forms of 'slipper', 'use me quiet', 'in hidden place' and 'withouten' need touching on, even if all these usages are probably comprehensible at first sight. But it is not simply that the difficulties are negligible and easily overcome; the poem itself will prove to the students that 'archaic' language in a good poem can be more living, more expressive, than familiar language in an inferior poem—a fact of the greatest importance in the study of literature.

There is no problem at all over the question of the original poem which has been translated by the five poets. We can simply ignore it, forgetting that the poems are translations and regarding them simply as comparable poems on the same theme. The accuracy of the translation, the question of whether it renders an original faithfully or not, does not concern us: we are to regard the translations as poems in their own right, which was, I believe, the intention of all the authors. The theme of the poems is the desire to escape from the rat-race of power. Other people can live at the top, with the anxieties, the strain, the intrigues, the coups, the general uncertainties of politics, high society and success; the poet wants a quiet peaceful life, which he can organise to his satisfaction. Only after such a life, he says, will he know how to face death. The grounds for comparison are not dissimilar to the grounds for comparing the Herbert poems we have just looked at. The question that practical criticism must decide is, which poet has written because he feels this theme has a real, personal meaning for him, and which poet is merely 'translating', i.e. providing a neat exercise which 'talks about' the theme in a cold, routine way. In other words, which poet 'talks about' the theme, and which 'actually presents' his emotions and experience? Perhaps the weakest of all the translations is B; insipid, mechanical movement, into which it is almost impossible to inject expression while reading, facile epithets, tautology, all are signs of lack of inspiration. 'Mighty mace', 'sweet and quiet rest' ('obtain' seems to me put there to meet the needs of the rhyme), 'place obscure and low degree', 'pleasant rest', 'over past', 'troublous tumult spent', 'full well content' are examples of feeble diction and tautology which no poem can survive. It would be difficult to like or even remember a poem written in such limp language; clearly the theme of escape from 'the top' did not mean very much to the poet. He tries for metaphorical interest in 'the step of secret silence', though in view of the insipidity of 'secret silence' ('step' seems dictated by the alliteration) the contrivance doesn't really add anything to the poem. He is also attracted by the opportunity of producing a neat ending; his conclusion is carefully turned. Much of what I have said about this, the Elizabethan version, applies almost equally to the eighteenth-century version, D. The writing is hardly less facile. The eighteenth-century couplets have neatness,

> Happy the Man who thus retir'd from sight
> Studies himself and seeks no other light...

but this is neatness of a habitual kind. Nothing, that is, is unusually strongly felt on this occasion, and the diction has nothing of the trenchancy, point and felicity which we know in the great eighteenth-century poets. 'Worldly Luxury and Pomp's allure' is cliché; the language is stale throughout. On the evidence of this poem no reader could believe that the poet ever seriously considered the kind of retreat contemplated, or had any genuine horror of the rat-race of politics and high society. The poet sounds far too comfortable for that. It is a literary exercise by an elegant eighteenth-century peer, and I suppose a number of 'rhyming peers' could have turned out something as good. C, on the other hand, is oratorical and expansive. This poem is almost twice the length of the others, but it takes no very long inspection to see that much of the language is redundant. The poet is intent on being 'classical' with a vengeance—he sees himself in the orator's toga—and he brings in seemingly as many classically flavoured tropes as he can think of (e.g. 'The guilded pinnacles of fate'). The metaphors are wordy, redundant ('wrapped in th' arms of quiet', 'embroidered', and so on) and the orotund phrases grow a little absurd ('O ye gods'—they aren't real gods). No one, I believe, could communicate a real desire, a real thought, in a manner such as this.

From the pompous verbiage of C it is a relief to turn to the much more effective and restrained poem E. It is not just that E avoids the faults of D, with neat, compact expression and modest, composed tone. The poem has in places real imaginative felicity. Notice how well appropriate suggestions are caught in 'secret nest'; and notice the naturalness of diction, a naturalness which none of the poems previously looked at has shown, in 'I shall die without a groan' and 'An old honest country man' (a useful contrast with the absurdly unreal 'old plebeian' in C). Most of all, the ending is more successful and interesting than that of B, C or D. 'Pries' is neatly, almost elegantly felicitous, suggesting the care that we need to take in self-examination if we are to discover the secrets we hide from ourselves, and 'strange surprise', in its unforced way, conveys the strangeness and suddenness of death for a man who is morally unprepared for it. Instead of resorting to educated cliché, this poet has done something to make a new, individual poem of his translation.

The higher quality of poem E is not perhaps surprising, as the poet is Marvell. But the poem pales in comparison with poem A, which, alone of all these examples, seems to me to have been written by a man for whom the theme held a vital importance—a man who really feared the life of the court and desperately wanted to leave it. Looking back at poem E, I feel the rhythm is a bit perfunctory, the poem *too* neat. Marvell has managed to do something with it, but there are no signs of strong emotional or intellectual pressure behind his poem. It is, at a higher level certainly, another literary exercise, of a sort that the educated gentleman in the seventeenth century habitually practised. I think it is relevant, once we have made these observations about the poem, to recall that Marvell was a professional politician, and a very intelligent one, who disliked the political events of the age he lived in, and that many of his surviving statements about his age show a strength of character and integrity that, having read his best poems, we would expect of him. But he never had a real *revulsion* against politics and the life of a politician, and this poem shows it. Passionate conviction lies behind every phrase of poem A:

> And use me quiet without let or stop,
> Unknown in court that hath such brackish joys.

Only a man who had tasted the 'brackish joys' of court could have found that phrase for them, with its vivid physical impact (the phrase seems to have, rhythmically, the weight of the first four lines in it). He would prefer to die 'aged after the common trace'. As none of the other poets quite does, he fervently desires the ordinary, the commonplace, and he is the only poet for whom the ending is more than a generalised, abstract moral statement. Death in this poem is not something that conveniently comes to underline the moral for us, it is an appallingly violent physical fact. As Mr Mason says, commenting on this poem in his *Humanism and Poetry in Early Tudor England*, in

> For him Death grippeth right hard by the crop

'every word is active'. This is the savage shock of violent death, which, the poet knows only too well, awaits those who live the uncertain, dangerous life of court intrigue. The last line, far from giving us a sententious warning to 'know ourselves', carries the terror-stricken bewilderment of the victim of an execution and the horrified gaze of the onlookers ('unknown' has almost the effect of understatement: this is so much worse than moral self-ignorance, and 'unknowing' takes on a new and terrible sense). It is tempting to relate this poem to the fact that in 1536 (see Mason, page 182) Wyatt, the poet, was forced to witness the execution of some of his friends in the Tower of London, and to the fact that everything we know about Wyatt tells us that he destroyed himself in an exhausting life of uncertainty and danger as courtier and servant of Henry VIII. But the poem itself doesn't need this gloss. Whatever the actual circumstances of its composition, it is itself a terse, charged private outburst, forced from the poet by an uncontainable desire to escape, as he recoils from the life in which he is trapped. The original poem is a famous one, and has been translated many times, but the most remarkable thing about Wyatt's poem is that it *is* a translation, so different is it from the polite renderings of foreign verse that we usually associate with the term.

CHAPTER 12

Shakespeare's Verse: Additional Exercises

As these examples (Exercise 11) are intended to follow up the material discussed in chapter 5, only brief commentary will be necessary. There is immense variety in Shakespeare's verse, too immense to be suggested in any short selection, and I do not pretend to have defined, in any inclusive way, the characteristics of Shakespeare's mature verse. Only the early verse (except for lapses in the later plays) is stereotyped and therefore easily categorised. The notion that pieces of Shakespeare's verse can be 'dated' by external signs, such as the number of end-stopped lines, is largely mistaken. The exercise of 'dating' or (a better term) appraising Shakespearean verse, is a genuine and useful one because we have to respond to recognise; the test must be an internal one, and we cannot know a good piece of Shakespeare by checking against a memorised list of characteristics, 'in an imitation botanical fashion'. Bearing in mind the limitations involved in this sort of exercise, which I have tried to discuss on page 28, it will not be difficult for the reader or teacher to find further exercises for himself—though of course it is hoped that this will also be the case with the other exercises in this book.

1. This is a simple and straightforward case which might be used for a first exercise. In A the horrific and sinister are done with a naive relish; the poet is really laying it on thick. Compare this charnel-house stuff to the extract from *Macbeth*. There is expressive control of the voice here; the violence of the forces Macbeth invokes is felt in the intensity of 'scarf' (the suffocating, choking quality of the thick darkness is vividly suggested) and in 'Cancel, and tear to pieces'. This is not just a story-book shudder. A powerful and perverse desire is felt in the fierce pleasure with which Macbeth envisages the tearing up of the great bond—and it is the pleasure of self-destruction.

'Light thickens'; such an expression would have been impossible to the Shakespeare who wrote the piece from *Titus Andronicus*. The sinister beings who rouse to their prey can really rob the 'good things of day' of their influence on man. Even the rhyme, which ends the speech, is more than a stage convention—it helps to get the full threatening value of 'rouse'. The speaker clearly feels that 'paleness' is useless to him. Reference to the scene, which should be made after the exercise is done, will show how dramatically effective the note of invocation is here. Macbeth, at this stage of the play, speaks almost in the language of a devotee—he can draw comfort, almost, from the images of darkness, naively believing that he can rely on them for his ends.

2. This passage—it might be compared to the famous 'To-morrow and to-morrow and to-morrow' speech from *Macbeth*—is clearly early. One notices this in the neat arrangement of metaphors, which follow one another as a kind of decoration of the main thought (Traversi has some good discussion of this speech, *Scrutiny*, vol. xv, no. 2, pp. 120–1). A character, feeling world-wearied, thinks that could we but see the future we would not think life worth living. There are plenty of conventional figures to illustrate this thought, and out they come: the book of fate, mocking chance, changes filling the cup of alteration with diverse liquors (a very characteristic bit of elaboration), the happiest youth (it had to be him) reading in the book of fate that life will be miserable and shutting the book and giving up. The *Macbeth* speech too, however, contains conventional figures: the poor player for instance is an adaption of a trope which occurs elsewhere in Shakespeare and, in various forms, in other Elizabethan literature. Plainly the trope was one of those at which, as so frequently happened, everybody tried his hand. But a great writer can raise a conventional thought to the highest intensity, and in this speech, full of Macbeth's jaded despair, his total spiritual and emotional bankruptcy, the figures are unforgettable. In fact, we have to remind ourselves that they are, in origin, conventional (an

illustration of the point made earlier, that conventionality is a quality we can sense, not something we recognise by knowing a check-list of the tropes of a period). And of course analysis will show that the language is working ('struts and frets') in a way it is not working in the passage before us, with its conventionally rounded cadences and stale phrasing. The verse here moves in terms of maxims and clichés, and it is undramatic in the sense that there is no fully realised human being behind it; this is simply a recitation of noble thoughts. In the *Macbeth* speech, Shakespeare is, as several critics have pointed out, not expressing his total view of life, but only Macbeth's at this particular moment of his tragic career. Yet the speech has such conviction that it is not surprising that other critics, looking mistakenly for a statement of 'Shakespeare's philosophy' from one of the characters, should have fixed on this passage. Their heresy has this excuse, I think, that we can easily believe Shakespeare may have felt like this at certain moments, so fully does he understand Macbeth's despair.

But what has been said so far is not quite true of passage 2. Mr Traversi points out that in one place we do seem to be reading something more than conventional Elizabethan rhetoric.

> And see the revolution of the times
> Make mountains level, and the continent,
> Weary of solid firmness, melt itself
> Into the sea.

'Make mountains level' is expected, but the lines about the continent, 'weary of solid firmness' melting into the sea seem not to 'talk about' the meaning, but actually to suggest it—to present something directly to the imagination. 'Weary of solid firmness' (the rhythm is more alive here), with its generalising power of suggestion, makes King Henry IV's weariness far more real to us than

> O God! that one might read the book of fate...

and 'melt itself', effectively placed, develops the metaphorical suggestions of 'weary of solid firmness' in a way that is reminiscent of the creativeness of the later Shakespeare, not the simple devices of the early dramatist.

3. This is very clearly a mature passage: the rhythm tells us this straight away. Notice, for example, how the first sentence seems to gather itself together for the shattering blow of the onslaught in 'struck/Corioli like a planet', where the break we are forced to observe between the last syllable of 'struck' and the first of 'Corioli' makes it impossible for the actor to slur over the lines limply and unexpressively. This is what is meant by saying that Shakespeare's verse 'embodies' its meaning. Consider too the effect of the last line—it is as though the speaker, re-enacting the fight in his description, doesn't pause for breath until the onrush of his language has finished. The opening phrase, 'From face to foot/He was a thing of blood' has a vivid directness that could not have come in the early plays, and, reinforced by the movement, the imagery throughout carries hints of larger-than-life, horrific feats of carnage. 'Tim'd with dying cries' gains part of its effect from the almost eerie overtones, and, after Coriolanus (the hero) has, with a supreme effort of vitality and courage, 'Re-quicken'd what in flesh was fatigate', he runs 'reeking o'er the lives of men'; the horrific note becomes explicit. The speech succeeds, without conventional superlatives, in conveying the super-human. What this sort of exercise cannot tell us is that super-men are finally rather boring, even when they are presented critically, and that Coriolanus never seems to matter to us as much as Macbeth or Hamlet. Nor can it tell us that too much of this sort of poetry, however superbly done, is liable to defeat its own end, for Shakespeare is less deeply engaged in this play, and, compared with *Macbeth*, *Coriolanus*, in verse as well as in characterisation, lacks subtlety, variety and depth. We might compare the famous speech of Posthumus in *Cymbeline*, which reports the battle, and this, though it is an isolated speech in an uneven play, has ultimately more subtlety and life than the Coriolanus speech, and its resources are less limited.

4. This, like no. 1, is a very straightforward case. In both passages a young man speaks idealisingly of a lover, but Romeo, in A, speaks in the language of Elizabethan love poetry. There is quite an extravaganza of conceits, not without a slender, very 'dated' charm. But in B the language is real. The tone is beautifully controlled in this little outburst of lively affection by a young man—who really does seem young. Both the enthusiasm he feels and the grace he admires are attractively present in 'I wish you/A wave of the sea'. He is carried away; but the speech is not merely cheap hyperbole, and the idealising quality of his affection, which delights in everything she does, is pleasingly caught. Perdita in reply tempers his enthusiasm: she shrewdly suspects that he doesn't express himself like a shepherd. But there is nothing of the frigidity of courtly compliment in this fresh, youthful speech. In discussion of these passages, it is useful to add, as a further contrast, Troilus's 'I am giddy, expectation whirls me round' speech from *Troilus and Cressida*, Act III, Scene ii. In view of Shakespeare's intentions here, it seems to me impossible to include this speech in the exercise; it would be too difficult to introduce. But some of the astonishing effects of imagery are very discussible in the present context, and the difference in attitude, as Shakespeare here is almost brutally cynical about youthful, idealising love, is illuminating.

5. There is a catch here, though I believe it is a fair one. Those students who recognise this as a piece of *Hamlet* will, unless they are very independent, say this is a piece of mature and successful verse. Those who don't recognise it will almost certainly see its quality, for this speech by the Ghost is a piece of sensational charnel-house stuff, a lapse into an earlier manner. The crudeness is quite unbelievable as the Ghost dwells, with maximum grisly effect, on the impact on Hamlet of the tale he *could* tell, if he wanted.

CHAPTER 13

A Case of Idiosyncrasy: Two Poems
by Hardy

These poems (Exercise 12) introduce a series of more difficult exercises. The difficulty of practical criticism exercises is not always easy to grade, but what follows here does, I think, call for a greater sophistication in reading than what has gone before, and should only be attempted by students who have acquired some experience in dealing with poetry.

The critical problem with the Hardy poems lies mainly in the highly personal idiosyncrasies of language which are so characteristic of this poet. Any poet who matters must be idiosyncratic; this is one of the sure signs of creative talent, evidence of a power to force language to express something new and individual. The idiosyncrasies of most great writers we can accept without difficulty. They are, to adapt a phrase of Johnson's, that which 'is at once natural and new, that which, though not obvious, is, upon its first production, acknowledged to be just'. But Hardy's poetry contains eccentricities of language of a sort we are not always ready to accept in this way. In the present poems, 'in my imagining', 'unvision', 'this old track', 'Let me view you then', 'existlessness' and 'wet mead' are among the instances of unusual diction over which the reader may be inclined to hesitate. The oddness looks as though it might be sheer clumsiness, or sometimes as though it might be quaintness relished for the sake of quaintness, something which the poet has cultivated because he believes it has a 'poetic' flavour. Nothing is more irritating in poetry than what we feel is a deliberately cultivated mannerism, though Hardy's mannerisms seem always to be offered unpretentiously and naively, and the reader who knows Hardy well can even find something endearing about them. But if this were true of the language of both poems there would be little point in this exercise. Dr Leavis was, I believe, the first to point out that in Hardy's best poems the characteristic oddnesses of diction are remarkably transformed into felicities. When Hardy's poetry has real pressure behind it—and, with him, this is almost always the pressure of certain personal experiences, which invariably form the subject-matter of his greatest poems—the eccentricities of language become both natural and new, as the reader who has got the 'feel' of the poetry and overcome his initial hesitations will recognise. The present exercise asks us to consider the differences between the mere mannerism, the habitual amiable clumsiness or the 'poetic' word put in to add spice to the style, and the unusual coinage which is the product of a creative invention seeking ways to convey new and strongly felt experience.

In both poems the poet recalls a woman long dead. In the first he imagines he sees her shadow, and refuses to turn his head and see that there is nothing there: he prefers to nurse his illusion. In the second, he thinks he hears the woman's voice carried by the wind across the autumn countryside, but is unsure and is left with his memory and a feeling of intensified loneliness. I think that even our first, unconsidered impression will probably be that B is the more powerful poem. The difference between the best Hardy and the routine Hardy is great enough to begin to show through from the start, even though the reader may not yet have reconciled himself to all the language in B.[1] The first poem seems to have something heavy-handed, less spontaneous about it. It makes its point about nostalgia, but the experience does not seem as fully and poignantly evoked as in the other poem. And, when we look more closely at the poems, these first impressions are confirmed. In A, Hardy's customary frank directness suggests that the poem may have originated in an actual incident—it seems 'authentic' in this sense—but the details do not tell in any very precise, vivid way,

[1] Here, of course, the reader is challenged to make the specific comparison and the difference is much more immediately obvious. Reading through the volume of Hardy's collected poems, as has often been pointed out, it is sometimes possible to miss one of the good poems, i.e. to be deceived by mannerisms into making a hasty judgment.

either individually or cumulatively and, when the poem is particular, the particularity is awkwardly, insensitively or ineffectively handled: it, too, represents a failure in creativeness in the poem. There is, as we say, no fine organisation present, such as there is in the second poem. Despite the fact that the themes of the poems are so close, and that this is the theme of Hardy's greatest poems, he seems on this occasion not to have been unusually or deeply moved.

The detail in the first lines,

> I went by the Druid stone
> That broods in the garden white and lone...

is not distinctive enough. 'White and lone', 'broods': there is something a little ready-made in the atmosphere. The Druid stone opens the poem, but it doesn't seem a very necessary part of the experience, and something else of a loosely 'atmospheric', mysterious nature might have done as well; neither the stone nor the glade is sharply relevant, but merely 'suitable'. The failure in the remainder of the stanza is of a different kind. The stanza labours rather in getting its details out, and the likeness between the shadow of the branches and the woman's shadow which is 'shaped' in the poet's 'imagining' seems freakish rather than poignantly evocative. It is partly, I think, a matter of the unfortunate explicitness. 'Rhythmic swing' is rather worrying: the woman hoeing or raking the garden may well be making rhythmic movements, but the word seems a very arbitrary one to apply to the movements of the branches of a tree in the wind. The fact that the poet says the shadows shaped in his imagining to the shape of the woman, i.e. his imagination 'worked on' the shape and movement to produce the likeness, does not quite do away with this embarrassment. In the 'well-known head and shoulders' we again feel the rather awkward explicitness which gives the incident a slightly bizarre pedestrian quality, robbing it of any poignancy it might have had. 'Shaped in my imagining' seems just a curious locution. The phrase has none of the inwardness with the experience of recollecting deeply moving things which we find in the language of Hardy's best poetry.

The failures we have noted in the first stanza (and, though this poem is a respectable enough performance in its way, what we have been discussing does represent, comparatively, a failure in creativeness) are characteristic of the whole poem. In the second line of the second stanza, though one is a little irritated by the mannered, 'poetic' 'Yea', Hardy does use alliteration with effective naturalness,

> Yea, her I long had learned to lack,

but the poet's speech to the supposed apparition,

> And I said: 'I am sure you are standing behind me,
> Though how do you get into this old track?'

is so insistently unnatural in its clumsiness that it is virtually impossible to read out convincingly. Is 'this old track' there mainly because Hardy was looking for a rhyme for 'back' and 'lack', and, mistaking clumsiness for 'poetic' flavour, accepted this phrase which was suggested by the need for a rhyme? Whether this is true or not, the lines are quite without that emotional sense of the lapse of time that Hardy elsewhere creates so wonderfully, and in fact they are without any emotional quality whatsoever. The leaf falls as a sad response (we can compare this with the evocations of loneliness in the second poem), and the poet refuses to 'look and see' and disillusion himself—though in these lines Hardy has surely mistaken slight eccentricity of phrasing for poetic character. Hardy's rustic straightforwardness of manner, which can offer these eccentricities so naively, is in this poem in danger of descending to something it cannot afford, the prosaic, and in the last stanza there seems to me a banality in his handling of his feelings. The pathos is lessened because it is too explicitly insisted on; the poem makes its 'point' too deliberately for us to feel the underlying currents of emotion and recreate the experience for ourselves. The poem hangs a bit too heavily on that 'somehow': Hardy is underlining this little irony for us. The banality is reflected in the diction ('look and see', 'at the back of me'). 'Unvision' is typical of the kind of invention that, in other poems, can be marvellously successful, but here, where the 'vision' is so thinly, so externally evoked, the word sticks out clumsily. 'Visioning' is not, in this poem, the process that it is in *After a Journey* or in the poem that follows here. *The Shadow On The Stone*, that is, fails to suggest a deeply moving memory brought to life unexpectedly in a chance moment.

The second poem starts uncertainly. There is, as several of Hardy's critics have noticed, something of a jingle in the first two lines (not unreminiscent of the banality we have been complaining of in the first poem and another instance of a naively 'poetic' device). But by the third line the poet is beginning to bring the rhythm under control; the emphasis begins to come more naturally and expressively, and the last line has what we feel at once to be a specially significant overtone:

But as at first, when our day was fair...

Nothing is defined as yet, and 'changed' is left entirely unexplained, but this momentary allusion to an unknown personal history is curiously effective in giving us the sense that a deeply important moment, the one which of all his experiences matters most to the poet, is going to be recalled. Several of my student readers have found this detail pointless, but what it is doing, I think, is to put the poem in perspective for the reader; it helps to introduce him to the very private atmosphere, an atmosphere full of special, heightened personal resonances and associations. For this poem, unlike poem A, can really take us into the world of intimate personal recollection, in all its distinctive individuality. The 'original air-blue gown', which, until we have responded to the poem, may seem rather arbitrary, has a special personal resonance for Hardy. It is one of the things through which he can recall the emotional exaltation of many years ago. But, if this is a 'private' meaning, there is no failure of communication such as the word 'private' might suggest. The poignancy that the air-blue gown has for the poet we can recognise without difficulty as the feeling which, as we know in our own less fine and passionate way from our own introspection, grows round a detail we associate with a strongly moving experience. We recognise at the same time that only exceptionally sensitive poetry can present the quality, the flavour, the sensations of this level of intimacy so faithfully and convincingly.

The intimate personal quality is there too, of course, in the movement. Compare the ineptitude of

> I am sure you are standing behind me,
>> Though how did you get into this old track?

with

>> Can it be you that I hear? Let me view you then,

in which we seem to be overhearing an inner conversation in the poet. The words are not, as it were, spoken aloud. Hardy, whose manner has something of straightforwardness in it which is very characteristic (the naivety we noted in the other poem transformed into a solid sincerity and directness), is addressing a memory, a recollection which he can only for a moment incredulously believe is a reality, and the tones of inner conversation are beautifully caught. 'Can it be you that I hear?' As the memory, brought unexpectedly to life in a chance moment, gathers strength, the rhythm gathers momentum and warmth. 'View' means so much more than the deliberate 'vision' of poem A:

> Let me view you then
> Standing as when I drew near to the town,
> Where you would wait for me...

There is no awkwardness about the double rhyme; a passionate stress is gained by it, and it seems to have nothing to do with the little poetic devices Hardy is so fond of elsewhere:

> Yes, as I knew you then,
> Even to the original air-blue gown!

I have tried to explain something of the effect of this phrase, which must imprint itself indelibly—like so much else in this poem—in the mind of anyone who reads responsively. It has—

though I doubt very much if this is the result of a conscious calculation by Hardy—both the distinctness of a vivid, accurate recollection and the thin, airy, disembodied character of a memory, an image in the mind. Even when Hardy speaks, with reawakened passion, of the woman, we know that she is not a solid actuality; she is only something thought of, with the insubstantial life of the imagination.[1]

After the approaching elation of the second stanza, there comes the sudden disillusion of the third: the sound of the voice may only be the breeze. The poet feels his loneliness with unparalleled intensity, 'unparalleled' because, although other poets have expressed fairly similar sorts of loneliness, only Hardy has expressed this penetrating sense of desolation, of distance from the loved and valued in an indifferent world. When we realise the truth and power of this mood, and understand how it can show us, in a way we never felt before, what loving and valuing can mean, we realise at the same time that it is very much Hardy's own, and only he could have written about it like this. The utter indifference of the surroundings is evoked as only Hardy could evoke it:

> Or is it only the breeze, in its listlessness,
> Travelling across the wet mead to me here...

The unmoved, impersonal neutrality of the breeze is unforgettably caught in these lines, especially in the superb 'listlessness' which so wonderfully suggests the apathetic caress of the light wind as it travels past the poet, who is a completely irrelevant object in this bleak autumnal landscape. 'Wet mead' has been found by some readers to be an eccentricity of diction, an affectation ('O may I squire you round the meads,/ And pick you roses gay?') but there is no 'poetic' glow here; the phrase has the exact despondent overtone Hardy needed to suggest the cold, dispiriting dampness of the autumn day. No other poet, probably, would have found this phrase, in which oddness has become felicity. The following lines modu-

---

[1] Dr Leavis has discussed similar effects in *After A Journey*, and readers are advised to look up his very close discussion of that poem in *Scrutiny*, vol. XIX, no. 2.

late from the bleak indifference of the landscape to Hardy's full sense of loss, and the sheer negative emptiness of absence:

> You being ever dissolved to existlessness,
> Heard no more again far or near?

There is no need to make detailed comparisons with the feeble and contrived attempts in poem A to convey this sense:

> And there was no sound but the fall of a leaf
> As a sad response...

The power of the lines owes a great deal to Hardy's coinage, 'existlessness' (compare 'unvision'), which, reinforced by and reinforcing 'dissolved', contains a general, all-pervading sense of desolation. The degree of generality, of abstractness in the language is perfectly right; the sense of void, of emptiness which fills this whole stanza is remarkably summed up in this one word. Hardy's later alteration, 'wan wistlessness', seems much weaker. It is a concession to 'poetic' feeling—at least there seems to me a little surge of self-conscious pathos with the phrase, and it altogether lacks the austerity of 'existlessness' which is so much more in keeping with the feeling of the poem.

In the final stanza, with what Dr Leavis calls 'superb modulation of tone' the poet makes his comment on himself. He is bewildered, lost and frail, 'faltering forward', in a cold impersonal landscape,

> Wind oozing thin through the thorn from norward,

in which even the raw, chilling wind seems to grudge its energy. The language of the line just quoted is completely natural and unforced. I find it difficult to explain just why 'norward' should be more effectively bleak than 'northward', but there is not the least incongruity in this unusual piece of diction. Finally, there is the woman calling, not the real woman he had hoped to see in the second stanza, but only the elusive, evanescent memory, which haunts and bewilders him, leaving him only with a greater sense of his separation from the real woman of forty years ago.

The Voice is in a sense a nature poem, in that it uses natural scenes to arouse the feeling the poet wants to convey to the reader, but there is nothing about it of the drearily ready-made emotions that we normally associate with term. Most of us probably regard 'nature poetry' as a sort of irrelevant luxury— a means of feeling sad or happy that has little to do with the life around us and which is thoroughly spurious in its workings. But *The Voice* doesn't strike us—unless we remind ourselves of the fact—as nature poetry at all. The desolation of Hardy's old age and the poignancy of his memories are too real. The poignancy is something we can envy, for it is the echo of a rare and developed tenderness, and the desolation is something we can fear. It is, though, a meaningful desolation—it could not have existed without the supreme moment of experience to recall and it is this which gives Hardy's poem its tragic depth and power. I have, in this discussion, been keeping in mind some representative reading errors I have had from students. One is that 'the poem is too private', another that 'the poet is full of self-pity and has lost his grip on reality'. I hope I have done enough in close commentary on the poem to dispose of these casual, erring descriptions. The suggestion that leaves in line 14 are 'symbolic' nicely illustrates how deadly an influence that term can wield.

CHAPTER 14

More Creation versus Statement:
Frost and Edward Thomas

Though both poems in this exercise (Exercise 13) are modern, they are not 'modern' in the sense in which the term will probably be understood by many students who are coming to twentieth-century poetry for the first time: that is, difficult and abstruse. They are, on the contrary, open and natural in manner, decidedly close to ordinary speech (it is well known that Frost's example helped Thomas to escape from the more stilted, stereotyped rhythms of their contemporaries) and neither is abstruse or obscure in conception. They should be perfectly accessible to students at the level presumed in this book. In each poem, the poet stands at a cross-roads wondering which road he should take, and, by a simple extension of meaning, he reflects on the uncertainty of our choices and decisions in life. 'Which way shall I go?' The first poet chooses one road out of sheer whimsy, and reflects ironically on how he will probably remember this decision in the years to come. The second poet hesitates, and sees his hesitation as an inescapable part of his life as a human being, though his conclusion is an unexpected and (I think we shall finally come to agree) an original and striking one. The questions which, as critical readers, we shall want to put to the poems (and, so often, if we can put the right questions to a work of literature, the right answers will suggest themselves) are not hard to find. Which poet has given the incident—which looks a promising one for a poem—a greater illuminating significance? Or, to put the question less broadly, and perhaps a little less portentously, since both poems are offered as documents of personal experience, in which poem is the incident of personal experience, with its accompanying self-realisations, more sensitively evoked and more fully entered into? Which has the greater moving vividness of detail? And which, on the other hand, leaves us with not very much more than a good idea for a poem, something stated only, rather than deeply felt?

Some of my student readers praised poem A for its 'subtle complex realism', a piece of jargon which, in the way jargon has, covers something important with ready-made terms and saves the user the labour of explaining exactly what it is that he feels in new phrases of his own. Jargon is an ever-present danger in practical criticism and we all know how a teacher's or critic's carefully chosen language can be served back mechanically, as a routine. Most jargoneers can be made to recognise their language for what it is, once it is pointed out (or better, read out) to them, and often a teacher can usefully place a temporary ban on words like 'complexity' or 'realism', if he finds they are being overused, or used as a means of avoiding explanations and descriptions which can and must be given. Perhaps the best general tip that can be given to students is that they should imagine themselves addressing a person of good intelligence who is not particularly sophisticated in literature, who hasn't yet seen their point but is willing to listen sympathetically. It is by developing a sense of the reader addressed that we learn to write lively and natural prose. But the comment that Poem A has a 'subtle complex realism' seems to me mistaken praise in any case. The poem by its very conception is not in much danger of fantasy, of addressing something other than a common situation in life. The danger is much more one of being pedestrian, of addressing a common situation without much subtlety or complexity. The poet sees two roads in front of him and chooses one of them whimsically, 'because it was grassy and wanted wear'—though he tells us that even this 'reason' is hardly a reason, as the paths were equally worn and no step had trodden the fallen autumn leaves that morning. He knows at the time that he will probably never return to explore the other road, and in the last stanza he tells us he will probably one day believe that this choice has had a profound influence on his life—it is so easy to attribute the important facts of our life to mere chance decisions, and perhaps it is comforting too. But when we put our critical questions to the poem, and ask what special qualities of insight and feeling the poet has brought, it is hard not to answer that he has done very little to raise the poem above a series of rather commonplace observations. There is a triteness in *The Road Not Taken* which makes real entry into the poet's state of mind impossible. 'In leaves no step has trodden black' shows some accuracy of observation, but otherwise the incident in the yellow (i.e. autumn—though there is no particular reason why it should be) wood does not seem sharply evoked in atmosphere or detail, and one feels that perhaps another incident might be substituted without making all that much difference, as long as it was one that rested upon a 'toss-up' decision. In the last stanza, perhaps, the poem tautens slightly with the ironic reflection at the writer's own expense. This is the kind of false satisfaction that we sometimes get from recalling random decisions; the poem does, in a way, try to *illumine* whimsy for us. But the writing is loose and heavy in gesture:

> I shall be telling this with a sigh
> Somewhere ages and ages hence...

(cf.   Oh, I kept the first for another day...)

and elsewhere the poetry, which seeks to make a virtue of simplicity of manner, verges on the prosaic, sometimes on the awkwardly, limply prosaic:

> Though as for that the passing there
> Had worn them really about the same.

The conception and the treatment are comparatively external. Not being unusually moved on this occasion, Frost has not taken us much beyond the level of the neatly (or not so neatly) turned commonplace.

Poem A, then, is deficient in creativeness: the content is never more for us than a stated idea with a few thinly imagined details clinging to it (the autumn wood, etc.). But in poem B the poet's hesitations and uncertainties, the inner misgivings he feels about himself and his direction in life, are entered into with a fullness which poem A doesn't approach. The difference may provisionally be put by saying that, when reading poem B, we seem to be in close touch with a distinct personality. The poem gives us a very good idea of what the poet's character is like, whereas in A we have no such strong impression of an individual person. I don't say that this is a reliable test for any poem, but I believe that for these poems, with their particular intentions, it is. The student who commented on poem A that '...there is a disappearance of private mundane experience beneath the more complex experience of having to make choices' has I think stated the exact opposite of the case. A is the weaker poem because it is generalised, disembodied, 'thought of'. In B there is the particular experience of a distinct individual—a man of great sensitiveness and integrity, whose experience is therefore truly representative and interesting.

The claim that in poem B we have a vivid impression of a distinct and interesting personality must, of course, be made good in detailed analysis; only then can the claim be properly understood. The poem opens with a bleak, wintry scene. The light is cold, suffused (beautifully caught in 'dim' and 'glint'), the sun is withdrawn, and the grasses are chill, frostily damp and barely alive. This is a cliff-top where only the hardier plants can grow, and this is the harshest season. The weeds are 'skeleton weeds'. Notice how effectively both rhythm and rhyme are used in

and the never-dry,
Rough, long grasses keep white with frost...

The intonation of the voice is perfect. Modestly, but precisely, the bleak, comfortless atmosphere is evoked for us, and unlike the 'yellow wood' in A this opening scene is essential to the poem and its themes, not an accidental stage setting. Only in such surroundings, we feel, could these particular intimations have come to this poet in this way. He reads the sign and doubts. A voice inside him answers readily—

> You would not have doubted so
> At twenty...

But this voice, which produces the immediate and instinctive answer (once you were young and therefore sure of yourself) is met by the retort of a second, much more disconcerting voice, which quietly reminds the poet of what he actually was like as a young man. His youth was anything but flourishing and confident:

> Another voice, gentle with scorn
> Says: At twenty you wished you had never been born.

'Gentle with scorn'—the phrase exactly describes the quiet but irresistible way some of our truer intuitions come to us, and deflate our easier, more reassuring conclusions. Thomas remembers himself at twenty: we know from the poem (there is other evidence too, if it were relevant) that Thomas was a sensitive, introspective young man, for whom life was liable to seem too great a burden. Just that quality of youthful melancholy seems to be hinted at, and it is a poet of rare integrity who can make this reflection so convincingly. Thomas is not thinking of his early melancholy with any pride or self-conscious satisfaction. It is very real misery, an unhappy time of life, that is being recalled.

The first voice, if it is more obvious in its thinking than the second, is still very human. It is human to cling to the illusion that we were once confident young men and, after the light but telling description of the hazel tuft which loses a leaf of gold (not 'irrelevant description'—the analogy is delicately insinuated), the second voice anxiously asks what the poet will feel like when he is 'sixty by that same post': will he be any more self-assured after so many years? The second voice, which is detached, intelligent, but not, we feel, hostile, is inclined to ridicule (gently) the folly of this wish. He laughs—'and I had to join his laughter'; the voice has a compulsion and a fascination for the poet and for the reader, as he reminds Thomas that death will be the final remedy for those troubles. The poem commands a remarkable physical immediacy ('mouthful of earth' has full shock value) without the least sensationalism.

> Whatever happens, it must befall,
> A mouthful of earth to remedy all
> Regrets and wishes shall freely be given.

It is not surprising that the second voice has gradually taken over the poem. But from this point onwards the tone modulates unexpectedly. There is—though when we look at the poem as a whole it is not inconsistent—a reversal of feeling. The second voice has been, in its non-hostile way, deflating up to now, and it doesn't at this stage begin to offer *comfort* (the term simply doesn't fit the poem); but it does begin to offer something much more positive than deflation. It goes on to say that if the grave is a heaven of rest from the problems and uncertainties of life, there may still be a flaw in that heaven, and that will be a yearning to be alive again, even in a life of uncertainty and indecision. Life will still be poignantly desirable, far more desirable than death. The verse rises on a powerful current of feeling:

> 'Twill be freedom to wish, and your wish may be
> To be here or anywhere talking to me,
> No matter what the weather, on earth,
> At any age between death and birth—
> To see what day or night can be . . .

as the poet's imagination comes burningly alive at the thought of the contrast between life and death. He would prefer to be 'With a poor man of any sort, down to a king'—the sudden kaleidoscoping of relations in that line is remarkably effective —he would rather be

> Standing upright out in the air,

which is the poem's culminating description of vitality, the final vision of human life as it might be envied by the dead. The poem, which has begun in despondency and disillusion, ends on an affirmation; to be alive is inevitably to be uncertain, but there is no melancholic's wish for extinction. There is a strong desire to live. The poem makes one realise the robust qualities, the sanity which went along with Thomas's melancholic sensitiveness. The essence of Thomas's poetry is its modesty, its unforced, unsensational demeanour. But the more one looks, the more striking and original this poem seems to be.[1]

[1] Another useful, though much simpler, comparison can be made between Frost's *Putting in the Seed* and Thomas's *Sowing*.

CHAPTER 15

Contrasting Poems:
Jonson's 'To Heaven' and Donne's 'Thou Hast Made Me'

Students who are being introduced to practical criticism for the first time should, as I have tried to suggest earlier, be encumbered as little as possible with the question of differences of kind and convention in poetry. The factors which may complicate first attempts at critical analysis, particularly comparative critical analysis, should be kept to a minimum. But a practical criticism course, to be of any real value, must try to reflect as far as it can the experience of the ordinary reader of literature, and we must soon begin to think more about the flexibility which, to be competent readers of literature, we must have. For some of the most important decisions we make about literature involve, not a comparison of similar things, but a balancing and contrasting of dissimilar qualities, without a rejection of either. Instead of asking 'Which of these two similar poems is the more successful?' we must often ask 'What has each poet, in his own different way and with his own different resources, been able to achieve?' A practical criticism course should certainly include at least a few exercises which ask this sort of question. In this way, students can be made more consciously aware, through the sharply focused concentration on particular examples which practical criticism affords, of the flexibility, the breadth of sympathy in response that literature often demands of us. The challenge here is to take into account more diverse factors than has generally been the case in the comparisons we have been making up to now: to compare unlikenesses as well as likenesses. An exercise of this sort is often a useful reminder that, in practical criticism, we are not learning any one 'method' or routine: it can, in a timely way, underline for us the need to keep alert for new and unexpected ways in which poets may expect us to respond.

The poems in Exercise 14 were written in the same period, they are both by great poets, and they seem to have been called forth by similar situations. In each poem, the poet, obviously in middle or advancing age, and no longer with the optimism of youth, feels acutely aware of his own weakness, his inability to lead the good life without God's help. He prays to God for 'grace', that is, for special strength and inspiration to overcome his frailties and live a life that will be crowned with salvation. The poems are concerned with misgivings and uncertainties about oneself, at a particular moment in life. But the ways in which the poets have reacted, and the ways in which they express themselves, are very unlike. In saying the poems are different in kind, I do not have any clearly defined, formal categories in mind (the seventeenth-century reader would probably have described the difference in terms of the plain style and the ornate style, but I see no point in complicating the discussion with these terms here). One way of putting the difference would be to say that Donne, as is evident at once, uses more metaphor than Jonson, and that his metaphor is more daring and original. And, after a further reading, we might add that Donne has the genius to recreate a high moment, a crisis of personal experience, while Jonson's genius seems to be more for summing up experience, for stating an attitude towards experience. This is, of course, as much as to say that Donne's poem is the more immediately striking one, and it is not hard to get most students to like it. The majority reaction to this comparison in fact is always in favour of the Donne. Jonson is often found to be 'dull', 'prosaic': after Donne, his poem seems rather tame, rather solemnly composed. This is, I think, because the Jonson poem reveals itself a little less readily. Mr Yvor Winters, commenting on Jonson's comparative restraint in this poem, says '...there is an exact correlation between motive and feeling which may easily be mistaken for coldness and mechanical indifference by readers accustomed to more florid enticements, but which impresses the present reader rather as integrity and nobility'. Perhaps behind the marked preference most readers feel for the Donne lies a belief that poetry and metaphor are the same thing, and that absence of metaphor means absence of poetry. We have met this belief before, and it is a clear sign of *undigested* teaching in practical criticism—of hints on how to deal with a poem applied ritually and unimaginatively. A great deal of poetry, including Donne's, depends on metaphor as a means of expression. But reading Donne should not disqualify us from reading and responding to Jonson.

The Jonson is more subdued, more regular and measured in movement, and this, together with the lack of metaphor, makes it less easy to analyse. Audacities of rhythm and metaphor almost always give us an opening for discussion, but it is another matter to comment convincingly on a poem which is as restrained in its effects as this one, and which makes its points by *understatement* as much as anything else. Yet I think a fairly convincing commentary is possible; and we can do something to show a doubting reader that Jonson's restraint, which is so foreign to Donne, does not imply a poverty of feeling. We need more time than usual, perhaps, to let the pace and inflections of the voice establish themselves. For instance, we must hear just the right insistence on 'disease', in the opening, which carries Jonson's slightly derisive but also awestruck sense of the disproportion between the courtier's shallow contempt for religious feeling and the real seriousness of what is troubling him. Such behaviour (his 'melancholy') may be out of place in a life of social events at court, and the opening of the poem is full of this change in perspective. The gloom or 'melancholy' is anything but a whim, and the lines

> . . . if I be sad for show
> And judge me after: if I dare pretend
> To aught but grace, or aim at other end

have Jonson's natural trenchancy of statement heightened by his awe and fear of the ultimate issues in life which he knows he

impact. There is little metaphor, but Jonson has nevertheless managed to capture the sensations of this moment of insight, the shock of realisation as the poet is recalled from the life he has been leading—a preoccupied life of the surface—to a sudden new consciousness of the more serious underlying truths of existence. Donne's power of metaphor is remarkable, but so is Jonson's ability to compress a great deal into a single brief phrase. 'Rap'd' seems, in this poem, to regain all the original force and vividness, all the meaning of being *transported* which the word has lost through loose, familiar usage. Jonson's ordinary everyday existence has been a dream, heedless of greater, more disturbing realities. This at any rate is the best explanation I can give for the unusual potency of the word here, and Jonson's terse intensity, which we notice everywhere in his best poems, his power to sum up a great deal in a brief, pungent phrase ('friendship of the spit', 'the wild anarchie of drink' are examples) is I think as clear a sign of greatness as Donne's metaphorical power, though it sometimes looks as though it were less remarkable.

The final section, from line 17 onwards, is really the centre of the poem, the statement (the word is scarcely adequate) of the insights which lie behind the poem and to which everything up to now has been leading. Not surprisingly, perhaps, it is this last part of the poem which usually appeals most readily to readers, and these lines above all make the poem, for me, one of Jonson's greatest. In lines 17–20 he is, of course, repeating a traditional, received truth, and in line 18 especially he is recalling traditional language. But there is never for an instant a doubt that this is Jonson's own belief, his own conclusions about life. The distinctly personal tone of voice, which, once we have read Jonson, we can recognise so easily, is never lost; and these lines are full of his personal pessimism, the deeply felt conviction of human frailty and the inevitability of misery and suffering which runs through much of his best poetry (we have already noted it in the poem *On His First Son*). Although the language of these lines is traditional and has a 'public' sanction, this section of the poem contains things which can only be realised by a man alone, in private. It is part of the poem's greatness that, in its subdued tone, it never loses the atmosphere of a private, intimate moment. The idea of a third person possibly being present, as it were to break the intimacy of atmosphere, at once strikes us as incongruous. Jonson, without the least trace of melodrama, approaches despair. This is not despair of the tempestuous, agitated sort, but the quiet, considered, convinced despair of a middle-aged man who has reviewed his life with the mature, balanced detachment that comes with middle-age, and finds the thought of continued existence difficult to bear. The handling of tone here is perfect: each phrase seems to fall with just the right unalterable certitude:

> Standing with fear, and must with horror fall,

the inversion in the line, the likeness of 'fear' and 'horror' and the unlikeness of 'stand' and 'fall' are used to the maximum in this compact summing up of the insecurity of life and the violence of death. The final 'after all' is a superbly trenchant concluding 'turn'. As if in the wake of this statement there comes a recollection of what his life so far has cost Jonson:

> I feele my griefs too, and there scarce is ground
> Upon my flesh t'inflict another wound.

This is not the cheap, half-meant self-abasement of so much religious poetry, as we can see from the close:

> Yet dare I not complain, or wish for death
>   With holy Paul, lest it be thought the breath
> Of discontent; or that these prayers be
>   For weariness of life, not love of thee.

I should like to refer to Mr Winters's remarks on this poem, which are among the most helpful criticism of Jonson I know:

The poem deals with love for God and the desire for death. God is perfect being, and therefore good; life, as the poet knows it, is being however imperfect, and therefore good only as a matter of theory. Ben Jonson, in middle age, does not fear death as Shakespeare professes to fear it, and as Donne apparently fears it in fact: his temptation is 'weariness of life';

his duty, which he accepts with a kind of semi-suppressed despair, is to overcome this weariness. There is recognition of reality here, distinct from a literary convention (as in Shakespeare) and from a gift for drama, or perhaps melodrama (as in Donne), which is very impressive. Much of the power of the poem resides in one of the elementary facts of life: the fact that a middle aged man of intelligence is often readier to die than to live if he merely indulges his feelings. Jonson deals with the real problem, not the spurious problem.

This is an admirable gloss on the meaning of the poem, particularly on the significance of the religious element.[1] Jonson knows that he must believe in the value of the struggle to live a good life, but it is only by the strongest effort of 'belief' that he can do this, and he fears that his prayers may be prompted by 'weariness of life' rather than a genuine desire for new strength to continue the struggle. In these last lines the 'semi-suppressed despair' (suggested most directly, perhaps, in 'breath/Of discontent' with its expressive movement across the line-ending, but present everywhere in the subdued rhythm) comes almost to the surface. In the final cadence, 'weariness of life', which sums up so much of the feeling that emerges in the poem, is spoken with something like a suppressed sigh. The distinction Jonson draws here between 'weariness of life' and 'love of thee' reveals an incisive clarity of mind which is moral self-knowledge (or 'strength of character') of a rare order. The contrast between what Jonson actually feels, and what he knows he must try to feel, and indeed cannot afford *not* to feel, is the essence of this moving piece of self-recognition. We feel that Jonson has seen his problem, his predicament, clearly and entirely; no aspect has been underrated or partially considered, and a 'real problem, not a spurious problem' has been summed up. Clarity of mind is certainly one of our chief impressions of this poem, but if the discipline of the poem is partly one of restraint (the despair has to be kept down, understated, and not given away to) there is no emasculation of feeling. There is, to use Mr Winters's

---

[1] And a reminder (if one is needed) that there is a complexity of feeling present here, although it does not show itself in the same way as complexity of feeling in a Donne poem.

terms, an 'exact correlation between motive and feeling' which impresses the reader as honesty and integrity.

The Donne poem, like the Jonson, could only have been written by a man at a particular time of life. Donne feels, not 'weariness of life', but the onset of physical decay, and he fears approaching death and possible extinction. He can no longer live on a fund of sheer vitality, as he did in youth. He must try to adjust himself to the new and horrifying circumstance of impending death. The constricting fear of the moment at which Donne realises that death is no longer something that can be felt as comfortably remote, and forgotten, is caught with a dramatic vividness and intensity we would not look for in a Jonson poem:

> Thou hast made me, and shall thy work decay?
> Repair me now, for now mine end doth haste...

In the opening line, Donne compares the assurance he ought to feel—for he has been made by God in His own image, a little lower than the angels—and his newly awakened anguish. Can it be God's intention that His own handiwork should perish? The following lines contain things we would never find in Jonson:

> I runne to death, and death meets me as fast,

A terrifying sense that the remaining space between the present moment and death is diminishing rapidly is conveyed in this line; the two runners approach one another on a collision course at full speed, and soon there will be a head-on crash. 'Runne' obviously calls for deliberate emphasis in reading: the effect is, 'This may look like hyperbole, but it is an all too literal truth'. Donne's conscience is fully awake: 'And all my pleasures are like yesterday' (Donne is sometimes accused of forced, eccentric audacities with language, but how natural in gesture and emphasis this line is). The poet's appalled sense of his own helplessness is given us vividly in:

> I dare not move my dimme eyes any way,
> Despair behind, and death before doth cast
> Such terror...

The control of movement here is superb. The poet is trapped between his 'despair' i.e. his sense of guilt for past pleasures, and his fear of death, and both are too terrible to contemplate. 'Such terror', placed as it is, has an agonised stress which only the most unresponsive reader could miss. It would be hard to think of a better example of what we mean when we say that the language of a poem 'enacts' its meaning. The language of Donne's poem enacts its meaning *in us*; we recreate for ourselves his moment of paralysed panic. He feels his ageing, weakened body is sinking towards Hell, and while the 'thought' is, in a sense, conventional enough (the body is sinful, will decay and may finally bring us to Hell) few poets have rendered this thought so convincingly in terms of actual physical suffering. The suffering, the physical weakness, are real, and Donne's belief that he is sinking towards Hell follows in such a way that we have no sense of a moral or sentiment artificially added on, as we certainly would have had if the poet had been feeling less strongly and writing more conventionally. The physical fear of death, and the moral feeling of guilt, are completely unified and blended in this poem.

There is a contrast in the following lines as Donne, who cannot bring himself to look steadily at his past and future on earth, looks towards Heaven. The downwards movement is replaced by an upward one, and again the moral analogy is felt as a physical sensation, this time the inrush of life and hope into a feeble ageing man. 'Our old subtle foe' still tempts him —to the sin of despair, one feels—and only God's grace can 'wing' him (i.e. give him wings) to enable him to soar above the abyss and out of Satan's reach. In the last line the movement seems to dwell emphatically on 'adamant'; this is the resistless power which alone can save the poet from perishing.

Looking back at Mr Winters's effectively tentative suggestion that Donne has a gift for personal drama or perhaps melodrama, we can say, I think, that this poem is drama, not melodrama. There is no trace of false heightening or rhetorical exaggeration. But the poem is incomparably vehement. As we read, the poet seems really poised over a gulf, helpless and ready to sink unless he is aided by stronger powers; his prayer is desperately urgent. This immediacy in portraying extremes of feeling in a crisis of experience is something we do not get, or do not get in the same degree, from Jonson, whom we cannot even imagine attempting to produce the sort of impact which Donne produces here. In a similar situation, although both poets are very much in the Christian tradition, Jonson's experience is different, and he confronts it differently. The unlikeness in language between the poems is directly traceable to these differences. Jonson is a less original and inventive poet than Donne, but in his more restrained way he is still original and inventive enough to be vividly individual. We pay for Donne's greater originality, perhaps, in his larger number of less successful poems, in which originality has become a fetish, or eccentricity leads to ambivalent results. Jonson is rich in representatively human qualities, and with his clarity, his power to resolve so much experience into incisive generalised moral statement, he matters to us scarcely less than Donne. To reflect on the differences between these poems and their writers is to realise yet again how useless and stultifying hard and fast definitions of what poetry is, and how the language of poetry works, are liable to be. Receptiveness and flexibility are what the critic really needs, and these things can only be developed by actual contact with literature, in all its variety. It is this contact, rather than a 'method' of reading, with fixed definitions and a 'learned' procedure, that a practical criticism course must try to provide.

CHAPTER 16

Prose

Although for the sake of convenience in exposition prose and poetry appear under separate headings in this book, I do not want to give the impression that they are separate entities, or that they are different and divided parts of our concern with practical criticism. The criticism of poetry and the criticism of prose are not separate activities, and to devote one half of the course to poetry and the other half to prose would be absurd. The exercises should be studied concurrently. The earlier chapter on practical criticism and method was directed primarily at the criticism of poetry, but almost everything said there, if it is valid, applies equally to prose. There is, of course, a purely scientific kind of prose, which aims only to put across fact, and this prose does not call for practical criticism (though it is notorious that scientific prose can sometimes be anything but impersonal). But most other kinds of prose yield themselves to analysis of 'prose-quality' in a way strictly analogous to the way in which we have been analysing poetry. This is most obviously true of the novel—where much the same limitations to analysis of particular passages hold good as with analysis of extracts from plays—but it is also true of most kinds of discursive writing; of criticism, philosophy, letter-writing, journalism. A prose writer reveals the quality of his mind in the way he uses language. His control of tone, the note he strikes, the choice of idiom and metaphor, all tell us important things about what he is saying. Prose is anything but a series of impersonal ciphers. One of the main general truths which we need to grasp (not simply 'learn') is that it is impossible to regard 'content' or a paraphrasable summary of the things said as something separate from prose-quality—unless the content is not worth worrying about, for a writer who consciously tries to draw attention to 'style' for the sake of style almost invariably strikes us as trivial and irritating. What we will grow to recognise is the close, distinctive sharpness of language which, in any age and in any idiom, reveals the writer who has something urgent and something precise to convey, and who has the flair for language which enables him to find the vocabulary and phrasing he needs to express himself.

But, first of all, I think we should begin by looking at extracts from novels, for they form the best starting-point for an exploration of the practical criticism of prose.

CHAPTER 17

Extracts from Novels: A Passage
from George Eliot's 'Daniel Deronda'

As I have just pointed out, much the same limitations apply to extracts from novels as to extracts from plays as pieces of practical criticism; only perhaps more so. We have an extract from a very long work before us (Exercise 31) and in discussing it we can only appreciate the greatness of the novel in a partial, qualified way. These exercises will only be useful if this condition is kept clearly in mind from the start—again, it will be a big advantage if work in this course can be related to work in other courses. There is, too, as with speeches from dramas, the often tricky problem of acquiring, in a sentence or two, the necessary information about the context of the passage. But this kind of work can be of real value in learning to read novels. The amount of careless reading that our first efforts usually show is an indication of what sometimes happens when we are reading on our own, and it is an interesting commentary on what probably lies behind the typically derivative essay that must be familiar in some degree to all teachers of literature whose students have much access to criticism. Exercises of this sort can help to show how lively an attentiveness the great novelists expect in their readers. They can play an important part in bringing to life and action the flair for responding to language, as opposed to merely reading language, which the student of literature must possess and develop if his courses are to be more to him than academic exercises.

I have included the Scott/Conrad comparison as a possible first prose exercise (Exercise 30). It should enable the teacher to enforce at the simplest level the elementary fact that the language of prose, in the novel, 'creates' its meaning in much the same way as the language of poetry, and that this meaning can be analysed in much the same fashion. The passages both describe sensational events, a crisis of physical danger, but in the first passage nothing is done to bring these events vividly before us. The limp, tired phrasing, the conventional epithets, the lifeless, routine prose movement, all tell us that Scott is not seriously involved in what he is writing about; we could even say he is not seriously interested. There are better things in the novel than this extract, but what we have here is an example of Scott's writing at little more than book-making level, the kind of thing he could turn out at speed and more or less to order. Conrad's language, on the other hand, really works to make us feel the sensations of the ship's crew in the typhoon. Notice the far greater exactness of detail, and the way in which different kinds of movement and sound are contrasted as Conrad describes the particularly vindictive violence of the storm's attack on the ship, especially the contrast between the noise of the storm and the 'frail and resisting' voice of the captain which reaches Juke's ear. The passage is attempting something fairly simple, and so the effects are of a limited sort. But the writer has felt and conveyed the frenzy of a typhoon at sea, and a class should have no difficulty in working out the comparison with the Scott in more detail than I have thought necessary in the present context.

The George Eliot passage is less simple in intention, but it should present no real difficulty to students who are, at the same time, tackling Jane Austen in another course, and there is nothing in it which, with careful prompting from the directions, will not be readily understandable. I have read many uncomprehending, or partly comprehending accounts of the passage, but the trouble comes from other causes than these. Students who go wrong on the passage may just not be lively enough to follow George Eliot; this writing demands an alertness of mind in the reader which many students, unprompted, are not ready to give. To appreciate George Eliot's total attitude—her admiration for Klesmer, her contempt for the philistine complacency of the English ruling classes as represented by Mr Bult, and, most of all, the way in which her views are not simply stated but presented in undistorted dramatic terms, to speak for themselves—we must recognise and respond to the wit of the passage. We must know how to take, for instance, the wit of 'A healthy Briton on the central table-land of life', which conclusively sums up the commonplace dullness of Mr Bult. His youth is brief, he reaches a stodgy middle-age in his early twenties, and remains drearily changeless until old age, stolidly fixed in personality (and physique). Only a prosperous man, we feel, could reach middle-age so quickly, and stay preserved in it for so long. His attitude to women is beautifully hit off in a few phrases: '...he did not mind Miss Arrowpoint's addiction to music any more than her probable expenses in antique lace.' To respond to this writing is like, on a higher plane, being able to understand and enjoy witty and vivacious conversation—we have to feel the innuendoes, enjoy the humour and take the force of the critical jokes. My readers who thought Mr Bult 'haughty, pompous, loud, overbearing' were not able to do this. The comedy of this exchange turns upon the fact that Mr Bult so blandly, unconsciously assumes his superiority to Klesmer; he is no bully—in fact he can easily afford good temper, because he has no inkling that any other values but his own can matter. He doesn't even need to assert himself. This is the point behind George Eliot's deflating wit, and this is why Bult is, for Klesmer, so maddening.

The passage might be described as a piece of international comedy, but, though we may feel we have nothing directly to do with the obtuse complacencies of the Victorian ruling class, we know equally well that what is going on here has a representative importance. George Eliot's liveliness and intelligence can tell us something about our world. Indeed, Bult and Klesmer are representative human types—the rich philistine and the creative artist—as well as being completely convincing dramatic beings. We are introduced to Mr Bult, whose name has a very appropriate stolid gracelessness, as an earnest cultivator of his own career, entirely satisfied with the world as he finds it, and a thoroughly dull man. The sort of competence which has enabled him to succeed is of the narrowest: he is a specialist in colonial affairs, and, as with many nineteenth-century English politicians, understanding colonial 'affairs' means understanding the international market. George Eliot gives us the quality of his interest when she speaks of his 'strong opinions' about distant countries. His idea of what concerns the serious politician is so narrow and blinkered that he has no more than the vaguest caricature of a notion of the kind of interests a more intelligent and enlightened politician might have. This caricature element in Mr Bult's mental vision of ideas and cultures other than his own is given us in the wonderfully deflating remark (deflating of Mr Bult, that is): 'Klesmer he hardly regarded in the light of a serious human being who ought to have a vote', and it is given us, too, in Mr Bult's assessment of Klesmer a few lines later: '...to be accounted for probably by his being a Pole, or a Czech, or something of that fermenting sort, in a state of political refugeeism which had obliged him to make a profession of his music'. Nothing could more effectively or wittily suggest Bult's utter imperviousness to anything outside his own philistine, materialistic creed. Foreigners are clowns to him; so, too, are musicians and, we feel (remembering George Eliot), writers as well. Bult's dismissal of Klesmer's political views is nicely linked to his dismissal of Klesmer's music. Music is a decorative accomplishment for young ladies, and no doubt it needs appropriately odd, 'artistic' foreigners to teach it, but it cannot claim the attention of a serious man of affairs for long. The mentality is captured completely.

Klesmer, of course, is foreign and excitable; his manners do not follow the pattern of English decorum. But George Eliot's art doesn't make us see this foreignness as clownish. Rather, she makes us realise just what staid English politeness and reticence can sometimes mean—not how admirable and civilised, but how deadly it can be. She is amused at the collision which takes place between Klesmer and the other guests after dinner: 'He was consequently a little amazed at an after-dinner outburst of Klesmer's on the lack of idealism in English politics...On this theme Klesmer's eloquence, gesticulatory and other, went on for a little while like stray fireworks, accidentally ignited, and then sank into immovable silence'. She is amused, that is, at the contrast between the demonstrative foreigner and the reserved Englishmen. But her sympathies are clear: Klesmer's idealism in politics is generous and imaginative, the English are obtuse, stuffy and complacently disapproving. The real clash comes in the evening, when Mr Bult approaches Klesmer at the piano, Miss Arrowpoint being near. Mr Bult doesn't want to be offensive, nothing is further from his thoughts, but the conversation is doomed from the start. 'I had no idea that you were a political man' has the tone of the professional speaking with kindly condescension to the bungling amateur, and Mr Bult's unconsciously patronising good intentions soon get him in trouble. Klesmer knows at once that there is no hope of a serious mutual understanding, and, icy politeness not being part of his nature, he first of all reacts with truculent rudeness and then relieves his irritation in high-spirited fooling. Miss Arrowpoint, however, is present. Mr Bult regards her as his intended, and Klesmer feels a natural link of sympathy and interests, and, in spite of her desire to keep the peace, her presence acts as something of a catalyst. She understandably feels embarrassed and makes a placatory remark, but Mr Bult, willing to help, unluckily reveals his real feelings about music and musicians. Nothing is worse than an intended compliment which misfires. It is Mr Bult who is the real clown here. George Eliot is completely behind Klesmer's outburst, which is the protest of the creative artist against the rich world which wants to use him as its toy. Klesmer's language is forceful, direct and dignified. But it is all lost on Mr Bult, whose comment, after Klesmer has 'wheeled away', is meant to be amiably shrewd and manly, but is only amiably dense and uncomprehending. The whole passage is sharp and sure in its judgments, but it has at the same time the sane wholesomeness of good humour. No one who reads it carefully could accuse George Eliot of a distorting or simplifying bias; she moves with the ease and precision of a writer who is in perfect possession of her materials.

CHAPTER 18

Extracts from Novels:
A Comparison of Passages from Thackeray
and Lawrence

This comparison (Exercise 32) asks us to consider a representative difference between the great novelist and the lesser novelist, one which we shall remember having met with, in a closely analogous form, in the critical analysis of poetry. This is the difference between writing in which something is 'actually presented', that is, created with a complete coherence and fullness of the imagination, and writing in which there is a failure of creation, where loose, weak writing reveals that the contents of the passage were never sharply imagined or closely, inwardly understood. To sum up these rather generalised, abstract phrases, this is the difference between the genuinely dramatic and the falsely dramatic in a novel. Both passages describe a clash between a wronged husband and an unfaithful wife; both are tense, and violence takes place in each; and, in each, the wife has been attracted to the lover by the cheap glamour of an affair with a rich man. But which novelist is rendering life with perceptiveness and penetration? Which gives us convincingly real human beings, and a piece of actual suffering? In which is the significance of details, of individual actions as well as of 'stage furniture', tactfully and sensitively taken? And which passage is conceived externally, with people who are merely clichés, and a situation cheaply contrived for effect? The difference between the genuinly dramatic and the pseudo-dramatic is always one which, in specific passages, we can 'prove' in detailed analysis. Both extracts are, I think, sufficiently long for there to be no misconception of intention, and no unfairness to the novelists concerned.

The comparison is a fairly straightforward one; it can be used early in the course. In passage A, everything is played up to the hilt for effect, and the art we can recognise as that of the sentimental melodrama. Rawdon Crawley returns unexpectedly to catch his wife red-handed amid all the corrupt glamour—the particularly wicked hilarity—of an illicit affair. 'Laughter and singing', the 'hoarse voice' of the ageing lecher, Lord Steyne—not one ingredient of the melodramatic confrontation is left out. The expensive immoral luxury is indicated with a heavy hand:

A little table with a dinner was laid out—and wine and plate...The wretched woman was in a brilliant full toilette, her arms and all her fingers sparkling with bracelets and rings; and the brilliants on her breast which Steyne had given her...

The characters don't behave naturally; they make a series of theatrical posturings:

Steyne was hanging over the sofa on which Becky sat...He had her hand in his, and was bowing over it to kiss it, when Becky started up with a faint scream as she caught sight of Rawdon's white face.

The attempts to suggest tension and consciousness of guilt are equally clumsy:

...she tried a smile, a horrid smile...Steyne rose up, grinding his teeth ...the nerves of his mouth twitching as he tried to grin at the intruder...

The guilty one, the scarlet woman, makes a desperate, dishonest plea of innocence,

She clung hold of his coat, of his hands; her own were all covered with serpents, and rings and baubles...

The old lecher turns nasty, and utters some unparliamentary language,

Innocent, by—!

There is a fight, in which the arrogant peer—who begins to look more and more like the Sir Jasper of the song—is easily overpowered by the superior strength of the upright hero:

...Steyne, almost strangled, writhed, and bent under his arm: 'You lie, you dog...'.

The villain is flung bleeding to the ground, and the guilty

Becky looks on terrified, but—oh subtle insight into female nature!—at this moment she admires her husband,

strong, brave, and victorious.

The scarlet woman is made to take off her lendings, a gem is thrown at the villain, which cuts him on his bald forehead (serves him right for trying to make love when he's gone bald), and leaves a scar which Steyne wears to his dying day. After more terrified pleas, and savage laughter from the hero, they go through Becky's things, through 'the multifarious trumpery' of the contents of her boxes and wardrobes, which we now realise are the false idols of a capricious feminine world which is so unstable, so—without the right guidance—prone to moral collapse. A brief, dignified reproach from the hero ('You might have spared me a hundred pounds, Becky, out of all this'); a further protest of innocence—these protests are pretty repetitive, and show the poverty of the writing rather than Becky's feeble panic—and he leaves her.

I do not think this account misrepresents the level of the appeal. No conceivable ironic intention on the part of the author could make this writing appear anything more than I have suggested.[1] The contrast with passage B is, I believe, obvious enough to be apparent at once to most people on first reading, but my aim here is to show the difference in detail—to appreciate the qualities of the second extract in detailed analysis, using A as a foil. B, it seems to me, is genuinely dramatic. There is no secondary sense on the writer's part that these happenings are noble and striking. The novelist is much more deeply moved by the events he is writing about, but melodrama is absent, and there is hardly a false touch in the whole passage. The events are presented with a vivid distinctness at every point; the people are incomparably more real; and each shade of feeling and atmosphere is sharply rendered. This novelist, unlike the writer of A, can really tell us what an emotional crisis between husband and wife is like.

[1] This, of course, is not the whole truth about Rawdon Crawley, but I believe I have not misrepresented him as he appears in this particular episode.

In the opening lines of the passage, the husband, who 'has a long score' against his wife, is being roused to fury by her. His reproaches are angry, direct: she is partly defensive but, anxious to retain that bit of her vanity (the word seems to fit) which has been flattered by the affair, she wants to win this battle, and she taunts her husband in an exaggeratedly 'superior' way for being dull, stupid, insensitive, and so on. The pert, bitchy, I-know-better-than-you tone of her replies is caught in

'I've just spoken to him when I've seen him', she said. 'He's not as bad as you would make out.'

We don't doubt, though the tenor of the passage is so serious, that this writer has a lively, even mischievous sense of humour. The contrast with the husband's angry directness (he has no 'tactics') is excellent:

'Have you been having owt to do with him?'

and those who know Lawrence can perhaps reflect on the difference between the handling of common, dialect speech here and in Mellor's speeches in *Lady Chatterley's Lover*, a difference which will, I believe, be clear to those who don't normally hear northern English speech. The tension mounts perceptibly as the wife, secretly afraid but still believing she can win the battle of wills, continues to mock.

A curious little grin of hate came on his face...
  'What am I frightened for?' he repeated automatically. 'What am I frightened for? Why, for you, you stray-running little bitch.'

Contrast this with Steyne's mouth, twitching as he tried to smile in the first piece, and it becomes clear which writer knows how people behave in a crisis. 'Automatically' is no facile sensational device: it suggests one of the odd ways in which speech comes to us at a moment of emotional tension, the slightly uncanny tones of voice. This coarse description of her behaviour—so unlike the description *she* has worked out for herself—goes home. But she hangs on, still hoping not to have to give in, still sticking to her line of defence: you are a coarse, clumsy bully, you're not fit to be let into something as far above you as my private thoughts. This is actually feminine (compare 'There was that in Rawdon's face which caused her to fling herself before him', etc.), this is the way a woman can really torment her husband. Notice, too, how well the description of the woman 'fits'. The husband goes out of doors, amid suggestions of an approaching paroxysm ('Below him, far off, fumed the lights of the town. He still stood, unconscious with a black storm of rage, his face lifted to the night') and returns to find her still defiant—

She stood, a small, stubborn figure with tight-pressed lips and big, sullen, childish eyes, watching him, white with fear.

Even if we haven't read the short story of which this passage forms the climax we know that this is a young married couple and that this is the first crisis, the real crisis, the outcome of which decides the nature and quality of their future relationship. And we can recognise, in the phrase 'big, sullen, childish eyes', exactly the kind of petulance which has helped to bring on this crisis; she is stubborn in a 'childish' way, a way which is mostly blind wilful disobedience to a tacitly acknowledged authority. There is something childish, not adult, in her spitefulness:

'How I hate your word "break your neck"', she said, with a grimace of the mouth. 'It sounds so common and beastly. Can't you say something else—'

There is, certainly, a girlish spite in 'What do you know about anything?' in the fatal sentence which brings on the crisis. And how differently this writer manages the physical violence. Compare the absurd theatrical posturing of the figures in passage A with this:

He seemed to thrust his face and his eyes forward at her, as he rose slowly and came to her. She watched transfixed in terror. Her throat made a small sound, as she tried to scream.

Then, quick as lightning, the back of his hand struck her with a crash across the mouth, and she was flung back blinded against the wall. The shock shook a queer sound out of her...

Mad with terror, she raised her hands in a queer clawing movement to cover her eyes and her temples, opening her mouth in a dumb shriek. There was no sound...

This writing manages to capture the oddly heightened un-naturalness of such a moment: the awkward movements, the strained nightmarish impotence of her actions, the unusual vividness of certain impressions.

And his lust to see her bleed, to break her and destroy her, rose from an old source against her. It carried him. He wanted satisfaction.

But he had seen her standing there, a piteous, horrified thing, and he turned aside his face in shame and nausea...

The way in which this visual impression imprints itself on the man's brain, and prevents him from giving a second blow—normality asserts itself just in time over the lust for violence—seems to me a success which only a major writer could pull off. This is real violence, and, as the husband is not a brutal man, it produces inevitable revulsion:

He could see it, the blood-mark. It made him only more sick and tired of the responsibility, the violence, the shame...

After the crisis, he feels wearied and sick of the whole business. The woman resists—she forces a few tears of self-pity—but she now feels helpless, and her protests ('she wept with rage') have a different tone. In the aftermath of the violence, they tremble in the balance for a while, and returning normality begins to have its effect as they sort themselves out. The man is quietly determined, the woman is no longer interested in the trinkets. She finally gives way before his determination, and the passage ends with the reconciliation it has been leading to—for this is a crisis of wills between a couple whose quarrels mean something; it has been a productive clash. The 'great flash of anguish' affirms something which has been, in a way, implicitly behind the whole incident. How faultless is the touch in the concluding lines:

'My love—my little love.'

The sentimental awkwardness of the phrase is the authentic note of real tenderness here. We might notice, as a last observation, how nicely Lawrence has handled one detail, the jewels. Compare the heavy-handed attempt to make the meaning of the corrupt, glittering jewelry clear in passage A:

...brilliant full toilette.
...her own were all covered with serpents and rings and baubles.

In B, the husband notices the jewels so naturally when, weary but clear minded after the quarrel, he packs them up to send them back to the man who has flirted with his wife (and again, we know this has been a flirtation, trivial in its vanity):

He looked at the little jewels. They were pretty.
  'It's none of their fault', he said to himself.

I hope this analysis has been sufficient to show that, as Dr Leavis points out, in this story we are not given a violent view of life; and that I have managed to show, too, that it was written by a novelist who, unlike the writer of A, understood and could represent the differing ways in which emotion ebbs and flows at a critical moment in human relationships. 'He looked at her in contempt and compassion and in rising anger'; 'they trembled in the balance for a while'; 'she was yielded up to him'; the reader who ponders the meaning of these (and other) key-phrases from the extract will know what is meant by 'the richness and complexity of the great novelist's presentation of life'.

CHAPTER 19

Two Passages about Belief:
Foerster and Forster

The transition from analysis of the prose of novels to analysis of other kinds of prose need not be a difficult one, if it is managed sensibly. Novels, of course, normally require no specialised skill or knowledge to be understood. But in making our decisions about other kinds of prose, we must often bring other factors into account, and the place of analysis of the prose-quality in the final decisions we make about a passage is not always so easy to recognise. The greater the number and variety of other factors we have to consider, the greater the flexibility of mind we will need in making decisions. For to know how to use his literary critical training in language along with other factors, and relate it to them, is one of the great tests of a literary critic's ability. He must know, for example, when a writer is stating a truth that he himself is in sympathy with and believes to be important, whether the writer is realising this truth, or whether he is merely repeating it in a stale, loose way; and, when a writer is stating something the critic disagrees with, he must still be able to find a coherent place for his judgment of the writer's language in his final decision. He needs to appreciate just what a failure with language can mean at a certain point in a discourse. I do not think there is any formula here which will simplify these questions for beginners, nor do I think general discussion of the problem in abstract terms will serve our purpose very much. Demonstration, and tactful choice of exercises, seem to me the only ways in which we become aware of the importance which the literary critic's sense of language can have in appreciation of a writer's thought. It is an importance which most people are unlikely to grasp without help (or with only the kind of training that is sometimes provided in other subjects); and it is an importance which, I believe, increases in proportion to the depth, penetration and value of a writer's thought.

The present comparison (Exercise **33**), it is hoped, is fairly obvious in what it suggests about the importance of prose analysis. The passages are both about humanism or, if that word is likely to cause difficulty, they are both statements of their writer's position *vis-à-vis* belief, particularly religious belief. The humanist's position is the one which recognises the importance of human values—which believes in human values —but which denies the need for religious sanctions. Both writers are humanists, but I hope this comparison will help to show why one of them is a great humanist.

The passages are statements about belief, but there is very little similarity between them and the differences are not explainable simply as differences of intention. We notice at once a difference in flavour between the passages, and, however vague a distinction it may seem at first sight, this sort of perception is liable to grow in importance as we get closer to the prose of each writer. The manner, the tone, is not something we notice *after* taking in the 'prose content' (the cliché neatly embodies the prejudice we are trying to get rid of); it conditions what the writer is saying, and in fact *is* part of what the writer is saying. The first passage is decidedly professorial, decidedly academic in tone, and its manner impressed some of my student readers: 'A is more intelligent, profound and objective'. The description 'impersonal' for this piece and 'personal' for the second occurs to most people who compare these passages, and the implied distinction seems to me an important one. But we must ask what this impersonality amounts to. What are its conditions, and what kind of an achievement does this impartiality represent? Is it the kind that, by detaching itself from the matter discussed, manages to say something new and important about it? If it eschews emotion in discussing emotional matter, is this a really difficult effort of disinterestedness, or is this an easy thing because the writer has no very strong feelings about the question anyway?

Close examination of the writer's langauage will enable us to answer these questions, and decide whether the writer's tone, which impressed my readers as having authority, is really a distinguished one. Those of my readers who got beyond the stage of being impressed by the manner were usually ready to comment on the extremely abstract character of the language. If 'humanism', as envisaged by this writer, is to be a creed we live by, then it is very abstruse; and the writer's language, despite the professorial air, is, when we look at it, anything but precise. One wonders if that opening sentence, with the 'centripetal energy' and the 'centrifugal impulses' is much more than a convenient scientific metaphor. Judging by the way the writer later tells us that humanism describes it *thus* in physical terms, he appears to imagine that he is describing actual physical phenomena. But he is not, and his use of pseudo-scientific language reveals a disturbing confusion of mind. If he had clearly worked out his meaning and seen that he was discussing a moral sensibility, not a scientific fact, then he might have found the right language in which to express himself. It is plain, though, that this pseudo-scientific language has a glamour, a prestige value for the writer that prevents him from seeing its confusions. He continues in similarly ready-made, glib formulations: 'It cannot bring itself to accept a formal theology (any more than it can accept a romantic idealism)...' The phrase 'romantic idealism' means nothing precise, and the writer has plainly never thought about the process that he names 'accepting' a romantic idealism; it sounds more like accepting or rejecting a conclusion to a seminar than discovering or embracing a personal belief. Similarly 'the too harsh dualism of the flesh and the spirit' is another synthetic phrase which smacks too much of glib, second-hand generalisation. The language is not precise enough, nothing is grasped in the phrase (which religion? isn't there usually more subtlety in many traditional religious views of the relation of the flesh and the spirit—more subtlety, at least, than this summary dismissal suggests?). We don't need to be religious believers ourselves to want to question whether religions uniformly believe that supernatural intuition must not be 'tested by the intellect', or whether religion doesn't assign an important place to both science and art (and where art is concerned, a number of the poems already looked at in this book can tell us something). In what way do religions (or some of them) *not* call for completeness? The phrase 'wishing to use and not annihilate dangerous forces' certainly doesn't suggest that 'completeness' is a full or developed conception of the writer's. Then follows a definition of common ground between religion and humanism, the 'perception of the ethical will', and it is here above all that the writer's language betrays him. There is no trace of warmth in the writing, no current of strong feeling, no air of personal conviction. The terms are abstruse, unfelt, the prose is anaemic, and we have to remind ourselves with an effort that this is meant to be a statement of a truth felt (or claimed) to have great importance for the writer. Important truths, we might say, never feel like this. There is none of the distinguishing incisiveness of language that goes with real thought—that is, thought that is first hand, searching, and rigorous. The prose moves in a series of shallow, ready-made phrases. We might add that this writer is only interested in ideas *qua* words. He manipulates phrases, but fails to engage with anything; his expression is a barrier to thought, rather than a means of thinking. No one, we are tempted to conclude, ever thought effectively in this idiom.

In B we can sense the involvement of a particular personality. To recall the sentence from George Orwell quoted earlier, somewhere behind any really individual piece of writing we always have an impression of a face, and this is true of the present passage. The idiom and the manner are spontaneously personal; we are utterly free from the jargon of passage A. The quiet, firm, unpretentious manner could hardly form a greater contrast; this really does sound like a statement of beliefs which are vitally important to the writer. In 'But this is an age of faith, and there are so many militant creeds that, in self-defence, one has to formulate a creed of one's own', the characteristic 'in self-defence' is not a stale affectation of modesty, a cheap trick to get on good terms with the reader.

The sentence, and in fact the whole passage, tells us, in a way abstract language could never do, of the difficulties and perplexities of a liberal mind in an age which, more than most, denies liberal values. It reveals the determination, as well as the distaste, with which Forster looks at the modern world; he is determined to adjust enough to be effective, but not to adjust too far and be drawn into conflicts on the age's own terms;

Tolerance, good temper and sympathy are no longer enough in a world which is rent by religious and racial persecution...Tolerance, good temper and sympathy—they are what matter really, and if the human race is not to collapse they must come to the front before long...

'Tolerance, good temper and sympathy', unlike the abstract 'completeness' of passage A, are real and instantly recognisable; they are not part of the jargon of a history of religion course, bookish terms which have no living relation to conduct and action, but something we can readily relate to life as we know it. The gentle insistence with which these words are offered saves the writing from any hint of platitude or obviousness. These things, Forster seems to be saying, are such ordinary, simple qualities to talk about in the complex, scientific modern world, but I am asking you to reconsider your attitude towards them. He is restating these truths, and gives them a new freshness and force as he asks us to ponder their relative importance. He is readjusting our view of things, which is something platitude can never do. Most of all, this passage, unlike passage A, has actual, urgent problems behind it. It shows a mind trying to grapple with the difficulties of civilised survival in the modern world, trying to work out its own position and clarify some simple decencies which the writer feels he cannot take for granted, and which he believes must begin to leaven life if we are to survive. Writer A does not address himself to any real situation or problems; he writes 'in the abstract', without any strong compulsion or concern. We know that he does not really fear the 'too harsh dualism of the flesh and the spirit', nor does he feel that the forces inside himself are potentially dangerous—or, if he does, his pallid language gives no evidence of it. He is not strongly moved by the thought of an 'impersonal reality' transcending his ordinary self. But the military jack-boot in passage B is actual and sinister (the passage was written in 1939) and the writer truly fears the worship of political power and violence. He feels, too, a real contempt for the people who have debased the pursuit of knowledge into a race for weapons (science now 'plays the subservient pimp'). He distrusts creeds and dedication to creeds, but he knows that he must formulate something in the shape of a creed out of his own views if he is to get an effective hearing. Compare this to the seminar-room inspiration of writer A, and it is not surprising that B writes the better, more vital prose. The note of personal first-hand directness, which is completely the writer's own and yet so different from 'style' or cultivated mannerism, is one of the most enviable features of passage B, and the one which, probably, it would be hardest to reproduce or imitate.

CHAPTER 20

Aphorisms by Franklin and Lawrence

This exercise (Exercise **34**) is included for the sake of showing that, even in these brief, terse moral directives, which look so devoid of all 'literary' intention, prose quality is as much a part of the meaning as it is in the continuous passages we have been studying. Prose analysis, as students need to be reminded from time to time, is not some solemn, formidable process which critics employ only when they are assessing passages of full, formal classical dignity; it is not a specialised, esoteric skill which we learn for the purpose of reading established works of literature alone (or of passing examinations on them). It is, really, nothing more than a detailed consideration of the effect other people's words have on us. We respond to the language of literature as we respond to the language we hear in ordinary life, except that with literature our responses are more ordered, less casual and more significant; and analysing literary language is perhaps only something which we do, sporadically and half-unconsciously, with much of the conversation we are hearing every day. The words 'literature', 'literary' have such a power of conjuring up distinctions in most people's minds, that it needs a considerable amount of conscious effort, in general discussion and example, to rid a practical criticism class of the tacit assumption that critical analysis is like a special tool, carefully manufactured in order to do one partcular job and no other. The present exercise is intended to help in this effort to get the 'literary' feeling out of the phrase 'literary criticism'. The moral aphorisms have nothing overtly to do with literature. But analysis of them will show that our concern with language, which we have developed in discussing literature, is important when we consider any kind of expression; it is relevant to all uses of language, except perhaps the strictly scientific. To understand either writer in this exercise—his aims, his temper, his attitude of mind—we must take into account the way he uses words. We must, even here, respond critically to the language, not merely translate a series of signs on the page into abstract ideas or paraphrasable 'prose content'.

The readers who go through this latter process, looking for 'prose content', in my experience invariably go wrong with this exercise, reaching shallow, undiscerning conclusions. To an uncritical reader, A usually seems respectable, the sort of thing we expect to find in a series of moral injunctions and therefore reassuring. It all seems sound enough. B is more unusual, some of his statements, after A's, startle rather, and perhaps he is less to be trusted. But the conclusions a more lively, alert reader will reach are very different. A's advice may seem, in a sense, safe, sound and respectable, but he is also dull. His language is dry, the movement is stiff—there is something meagre and ungenerous about it. He has conveyed a good deal of fairly conventional morality, but he has conveyed the stale, insipid dullness of conventional moralising as well. Reading him, we are forced to ask if a moral injunction, when it is stated in a trite, insipid way, has any value, any real soundness or truth. For the mind that produced A seems, on the evidence of these aphorisms, to have been a pedestrian one, and the description has more force when we know that the writer used his rules to test his conduct at the end of each day. He likes order, he likes safety, caution, forethought, thrift, punctuality, and these virtues appear here at their most drab. It might be objected that his intention in making the list was not to provide rules for guiding the whole of life, but simply to check himself in certain details of his life where a practical, utilitarian spirit is harmless and in place, leaving the greater part to be organised in some other way. But a closer reading of the aphorisms will show that writer A is not thinking merely of one part of life that can be neatly severed from the rest. He is thinking of all that can come under the heading of conduct; the narrow spirit of his rules is of the sort that is liable to permeate our attitude to a great deal of our experience, as writer B sees. At this point, however, I would like to add a caveat. What has just been said has been said in criticism of the aphorisms and the attitude of mind they embody; we must hesitate to draw wholesale conclusions about the writer's character on the basis of them. It is so easy, in practical criticism, to frame our commentary as though we were giving a run-down on the writer, and students are only too liable to forget that it is the work only that we are discussing, or the writer as revealed through the work. The student commentary which reads like a character-assassination of the author of a bad poem is familiar to most teachers of literature, and it is something to be discouraged, for it is intemperate criticism, revealing a distorted sense of critical values. The poem or piece of prose may be bad, but the man may not be bad or even dull. We need only think of the number of interesting Victorians who wrote dull poetry to recognise the truth of this. Writer A is also a case in point: Benjamin Franklin has an interest of a sort we would never guess from these aphorisms. The caution is an obvious one, perhaps, but anyone who doubts its necessity should look at some of the denunciations that sometimes appear in student work, and reflect how easy it is to encourage a hard, intolerant spirit in criticism, and how difficult it often is to foster a flexible, tempered one.

Writer B—whom a number of my students always find more difficult to understand—produced his list of virtues, we must remember, because of his irritation with A's list. Otherwise, he would probably never have tried to sum up his thought (or part of his thought) in this form. Yet it is remarkable how much he manages to get into his injunctions, and how effectively his list criticises A's. If his meaning is less obvious than A's, and his nostrums have to be understood as a whole if they are to be understood individually, this is because his thought is more penetrating and profound. But surely the first thing we notice is that his language is so much more vivid and vital than A's. His manner is more immediate—by contrast A's seems feebly regular and tame, and this is not because B is a modern writer and A is eighteenth century. The first virtue, Temperance, is a good example.

A. Eat not to fullness; drink not to elevation.

B.   Eat and carouse with Bacchus, or munch dry bread with Jesus, but don't sit down without one of the gods.

'Elevation' is a comically prissy euphemism for drunkenness, and I don't believe this can be explained away as an archaism. The eighteenth-century had plenty of vigorous, racy language to describe drunkenness, and much of it in the vocabulary of the polite authors. B seizes on what is wrong with A, and is lively, witty and mischievous. Readers who are too dull to feel this invariably misunderstand him: 'Writer B wants nothing but extremes. His advice would put us all in hospital...' This pedestrian literal-mindedness will never communicate with writer B. 'It could be difficult to comply with this rule.' But writer B is telling us that, whatever happens, we must not work out our lives on a narrow utilitarian calculation. The really deep and moving experiences cannot be had in this spirit. On Silence, A is trite:

A.   Speak not but what may benefit others or yourself; avoid trifling conversation.
B.   Be still when you have nothing to say: when genuine passion moves you, say what you've got to say, and say it hot.

A's distinction between the beneficial and the trifling seems commonplace, unilluminating and naive (there is good deal that is naive about his list, when we look at it). He suggests to me a kind of serious-mindedness which would rob our speech of spontaneity and natural feeling, of that inspiration for finding the right word to embody our emotion in a passionate moment which gives our language life. B has understood this perfectly: he gets *behind* the cliché and all its staleness and ungenerosity. There is a control and economy to be observed in speech, but it doesn't hang on A's 'beneficial' and 'trivial'. It consists in the avoidance of unfelt, unmeant speech which blurs both language and emotion.[1] On Order and Resolution A begins to sound rather boy-scout-like, and as we read on we

---

[1] On Frugality, B again picks up the thought from A and transforms it. Frugality is not economy of possessions. 'Don't squander your emotion'— it is the quality of living we should be concerned most with, and sloppy feeling is worse than extravagance with money.

get the impression that he meets everything with a conscientious, dreary composure ('Be not disturbed at trifles, or at accidents common or unavoidable').

Much of B's language is, of course, metaphorical, and it has given trouble to numbers of my student readers. It seems to me that the less metaphorical and therefore presumably more readily understandable things said by B are clearly so much better than anything said by A that there can be no real excuse for rejecting B out of hand as eccentric or obscure. But the inexperienced reader typically goes for the more metaphorical parts of a poem or a piece of prose and loses his nerve if he draws a blank there, instead of trying to see the metaphors in relation to the rest of the text, and trying to work out their significance. There is no need to think that because B talks about gods he is 'a pantheist crank'. He is not concerned with exact theology, as we learn from the very first aphorism. But he is very concerned that there should be something in our experience which needs to be called 'religious'. His gods are, in a sense, metaphors, and so is his Holy Ghost; but it is not hard to understand the dimension he means to bring in to his thought by using them, especially when we remember that he is reacting against the canny, materialistic common-sense of writer A. It is a question of sensing the charge and weight of meaning behind B's phrasing—of responding to the outgoings of feeling. Only if we do this (and it would be difficult to sum up in a phrase what B means by the Holy Ghost) can we understand what is meant by 'Lose no time with ideals. Serve the Holy Ghost; never serve mankind.' The writer is not telling us to live in rapt contemplation like hermits. He is telling us not to accept the narrow, commonplace morality of writer A, with his enlightened self-interest and methodical 'do-gooding'. 'Resolve to abide by your own deepest promptings' is perhaps the essence of what B says, and the promptings must be deeper than the one which leads A to plan his little scheme for maximum efficiency and general benefit. 'Beware of absolutes, there are many Gods': this is a call to be flexible and generous in outlook and the wording is extremely effective.

The ideal of social efficiency which motivates A, writer B tells us, is only one way of looking at mankind, and a narrow way. The sentence 'To be sincere is to remember that I am I, and that the other man is not me' says the same thing rather differently. A believes that the same standards of efficiency apply to all men, B wants us to be conscious of the otherness of other people and to reverence it, not to bully them with our schemes of salvation: to know, in fact, that life is always larger than our ideas of it.

Most importantly, B is not advocating wanton individualism, or irrational abandonment to whim. To imagine from 'Follow the sincere intuition of the soul, angry or gentle' and 'Resolve to abide by your own deepest promptings' that he is, is to make a bad error of reading. As we become more aware of the importance of a writer's language in understanding his thought, we will become more scrupulous about our own descriptions and summaries of what he says. Language, in the hands of a great writer, is a very sensitive instrument and conveys delicate shades of meaning. 'Irrational abandonment to whim' is a hideous parody of B's meaning: the conventional, clumsy distinction between reason on the one hand and feeling on the other, which was obviously in the mind of the reader who made this comment, prevented him from understanding B at all. His own vocabulary, if you like, with its bigoted, narrow meaning for 'reason' and 'emotion', prevented this reader from thinking flexibly enough. It is odd how students, whose writing in previous literary exercises could, one might imagine, be taken as proof that they were above such an error and could recognise subtle differences in emotion, should be able to make comments like these. Perhaps it is evidence again of how the word 'literary' can precondition our reactions to what we read. Actually writer B makes it quite plain that he is not thinking about *whim*. He never suggests that the 'deepest promptings' are superficial intuitions. They are only to be found after the most careful self-scrutiny, the most searching effort of self-knowledge and they are very different from the easy indulgent satisfaction suggested by 'whim'. To see through shallow trivial surface emotion to our real feelings beneath is sometimes the hardest thing in the world. It is certainly one of the things that literature, and the study of literature, should help us to be able to do. The desires that A hopes to satisfy by following his scheme of things are superficial; they cannot attract us for very long. But B tells us to discover our deepest promptings, and his language, with its passionate conviction, tells us something of what these promptings are like. 'Never yield before the barren.' There is nothing here of the platitudinous 'Know thyself' of the conventional moralist. This aphorism—if the word applies to what we find in B's list—sums up his criticism of A. It takes courage, and faith in oneself, to live, for living involves a determined struggle against the 'barren', against the cheaper, falsifying alternatives which are always being presented to us in the day-to-day world. A preaches one of the cheaper alternatives that B dislikes most, a complacent and deadening doctrine.[1]

A's final aphorism, 'Imitate Jesus and Socrates', is rather comically naive, and it suggests that he has approached neither of these figures very closely. Although he enjoins us to Humility, his list, in its crudeness of touch, its lack of inwardness and general mediocrity is quite alien in spirit to the New Testament. Some of my student readers, who called themselves Christians, praised writer A for being a good Christian: 'Lose no time, be always employed in something useful; cut off all unnecessary action.' They had obviously forgotten that passage in the New Testament which begins: 'Consider the lilies of the field; they toil not, neither do they spin. . .' The passage may be looked up as a reminder of how much finer and more subtle New Testament morality is than writer A's; and, in the moving quality of the prose, it can also remind us that meaning, significance, is something more than paraphrasable 'prose content'.

[1] Lawrence's essay on Franklin, from which these extracts are drawn, should of course be looked at in connection with this exercise.

CHAPTER 21

Two Modern Passages on Literary Criticism

The writers of these passages (Exercise 35) have very different notions of literary criticism and of how it ought to be written. Writer A is an admirer of 'style'. A critic ought to take the trouble to make his books readable, that is, his way of writing must have a special value in itself, apart from the value of anything actually said. 'Style' is something that less civilised writers do not feel, and do not try to embody in their prose ('...the conceit which inspires some critics to expect to find readers...') yet it is essential to good criticism. Writer B doesn't concern himself with the attractions of style. To talk about literature effectively needs the most exacting precision and clarity in expression, and B feels that this is a large enough problem to take up all his attention. To avoid loose phrasing, and to make his judgments in a way that will give them maximum clarity and force, leaves him no time for style. The comparison will, I hope, give us the opportunity to analyse writer A's admiration for style, and to see what the preoccupation with style can lead to (the first passage in Exercise 38 and the first in Exercise 43 are comparable cases—see my comments in *Notes on Exercises not Discussed in the Text*).

Style, in passage A, is a species of eloquence, and, like all eloquence, it is self-regarding. *Le style, c'est l'homme même*: the writer's style is the man himself, and, we might add, style conceived as an end in itself always draws attention to the writer, not the content. Writer A is, of course, a stylist himself, and he has the trick of relishing his own language that Desmond MacCarthy has. His phrases, too, have the air of being 'picked'. But they have not been picked in the course of a discriminating search for precise meaning: '...But it is conversation glorified and transfigured and purged of its characteristic vagueness and diffuseness.' Most readers, if they haven't questioned the manner of the earlier sentences, will surely pause and question the manner here. Why these grandiose words? Isn't there some affectation here? Doesn't this writing suggest a false kind of awed admiration for MacCarthy's prose that rather embarrasses us? The word 'gleams' a few lines later is a revealing give-away. The word tells us a good deal about A's understanding of 'style'; it is his description of the way 'stylish' prose seems to be continuously congratulating itself on its choice of felicitous phrases. The lengths to which this narcissistic interest in one's own fine phrases can go are shown in the following, which is perhaps the most absurd of the treasures from Desmond MacCarthy: ...'the passion which smoulders in the dark impersonal eyes of Rembrandt's Jewish portraits...' The gleaming phrases are, in fact, pretty threadbare; as they inevitably must be, for when style is cultivated for its own sake it invariably leads to triviality and cliché. The phrasing is matched by the complete conventionality of the movement. Each sentence seems to follow a ready-made pattern, and we can predict its course in most cases before we read it half-way through. 'Style' seems in this case to be a game played with very well-used counters and along pretty rigid lines.

The writer notes how the 'steady, substantial good sense' of Desmond MacCarthy's discourse is 'lit up by the flicker of his playfulness'. But the joke isn't funny. It seems to me inanely flippant, and, importantly from our point of view, it turns on an assumption about literature and criticism without which, I suppose, writing such as we are examining would be impossible. Taste after all (so runs the tag) is relative, so if a critic has a taste which no one else shares, he shouldn't be inelegant enough to argue strongly for it. He must be archly non-committal. Only the boorish would feel strongly about it; the *literati* are charmingly—stylishly—diffident. The joke reveals that MacCarthy is taking seriously neither Swinburne's prose nor his own taste for it: he is striking an elegant pose.

B's views contrast strongly with all this. The critic does not write dogmatically, for critical judgments are not dogmas to be laid down as incontestable truths, and he needs to persuade the reader to form an independent opinion, not bully him into accepting something on trust. But the critic must write deliberately. The possibilities of misunderstanding, confusion and irrelevance being what they are, he must record his findings as clearly as he possibly can. Only then is he likely to call the reader to any similar clarity of mind about the literature, and, even if the critic is wrong, there is a real basis for discussion and a real interchange of views can take place. B's writing, after A, is refreshingly direct and concise: 'I think it is the business of the critic to perceive for himself, make the finest and sharpest relevant discriminations, and to state his findings as responsibly, clearly and forcibly as he can.' There is not a superfluous or unfocused word in this sentence. We notice, too, that B has a much more genuine respect for the reader than A. The reader is an equal, the critic will expect him to make the effort to work things out for himself. Contrast the way reader's approval is solicited in A: 'would-be critics to-day', 'himself an artist', the 'conceit that inspires some critics...', 'conversation glorified', etc., and the false modesty of MacCarthy's joke at the end. B knows that taste is certainly not absolute; that agreement must be reached with mutual co-operation; and that some disagreement is to be expected. But he believes that critical judgments *matter*, and that unless the critic feels passionately about them they are not worth making. If literature really bears on our inner—or outer—life, we can never affect diffidence; the most useful critic is the one who 'exposes himself as openly as possible to correction'. Only in this spirit can we hope to make anything clear in the often perplexed field of literary criticism.

Writer B believes he is bound to be misrepresented. Writing about literature in this way, he is certain to write things which are not immediately acceptable in some quarters—and he is certain, in academic circles, to upset a few apple-carts. I cannot help returning to that revealing sentence in passage A, 'For he was without the conceit that inspires some critics to expect to find readers, when they have taken no trouble to make their books readable...', asking what sort of critic is being de-

CHAPTER 22

Two Pieces of
Eighteenth-Century Literary Criticism

Literary criticism is apt to 'date' more than most kinds of writing, and the reasons for this are worth pondering to anyone who is engaged in that extension of criticism, teaching literature. They must include the fact that almost always more criticism is written than is actually needed; that pedantry almost always creeps in somewhere, or its apparent opposites, journalism and fashion; and that not many critics have been able to bring a wide range of interests and experience freely to bear in their criticism. It is this last characteristic above all that gives the writing of a great literary critic like Johnson its enduring interest; on nearly every occasion we can feel that a long and rich experience of life and literature is being brought to bear, and brought to bear pointedly and illuminatingly. Of the two pieces in the present comparison (Exercise 36), one, it seems to me, 'dates' very badly. A piece of mere book-making, it is interesting only as a reflection of a literary fashion, as a document of the less fine taste of its age. But the other passage is taken from a piece of criticism that will never 'date': Pope's remarkable Preface to his translation of the *Iliad*, which seems to me to contain some of the best writing in the language about any literature. Both passages are written in an idiom which is a long way removed from anything we would speak or write today, but Pope's writing, like all writing which has real pressure behind it, can communicate itself very rapidly even to readers who are not particularly familiar with eighteenth-century literature. The semi-archaic flavour of some of the phrasing quickly disappears in the irresistible warmth and vitality of the prose. The contrast with the trivially 'smart' piece by Addison could not, I think, be greater.

In extract A Pope is trying to say what it is that makes

Homer a great poet—a decisively greater poet than the other great classical epic poet, Virgil. The difference lies in the greater creative potency of Homer's language, its greater dramatic vividness. The eighteenth century was, as several critics have pointed out, poor at distinguishing the dramatic use of language—that is, language which creates what it talks about—from the language of statement. All the eighteenth-century critical canons, which were felt to have the full weight of scholarship behind them, tended to neglect this difference. The poet first excogitated his thought, and then found suitably tasteful expression according to the rules of polite learning, with metaphors and similes as illustration, decoration, and so on. It is true that much eighteenth-century poetry seems to have been written more or less according to this conception, and it is also true that eighteenth-century criticism could never quite bring itself to accept, officially as it were, Shakespearean audacities of language. But this passage seems to me clear proof that the greater minds of the eighteenth century could understand the difference between the 'creative' use of language and the prose-statement use (it is interesting to note that behind Pope's passage there lies a long, European debate on Homer and Virgil, and that the preference for Homer always indicates the emergence of a stronger taste in literature). Pope, in his own way, characterises wonderfully the creativeness of Homer and the thinner, more abstract, more sententious (if more 'Augustan' and 'correct') quality of Virgil. 'What he [Homer] writes is of the most animated nature imaginable: everything moves, everything lives and is put into action.' This is not an eighteenth-century critic formally stating an authoritative truth about polite letters (whatever the precedents for this passage), still less is it a classical scholar exhibiting a traditional piety towards one of the monumental works of the ancient world. Pope's language is utterly free from pedantry; it is fresh, lively and passionate, the language of a man who is powerfully moved by what he reads.

If a Council be call'd, or a battle fought, you are not coldly inform'd of what was said or done as from a third person; the Reader is hurry'd out of himself by the Force of the Poet's Imagination, and turns in one place into a Hearer, in another to a Spectator.

This is a brilliant description of what reading Homer feels like, and Pope's phrases sharply underline the difference between 'stated' meaning and created meaning in poetry: 'coldly informed', 'the reader is hurry'd out of himself'—there is no archaic quaintness about this prose. There is, too, none of the heavy, pompous ineptitude of metaphor which we are so familiar with in other eighteenth-century criticism: 'It grows in the Progress both upon himself and others, and becomes on fire like a chariot wheel, by its own rapidity.' The metaphor, which has naturally suggested itself to Pope as he read Homer, is genuinely functional; he contrasts this living immediacy of the characters and events in the *Iliad* with the more distant characters and events of the *Aenead*. Pope puts his finger on the effect of Virgil's immaculately worked surface with admirable penetration and point: 'This fire is discern'd in Virgil, but discern'd as through a glass, reflected, and more shining than warm, but everywhere equal and constant.' The 'correct' art of Virgil is what Ezra Pound called 'Tennysonianised Homer', and Mr Winters speaks of the 'slightly corrosive condescension' of the poem. Pope's criticism is all the more remarkable in that it was written in an age in which correctness and propriety were specially prized literary qualities (he says that poetical 'fire' i.e. strong inspiration, can 'over-power Criticism' in works where outward perfection of form is lacking). He notices acutely the dramatic failure of characterisation in Virgil: there is, for one thing, simply less action in the later poem, and the speeches 'often consist of general reflections or thoughts, which might be equally just in any person's mouth upon the same occasion'. But then, none of the characters are strongly individual in any case. We more often think of the author; that is, the consummate art of the versification is something of an end in itself.

Pope's prose is ordered and neat as all eighteenth-century prose is, but it is animated. We notice straight away that Addison's prose is not. It has a habitual elegance, but no trenchancy. The movement is feebler, and the phrasing is facile:

> ...the prodigies of Mankind, who...have produced works that were the delight of their own times and the wonder of posterity. There appears something nobly wild and extravagant in these great natural geniuses that is infinitely more beautiful than all the turn and polishing of what the French call a *Bel Esprit*...

'Nobly wild and extravagant' contains more than a hint of affectation: compare

> ...everything moves, everything lives and is put into action.

Addison is obviously using fashionable language, the sort that was ready to hand for a writer who had to produce copy for the next number of the *Spectator*. We cannot for a minute imagine that the literature of which he is speaking (he is never specific about it in the whole piece) is vividly present to him. In the sentence quoted above, the distinction between the 'nobly wild and extravagant' poets and the modern poets ('turn and polishing') seems too broadly and easily drawn—and why does that unnecessary 'infinitely' appear, except to give an elegant 'turn' to the sentence? Addison's language is carelessly loaded; none of the distinctions he makes seems sharp or telling. 'Innumerable flights', passages more 'elevated and sublime'—we don't doubt that these words were fashionable; but they are cheap critical coinage. There is nothing about this writing that suggests very strong convictions. When Addison goes on to discuss metaphor, he seems more interested in extracting a little whimsical comedy out of his material. Notice how easily he moves from Homer to the joke about the Emperor of Persia, and on to the conclusion, which doesn't seem (in spite of the cheery 'to cut off all cavilling') really seriously offered. The tone is chatty and relaxed. Pope talking about the difference between Homer's poetic power and Virgil's surface perfection is very different from Addison talking about ancient inspiration and modern polish. Addison gives us the impression of a writer moving easily through a series of current clichés, none of which, from the notion of 'wildly extravagant genius' at the start to the tedious idea about temperament and climate at the end, he has scrutinised closely. What Addison is doing, of course, is purveying to his readers the latest in fashionable criticism, the discussion about the merits of the ancients and the moderns. When it originated in France, this was a live issue which had seriously to do with public acceptance of new and important literature (the plays of Racine and Molière). But by the time it reached England it was a fashionable talking point, the sort of thing that would go nicely into a gentleman's magazine, and the sort of thing that, perhaps, made Pope, who felt that public reading created by the *Spectator* was not the ideal one for his poetry, say that 'not one gentleman in a hundred, even of a liberal education' would understand his *Essay on Criticism*.

I would like to end by quoting a sentence from elsewhere in the Preface to the *Iliad* which could never have come from Addison. It reveals a penetrating insight into literary critics and literary criticism such as few writers have possessed, and it seems, to a reader of modern criticism, to have an astonishing contemporary force:

And perhaps the reason why most critics are inclin'd to prefer a judicious and methodical genius to a great and fruitful one is, because they find it easier to pursue their observations through an uniform and bounded work of art, than to comprehend the vast and various extent of nature.

To study literature under academic conditions, as we do at the university, is always to be in danger of turning it into something we want it to be, instead of seeing it as it actually is; of suiting it to our own approach, and preferring the literature which fits our commentary most readily. As Pope so brilliantly saw in the criticism of his own day, literary critics are usually better at dealing with something 'judicious and methodical', something 'uniform and bounded' than with the 'vast and various extent of nature'. What applies to the critic applies yet more to the teacher. The class-room and lecture theatre— to say nothing of the academic paraphernalia of examinations and degrees—seem to demand us to handle what is 'uniform

Notes on Exercises not Discussed in the Text

16. A is insipid in movement and the sentiment is trite. The laboured construction suggests very strongly that the poem was written for the sake of the central metaphor. B is poignant and moving. The verse-movement has rare sensitiveness ('pause to breathe') and there are considerable subtleties of imagery in the second stanza.

17. Both passages are successful pieces of formal poetry. Some of B's best lines have exactness and 'weight' (e.g. the couplet 'Safe in his hands ...'), and the movement is actively used, not merely a stereotyped instrument of declamation. But B does contain some conventional diction ('panting for a happier seat') and A's verse, while not less dignified, is much more flexible. A's language is effortlessly exact, and the beautifully managed conclusion makes B's conclusion seem rather laboured.

18. Both poets complain of pedantry, but A, while he has a talented inventiveness with language, seems more interested in the search for striking, original effects than in what he is writing about. The ideas are too *trouvé*, however much we take into account the fact that this is a poem about boredom. The second poem is a natural and strongly felt outburst of irritation; the poet tries only to say what he has to say, and 'say it hot.'

19. A is merely a conventional rendering of a stock theme—the love-imagery makes the poem seem even more trivial. But despite its conventional outline poem B has at times a vividness of phrasing and a conviction in the rhythm which show that the poet, on this occasion, was really moved by what he was writing about.

20. The poets protest against artificiality and affectation in the name of simplicity and directness. But A has something artificial about him. His sarcasm isn't really incisive, and the hyperbolical self-abasement at the end is reminiscent of some of the more unreal extravagances of Elizabethan love poetry. The notion of writing poetry he introduces us to doesn't seem a very strong one. B has a refreshing masculine directness. 'Why can't you be ordinary?' is what he says in effect. His disclaimers in the last stanza are genuinely modest and attractively humorous and good-natured. Simplicity and directness are not a literary fetish here; they are part of the writer's own personality.

Note. Several scholars, notably Rosamond Tuve, maintain that poem B is simply a renunciation of secular poetry in favour of religious poetry, i.e. it contains no active criticism of affectation. This seems to me to rob the poem of most of its interest, to make it comparatively trivial. This suggestion can profitably be discussed in class.

21. It is well worth making the very small effort with archaic language which is necessary in introducing a class to these poems. The information contained in my directions for the exercise should suffice, and any further problems can be settled in a few minutes' discussion before the class writes the exercise. A has touches which in their telling brevity are typical of the ballad, but it is not the poem that B is. B is so powerful and immediate that it never fails to impress a class on first hearing—even a class which has read nothing more archaic than Shakespeare. No elaborate 'background' is needed to understand this poem.

22. Neither poem offers very much scope for discussion of 'complexity of imagery and metaphor' but if critical analysis is to be a properly free and flexible commentary on poetry it must be able to handle the sort of poetry which is represented here, and justify in critical discussion the discriminations we need to make. A quotation from Mr Winters may help. There is, he says, a kind of poetry the wisdom of which

lies not in the acceptance of a truism, for anyone can accept a truism, at least formally, but in the realisation of the truth of the truism: the realisation resides in the feeling, the style. Only a master of style can deal successfully in a plain manner with obvious matter...We are dealing with a poem which permits itself originality...only in the most restrainedand refined subtleties of diction and in cadence, but which by virtue of those subtleties inspires its universals with their full value as experience.

A has no such refined subtleties; the phrasing is facile, and the battle against the world seems to be won all too easily. The poet does not give the impression that he is contemplating something he really fears, and the poem is loose in organisation—the order of several stanzas might be changed without damaging it very much. The poet in B speaks *in persona*, and the quiet modest firmness of tone shows that the gentlewoman is more than a mere device. Her femininity and strength of character are real. She is genuinely horrified by those that 'blow away their lives'; Jonson gives her just the right degree of trenchancy and weight in her language. The ending, a collected and moving statement of the gentlewoman's attitude, reminds us of *To Heaven* and *On His First Son*.

23. B is a ripe specimen of late nineteenth-century verse, brimming with the 'poetic'. Most of the diction is strained and unconvincing, and the unctuous, vaguely ecstatic mood is entirely 'poetically' orthodox. A attempts to catch something difficult and elusive, but the language is more real and the attempt is free from the literary pretentiousness of B. The odd, wintry flowers are a really good inspiration. A's diffuseness is far more justified than B's unction.

24. Two metaphysical poems. Both are concerned with love and absence, both draw upon geometry and astronomy for their imagery. But in poem A the wit seems to be there for the wit's sake. We admire the dexterity of the poet, the cleverly clinching last lines of each stanza, the way in which each stanza makes a new ingenious variation on the central idea. But the hyperbolical love-situation seems to have been selected largely because it offers an advantageous starting-point for witty display; the poem is something of a *bravura* piece. B, a famous poem by Donne, has more serious content; unlike A, it can tell us something about our deepest, most intimate feelings. The 'metaphysical' imagery in stanza 3, for instance, is quite different in quality from anything in poem A: the contrast between the earthquake and the vast, cosmic phenomenon is like the contrast between our more superficial, easily expressed feelings and our profoundest feelings, which are not easily reached or readily articulated. The sense of awe at almost unimaginable cosmic events is perfectly matched to Donne's sense of wonder at the underlying truths of his relationship to the woman. The poem, it is important to note, is dramatically convincing: much more than A, it seems to be addressed to an actual woman, and the situation is convincingly authentic. The tone, with its gentle but sometimes also humorous tenderness, plays a vital part. There is a potently private atmosphere as the poet tries to recall the woman to a sense of the deeper realities of their relationship. The famous conceit of the compasses at the end is I think only properly understood if we have caught the tone of the previous stanzas. It is delicately, tenderly humorous, offered lightly, not as a deliberately profound piece of illumination.

25. A pleasantly amusing poem in which the old plumber is a distinct individual, not a conventional 'character'.

26. The poems use similar metaphorical devices, but in A the device is clumsily and externally handled. B, a strikingly idiosyncratic poem, is precise in language and vivid in its effects.

27. The extracts can, I think, be appreciated by a reader who has no previous knowledge of the figures satirised. A is full of stale epithets, the diction is trite generally and the humour is heavy and distinctly unfunny. The figure never begins to seem convincing. But in B the pedant is superbly created for us. The self-important, pompous old academician is genuinely 'mock-heroic', and the passage is full of penetrating satire of the academic mind and its stultifying effects on literary criticism. This exercise should be done by students with some previous knowledge of eighteenth-century poetry (e.g. *The Rape of the Lock*).

28. Both poems are in some sense 'satirical'. Mr Nixon is a successful careerist in letters, a cynical parasite on literature whose chief interest in

anything is purely in what may be 'in it', i.e. how well it will sell on the literary market. The irony is deft and incisive as the careerist speaks, condemning both himself and the literary world that approves of him. In B, Mr Apollinax introduces a disturbing new dimension into the genteel culture-vulture society of Boston. He is built up with whimsically humorous fantasy by the poet; a character of disconcerting and decidedly unpolite folklore associations, he mystifies the tea-party intellectuals, who are tellingly dismissed in the closing lines.

29. At first sight there might not appear much opening for close discussion of these terse, brief statements, but as soon as we begin to notice that some of the epigrams are more effective than others, we can ask why this is so and the grounds for comparison become clear. In some cases, the 'point' of the epigram seems a conventional one, made in an obvious way, e.g. in *Shock* and *Unknown Female Corpse*. Compare *A Son*, in which the father's bitterness (somehow we know it is the father speaking, not the mother) is not represented conventionally; or *The Beginner*, with its effective change of perspective, or *The Refined Man*, which is perhaps the best of the epigrams.

PROSE

37. A theme is being presented and considered here, but there is no sense of mechanical figures being used to represent a preconceived scheme of meaning. The contrast between Vanderbank's callow, smart fashionable talk with its underlying emotional hardness and insensitiveness (though we know he's not unintelligent) and Mr Longdon's warmth and sincerity is tellingly managed.

38. While A is not as factitious as some of the more blatant examples of 'poetic prose' which can readily be found in prose anthologies, it is not wiihout an element of eloquent fulsomeness; it seems 'external' when compared to the discreet, sensitive diction and more intimate movement of B. Discussion should not be confined to these extracts alone, but should certainly be extended to include the general differences between the stories, neither of which is unmanageably long.

39. A certainly touches on important issues, but the awful chirpy smartness of the manner, the looseness of formulation and the crass insensitive complacency of some of the things said make this an almost valueless statement about these questions. B—which is *not* a nostalgic demand for a return to past times—exemplifies a much higher quality of mind.

40. Another reminder that we cannot make any appraisal of a writer's thought without taking into account the way he uses language. This prose is mannered and inflated. The writer is being wittily, rather archly

knowing, not seriously trying to envisage and explore the problems of philosophy. Had he been serious, he would not have indulged in witty unclever verbal cleverness ('impure carbon', etc.). No valuable philosophy has ever been written in this spirit, though much bad philosophy has.

41. The writer of A feels that the life he is writing has a representative significance, but there is no unwanted sense of drama. The tone is direct, sensitive and manly. In B, the writer 'cloaks everything in a robe of rhetoric' (it is worth quoting Arnold's discussion of Macaulay's prose in the essay *A French Critic on Milton* in *Mixed Essays*). He is interested primarily in eloquent effects, in extracting the maximum cheap drama from what he is writing about. His prose derives from Johnson's, but it has become a 'style', not a vehicle for expressing something as clearly and concisely as possible. In C, the tradition has degenerated to vulgarity and journalistic sensationalism, history as melodrama.

42. Writer B is influenced by writer A. But writer A's humour is broad and unincisive: we enjoy the comedy for its own sake, as the writer himself is doing. B is also comic, but the writer is rendering life seriously, and we are asked to respond critically and intelligently. The humour is more intelligent, and it comes from a writer who has made a close and perceptive study of the society he writes about. A expresses uncomplicated exuberance.

43. In B there is an element of witty summing-up, and an impression of a lively mind eagerly sifting ideas. After the detached and slightly derisive first part, the writing becomes more warm and sympathetic at the close as the writer states his belief that one life is enough for any man. Even if we disagree with the view expressed, we know that we have been in contact with a strong and stimulating mind. A has no succinctness. It is full of unction and vague yearning. 'We know not how' is a lapse which no writer can afford to be guilty of. The clichés are inexcusable.

44. These passages are all recollections of childhood. A, B and C suffer from much the same defect. The authors make a dead-set at sensuous description. Supersensitive, Technicolour language meets us at every turn. There is, as Professor Hoggart puts it, 'a rhetorical spray of highlighted images'. None of these passages has very much to do with a child's mind; they have rather to do with the mind of the adult for whom rich, sensitive description has become a literary obsession. This writing is not spontaneous; there is, finally, something precious in it. Passage D is free from these distortions, and, alone of all the extracts, it explores the child's mind perceptively and inwardly. Dickens's remarks on the subject of childhood memories just prior to this passage (in chapter 2 of *David Copperfield*) are well worth quoting and discussing in class. Another passage which might be brought into the comparison is Paul's reminiscence of making

fuses with his father in *Sons and Lovers* (Penguin ed., pp. 82–3). This writing, with its natural unpretentious manner, is like a breath of fresh air after passages A, B and C.

45. The tone of passage A is 'official' and neutral enough, but this does not exclude emotional cliché; the piece could conceivably be used as propaganda. In B there is no cliché, and the description of the soldier's 'torrent of sentimental agony' allows us to make no obvious or ready-made reaction. The novelist knows too well that human beings can be reduced by unbearable grief or hardship and ruthless persecution to a state that is far from dignified or noble. He is concerned to show us, as exactly and completely as possible, just what the results of modern military persecution are in actual human terms.

46. A. The slackness of this writing reveals that the writer has not scrutinised his concepts very closely. Why all these overemphatic distinctions, except to provide a breezy sense of forthrightness and decision? Why should the scholar's virtues be so far, 'worlds away', from the critic's? Shouldn't accuracy, etc., be vital for the critic as well, and why does the historian *not* need imagination?

B. Doesn't this passage seem to misrepresent the relative importance of fact and opinion in relation to literature? The stress at any rate seems intemperate. A concern with 'facts', unless it is critically controlled, can prevent us from reading literature altogether. In choosing Coleridge's *Hamlet*, the writer has selected a big stick to beat criticism with. But 'corrupters' seems a sensational word anyway.

Exercises: Poetry

I

A ODE TO AUTUMN
    Season of mists and mellow fruitfulness,
      Close bosom-friend of the maturing sun;
    Conspiring with him how to load and bless
      With fruit the vines that round the thatch-eves run;
    To bend with apples the moss'd cottage-trees,   5
      And fill all fruit with ripeness to the core;
        To swell the gourd, and plump the hazel shells
      With a sweet kernel; to set budding more,
    And still more, later flowers for the bees,
    Until they think warm days will never cease,   10
        For Summer has o'er-brimm'd their clammy cells.

    Who hath not seen thee oft amid thy store?
      Sometimes whoever seeks abroad may find
    Thee sitting careless on a granary floor,
      Thy hair soft-lifted by the winnowing wind;   15
    Or on a half-reap'd furrow sound asleep,
      Drows'd with the fume of poppies, while thy hook
        Spares the next swath and all its twined flowers:
    And sometimes like a gleaner thou dost keep
      Steady thy laden head across a brook;   20
      Or by a cyder-press, with patient look,
        Thou watchest the last oozings hours by hours.

    Where are the songs of Spring? Ay, where are they?
      Think not of them, thou hast thy music too,—
    While barred clouds bloom the soft-dying day,   25
      And touch the stubble-plains with rosy hue;
    Then in a wailful choir the small gnats mourn
      Among the river sallows, borne aloft
        Or sinking as the light wind lives or dies;
    And full-grown lambs loud bleat from hilly bourn;   30
      Hedge-crickets sing; and now with treble soft
      The red-breast whistles from a garden croft;
        And gathering swallows twitter in the skies.

18) *swath*, the space cleared by the sweep of the mower's scythe   30) *bourn*, boundary

I saw old Autumn in the misty morn
Stand shadowless like Silence, listening
To silence, for no lonely bird would sing
Into his hollow ear from woods forlorn,
Nor lowly hedge nor solitary thorn;—   5
Shaking his languid locks all dewy bright
With tangled gossamer that fell by night,
   Pearling his coronet of golden corn.

Where are the songs of Summer?—With the sun,
Oping the dusky eyelids of the south,   10
Till shade and silence waken up as one,
And Morning sings with a warm odorous mouth.
Where are the merry birds?—Away, away,
On panting wings through the inclement skies,
   Lest owls should prey   15
   Undazzled at noon-day
And tear with horny beak their lustrous eyes.

Where are the blooms of Summer?—in the west,
Blushing their last to the last sunny hours,
When the mild Eve by sudden Night is prest   20
Like tearful Proserpine, snatch'd from her flow'rs
   To a most gloomy breast.
Where is the pride of Summer,—the green prime,—
The many, many leaves all twinkling?—Three
On the moss'd elm; three on the naked lime   25
Trembling,—and one upon the old oak tree!
   Where is the Dryad's immortality?—
Gone into mournful cypress and dark yew,
Or wearing the long gloomy Winter through
   In the smooth holly's green eternity.   30

The squirrel gloats on his accomplish'd hoard,
The ants have brimm'd their garners with ripe grain,
   And honey bees have stor'd
The sweets of Summer in their luscious cells;
The swallows all have wing'd across the main;   35
But here the Autumn melancholy dwells,
   And sighs her tearful spells
Amongst the sunless shadows of the plain.
     Alone, alone,
     Upon a mossy stone,   40

She sits and reckons up the dead and gone
With the last leaves for a love-rosary,
Whilst all the wither'd world looks drearily,
Like a dim picture of the drowned past
In the hush'd mind's mysterious far away, 45
Doubtful what ghostly thing will steal the last
Into that distance, grey upon the grey.

O go and sit with her, and be o'ershaded
Under the languid downfall of her hair:
She wears a coronal of flowers faded 50
Upon her forehead, and a face of care;—
There is enough of wither'd every where
To make her bower,—and enough of gloom;
There is enough of sadness to invite,
If only for the rose that died,—whose doom 55
Is Beauty's,—she that with the living bloom
Of conscious cheeks most beautifies the light;—
There is enough of sorrowing, and quite
Enough of bitter fruits the earth doth bear,—
Enough of chilly droppings for her bowl; 60
Enough of fear and shadowy despair,
To frame her cloudy prison for the soul!

Compare these poems.

Exercises **2** and **3** will be found on pp. 28–9 and 31–3 respectively.

4

A   ON MY FIRST DAUGHTER

Here lies to each her parents' ruth,
Mary, the daughter of their youth:
Yet, all heaven's gifts, being heaven's due,
It makes the father less to rue.
At sixe months end, she parted hence 5
With safety of her innocence;
Whose soule Heaven's Queen (whose name she beares)
In comfort of her mother's teares,
Hath plac'd amongst her Virgin-traine:
Where, while that sever'd doth remaine, 10
This grave partakes the fleshly birth,
Which cover lightly, gentle earth.

B   ON HIS FIRST SON

> Farewell, thou child of my right hand, and joy;
>   My sinne was too much hope of thee, lov'd boy,
> Seven yeeres thou'wert lent to me, and I thee pay,
>   Exacted by thy fate, on the just day.
> O, could I lose all father, now. For why   5
>   Will man lament the state he should envie?
> To have so soon scap'd worlds, and fleshes rage,
>   And, if no other miserie, yet age?
> Rest in soft peace, and, ask'd, say here doth lye
>   BEN. JONSON his best piece of poetrie.   10
> For whose sake, hence-forth, all his vowes be such,
>   As what he loves may never like too much.

Compare these poems, which are by the same poet.

5

A   LONDON

> I wander thro' each dirty street,
> Near where the dirty Thames does flow,
> And mark in every face I meet
> Marks of weakness, marks of woe.
>
> In every cry of every man,   5
> In every infant's cry of fear,
> In every voice, in every ban,
> The mind forg'd manacles I hear.
>
> How the chimney sweeper's cry
> Blackens o'er the churches' walls,   10
> And the hapless soldier's sigh
> Runs in blood down palace walls.
>
> But most the midnight harlot's curse
> From every dismal street I hear,
> Weaves around the marriage hearse   15
> And blasts the new born infant's tear.

B   LONDON

> I wander thro' each charter'd street,
> Near where the charter'd Thames does flow,
> And mark in every face I meet
> Marks of weakness, marks of woe.

In every cry of every Man,   5
In every Infant's cry of fear,
In every voice, in every ban,
The mind-forg'd manacles I hear.

How the Chimney-sweeper's cry
Every black'ning Church appalls;   10
And the hapless Soldier's sigh
Runs in blood down Palace walls.

But most thro' midnight streets I hear
How the youthful Harlot's curse
Blasts the new born Infant's tear,   15
And blights with plagues the Marriage hearse.

One of these poems is an earlier draft of the other. Consider the
changes made by the poet in the final version, saying what you think
is gained by them.

6

THE HUMAN ABSTRACT

Pity would be no more
If we did not make somebody Poor;
And Mercy no more could be
If all were as happy as we.

And mutual fear brings peace,   5
Till the selfish loves increase:
Then Cruelty knits a snare,
And spreads his baits with care.

He sits down with holy fears,
And waters the ground with tears;   10
Then Humility takes its root
Underneath his foot.

Soon spreads the dismal shade
Of Mystery over his head;
And the Caterpillar and Fly   15
Feed on the Mystery.

And it bears the fruit of Deceit,
Ruddy and sweet to eat;
And the Raven his nest has made
In its thickest shade.   20

> The Gods of the earth and sea
> Sought thro' Nature to find this tree;
> But their search was all in vain:
> There grows one in the Human Brain.

Discuss this poem. Is it obscure?

Originally the ending of the poem ran as follows:

> The Gods of the Earth and Sea
> Sought thro' nature to find this tree;
> But their search was all in vain
> Till they sought in the human brain.

> They said this mystery never shall cease;   25
> The priest promotes war and the soldier peace.

> .   .   .   .   .   .

> There souls of men are bought and sold,
> And milk-fed infancy for gold;
> And youth to slaughter houses led,
> And beauty for a bit of bread.   30

Did Blake gain anything by the alteration?

7

A   SONG

> Still to be neat, still to be drest,
> As you were going to a feast;
> Still to bee powdred, still perfum'd:
> Lady, it is to be presum'd,
> Though Arts hid causes are not found,   5
> All is not sweet, all is not sound.

> Give me a look, give me a face,
> That makes simplicity a grace;
> Robes loosely flowing, hayre as free:
> Such sweet neglect more taketh me,   10
> Than all th' adulteries of Art;
> They strike mine eyes, but not my heart.

B   DELIGHT IN DISORDER

A Sweet disorder in the dresse
Kindles in cloathes a wantonnesse:
A Lawne about the shoulders thrown
Into a fine distraction:
An erring Lace, which here and there   5
Enthralls the Crimson Stomacher:
A Cuffe neglectfull, and thereby
Ribbands to flow confusedly:
A winning wave (deserving Note)
In the tempestuous petticote: 10
A carelesse shoe-string, in whose tye
I see a wilde civility:
Doe more bewitch me, than when Art
Is too precise in every part.

3) *Lawne*, a piece of fine linen   6) *Stomacher*, a garment worn by women under the lacing of the bodice

Compare these poems.

8

A   IRREPARABLENESS

I have been in the meadows all the day
And gathered there the nosegay that you see,
Singing within myself as bird or bee
When such do field-work on a morn of May.
But, now I look upon my flowers, decay   5
Has met them in my hands more fatally
Because more warmly clasped,—and sobs are free
To come instead of songs. What do you say,
Sweet counsellors, dear friends? that I should go
Back straightway to the fields and gather more?   10
Another, sooth, may do it, but not I!
My heart is very tired, my strength is low,
My hands are full of blossoms plucked before,
Held dead within them till myself shall die.

B   LIFE

I made a posie, while the day ran by:
Here will I smell my remnant out, and tie
            My life within this band.
But time did beckon to the flowers, and they
By noon most cunningly did steal away,   5
            And wither'd in my hand.

My hand was next to them, and then my heart:
I took, without more thinking, in good part
        Times gentle admonition:
Who did so sweetly deaths sad taste convey,   10
Making my minde to smell my fatall day;
        Yet sugring the suspicion.

Farewell deare flowers, sweetly your time ye spent,
Fit, while ye liv'd, for smell or ornament,
        And after death for cures.   15
I follow straight without complaints or grief,
Since if my scent be good, I care not, if
        It be as short as yours.

Compare these poems.

9

A   NATURE

Full of rebellion, I would die,
Or fight, or travell, or denie
That thou hast aught to do with mee.
        O tame my heart;
        It is thy highest art   5
To captivate strong holds to thee.

If thou shalt let this venom lurk,
And in suggestions fume and work,
My soul will turn to bubbles straight,
        And thence by kind   10
        Vanish into a wind,
Making thy workmanship deceit.

O smooth my rugged heart, and there
Engrave thy reverend law and fear;
Or make a new one, since the old   15
        Is sapless growne,
        And a much fitter stone
To hide my dust, than thee to hold.

B   THE COLLAR

I struck the board, and cry'd, No more.
        I will abroad.
What? shall I ever sigh and pine?
My lines and life are free; free as the road,

Loose as the winde, as large as store.   5
   Shall I be still in suit?
Have I no harvest but a thorn
   To let me blood, and not restore
What I have lost with cordiall fruit?
              Sure there was wine,   10
Before my sighs did drie it: there was corn,
   Before my tears did drown it.
   Is the yeare only lost to me?
      Have I no bayes to crown it?
No flowers, no garlands gay? all blasted?   15
      All wasted?
  Not so, my heart: but there is fruit,
        And thou hast hands.
   Recover all thy sigh-blown age
On double pleasures: leave thy cold dispute   20
Of what is fit, and not: forsake thy cage,
      Thy rope of sands,
Which pettie thoughts have made, and made to thee
  Good cable, to enforce and draw,
        And be thy law,   25
While thou didst wink and wouldst not see.
      Away; take heed:
      I will abroad.
Call in thy deaths head there: tie up thy fears.
      He that forbears   30
  To suit and serve his need,
     Deserves his load.
But as I raved and grew more fierce and wild
    At every word,
  Methought I heard one calling, *Child*:   35
    And I replied, *My Lord*.

    1) *board*, i.e. the altar

Compare these poems.

10

A   Stond who so list vpon the slipper toppe
of court astate, and lett me here reioyce
and vse me quyet without lett or stoppe
vnknowen in courte that hath suche brackishe ioyes:
in hidden place so lett my dayes forthe passe   5

that, when my yeres be done, withouten noyce
J may dy aged after the common trace.
For hym deth grippithe right hard by the croppe
that is moche knowen of other, and of him self, alas,
doth dy vnknowen, dazed with dredfull face.   10

1) *list*, wishes; *slipper*, slippery   2) *astate*, order or class, i.e. court estate:
the court society   3) *lett*, hindrance   7) *trace*, track   8) *croppe*, top of the
head, cf. 'neck and crop'

B   Let who so list with mighty mace to reign
In tickle top of court delight to stand;
Let me the sweet and quiet rest obtain.
So set in place obscure and low degree
Of pleasant rest I shall the sweetness know.   5
My life, unknown to them that noble be,
Shall in the step of secret silence go.
Thus when my days at length are over past,
And time without all troublous tumult spent,
An aged man I shall depart at last,   10
In mean estate, to die full well content.
But grievous is to him the death, that when
So far abroad the bruit of him is blown,
That known he is too much to other men:
Departeth yet unto himself unknown.   15

13) *bruit*, fame, reputation

C   Upon the slippery tops of human state,
          The guilded pinnacles of fate,
Let others proudly stand, and, for a while
          (The giddy danger to beguile)
With joy and with disdain look down on all,   5
          Till their heads turn, and so they fall.
Me, O ye gods, on earth, or else so near
          That I no fall to earth may fear,
And, O ye gods, at a good distance seat
          From the long ruins of the great.   10
Here, wrapt in th' arms of quiet, let me lie;
          Quiet, companion of obscurity.
Here let my life with as much silence slide
          As time, that measures it, does glide.
Nor let the breath of infamy or fame   15
From town to town echo about my name.

Nor let my homely death embroidered be
  With scutcheon or with elogie.
    An old plebeian let me die:
Alas, all then are such as well as I.   20
    To him, alas, to him, I fear,
The face of death will terrible appear,
Who in his life, flattering his senseless pride,
By being known to all the world beside,
Does not himself, when he is dying, know,   25
Nor what he is, nor whither he's to go.

            19) *plebeian*, ordinary citizen

D   Whom worldly luxury and pomps allure,
     They tread on ice, and find no footing sure.
     Place me, ye pow'rs! in some obscure retreat,
     O! keep me innocent, make others great:
     In quiet shades, content with rural sports,   5
     Give me a life remote from guilty courts,
     Where free from hopes or fears, in humble ease
     Unheard of, I may live and die in peace.
        Happy the man who thus retir'd from sight,
     Studies himself and seeks no other light;   10
     But most unhappy he, who sits on high,
     Expos'd to ev'ry tongue and ev'ry eye;
     Whose follies blaz'd about, to all are known,
     But are a secret to himself alone:
     Worse is an evil fame, much worse than none.   15

E   Climb at court for me that will
     Tottering favors pinacle;
     All I seek is to lie still.
     Settled in some secret nest
     In calm leisure let me rest;   5
     And far off the publick stage
     Pass away my silent age.
     Thus when without noise, unknown,
     I have liv'd out all my span,
     I shall die, without a groan,   10
     An old honest country man.
     Who expos'd to others eyes,
     Into his own heart ne'r pries,
     Death to him's a strange surprise.

The above poems are all translations of the same original. Which
seems to you the most effective poem in its own right?

Note: The following version of poem A in modern spelling may be found helpful:

> Stand who so list upon the slipper top
> Of court estate, and let me here rejoice,
> And use me quiet without let or stop
> Unknown in court, that hath such brackish joys:
> In hidden place so let my days forth pass   5
> That, when my years be done, withouten noise
> I may die aged after the common trace.
> For him death grippeth right hard by the crop
> That is much known of other, and of himself, alas,
> Doth die unknown, dazed with dreadful face.   10

II

I A
> Here never shines the sun; here nothing breeds,
> Unless the nightly owl or fatal raven:
> And when they show'd me this abhorred pit,
> They told me, here, at dead time of the night,
> A thousand fiends, a thousand hissing snakes,   5
> Ten thousand swelling toads, as many urchins,
> Would make such fearful and confused cries,
> As any mortal body hearing it
> Should straight fall mad, or else die suddenly.

B
>   Come, seeling night,
> Scarf up the tender eye of pitiful day,
> And with thy bloody and invisible hand
> Cancel and tear to pieces that great bond
> Which keeps me pale!—Light thickens; and the crow   5
> Makes wing to th' rooky wood;
> Good things of day begin to droop and drowse,
> Whiles night's black agents to their preys do rouse.

> 4) *bond*, i.e the bond of humanity

Compare these extracts. Which seems to you to be the work of the mature Shakespeare?

2
> O God! that one might read the book of fate,
> And see the revolution of the times
> Make mountains level, and the continent,
> Weary of solid firmness, melt itself
> Into the sea! and, other times, to see   5

The beachy girdle of the ocean
Too wide for Neptune's hips; how chances mock,
And changes fill the cup of alteration
With divers liquors! O, if this were seen,
The happiest youth, viewing his progress through,   10
What perils past, which crosses to ensue,
Would shut the book, and sit him down and die.

Consider Shakespeare's use of his poetic resources in this passage.

3   ...from face to foot
He was a thing of blood, whose every motion
Was tim'd with dying cries. Alone he enter'd
The mortal gate of th' city, which he painted
With shunless destiny; aidless came off,   5
And with a sudden reinforcement struck
Corioli like a planet; now all's his;
When, by and by, the din of war 'gan pierce
His ready sense, then straight his doubled spirit
Re-quicken'd what in flesh was fatigate,   10
And to the battle came he, where he did
Run reeking o'er the lives of men, as if
'Twere a perpetual spoil; and till we call'd
Both field and city ours, he never stood
To ease his breast with panting.   15

Consider Shakespeare's use of his poetic resources in this passage.

4 A   But, soft! what light through yonder window breaks?
It is the east, and...is the sun.
Arise, fair sun, and kill the envious moon,
Who is already sick and pale with grief
That thou, her maid, art far more fair than she: 5
Be not her maid, since she is envious;
Her vestal livery is but sick and green,
And none but fools do wear it; cast it off.
It is my lady, O, it is my love!
O, that she knew she were!   10
She speaks, yet she says nothing; what of that?
Her eye discourses; I will answer it.—
I am too bold, 't is not to me she speaks:
Two of the fairest stars in all the heaven,
Having some business, do entreat her eyes   15
To twinkle in their spheres till they return.
What if her eyes were there, they in her head?

The brightness of her cheek would shame those stars,
As daylight doth a lamp: her eyes in heaven
Would through the airy region stream so bright   20
That birds would sing and think it were not night.

B   What you do
Still betters what is done. When you speak, sweet,
I'ld have you do it ever: when you sing,
I'ld have you buy and sell so; so give alms,
Pray so; and for the ord'ring your affairs,   5
To sing them too: when you do dance, I wish you
A wave o' th' sea, that you might ever do
Nothing but that; move still, still so;
And own no other function. Each your doing
(So singular in each particular)   10
Crowns what you are doing in the present deeds,
That all your acts are queens.

9–11) i.e. 'Everything you do, so peculiar to you in every detail, crowns what you are now doing...'

In A, a young man sees his lover come out onto a balcony at night; he is standing in the garden beneath. He does not yet know that she returns his love. In B, the young man speaks to the girl directly.

Compare the passages.

5   I am thy father's spirit,
Doom'd for a certain term to walk the night,
And for the day confin'd to fast in fires,
Till the foul crimes done in my days of nature
Are burnt and purg'd away: but that I am forbid   5
To tell the secrets of my prison-house,
I could a tale unfold whose lightest word
Would harrow up thy soul, freeze thy young blood,
Make thy two eyes, like stars, start from their spheres,
Thy knotty and combined locks to part   10
And each particular hair to stand on end,
Like quills upon the fretful porpentine.
But this eternal blazon must not be
To ears of flesh and blood.

6) *prison house*, purgatory   12) *porpentine*, porcupine   13) *eternal blazon*, revelation of eternity

Is this passage an example of Shakespeare's mature verse?

12

A THE SHADOW ON THE STONE

I went by the Druid stone
That broods in the garden white and lone,
And I stopped and looked at the shifting shadows
That at some moments fall thereon
From the tree hard by with a rhythmic swing,   5
And they shaped in my imagining
To the shade that a well-known head and shoulders
Threw there when she was gardening.

I thought her behind my back,
Yea, her I long had learned to lack,   10
And I said: 'I am sure you are standing behind me
Though how do you get into this old track?'
And there was no sound but the fall of a leaf
As a sad response; and to keep down grief
I would not turn my head to discover   15
That there was nothing in my belief.

Yet I wanted to look and see
That nobody stood at the back of me;
But I thought once more: 'Nay, I'll not unvision
A shape which, somehow, there may be.'   20
So I went on softly from the glade,
And left her behind me throwing her shade,
As she were indeed an apparition—
My head unturned lest my dream should fade.

B THE VOICE

Woman much missed, how you call to me, call to me,
Saying that now you are not as you were
When you had changed from the one who was all to me,
But as at first, when our day was fair.

Can it be you that I hear? Let me view you, then,   5
Standing as when I drew near to the town
Where you would wait for me: yes, as I knew you then,
Even to the original air-blue gown!

Or is it only the breeze, in its listlessness
Travelling across the wet mead to me here,   10

10) *mead*, meadow

You being ever dissoved to existlessness[1]
Heard no more again far or near?

    Thus I; faltering forward,
    Leaves around me falling,
Wind oozing thin through the thorn from norward,
    And the woman calling.

[1] This word Hardy later changed to 'wan wistlessness'. Do you think he gained anything by this alteration?

Compare these poems which are by the same poet.

13

A   THE ROAD NOT TAKEN

Two roads diverged in a yellow wood,
And sorry I could not travel both
And be one traveler, long I stood
And looked down one as far as I could
To where it bent in the undergrowth;   5

Then took the other, as just as fair,
And having perhaps the better claim,
Because it was grassy and wanted wear;
Though as for that the passing there
Had worn them really about the same,   10

And both that morning equally lay
In leaves no step had trodden black.
Oh, I kept the first for another day!
Yet knowing how way leads on to way,
I doubted if I should ever come back.   15

I shall be telling this with a sigh
Somewhere ages and ages hence:
Two roads diverged in a wood, and I—
I took the one less traveled by,
And that has made all the difference.   20

B   THE SIGN-POST

The dim sea glints chill. The white sun is shy,
And the skeleton weeds and the never-dry,
Rough, long grasses keep white with frost
At the hilltop by the finger-post;
The smoke of the traveller's-joy is puffed   5
Over hawthorn berry and hazel tuft.

I read the sign. Which way shall I go?
A voice says: You would not have doubted so
At twenty. Another voice gentle with scorn
Says: At twenty you wished you had never been born.   10
One hazel lost a leaf of gold
From a tuft at the tip, when the first voice told
The other he wished to know what 'twould be
To be sixty by this same post. 'You shall see,'
He laughed—and I had to join his laughter—   15
'You shall see; but either before or after,
Whatever happens, it must befall,
A mouthful of earth to remedy all
Regrets and wishes shall freely be given;
And if there be a flaw in that heaven   20
'Twill be freedom to wish, and your wish may be
To be here or anywhere talking to me,
No matter what the weather, on earth,
At any age between death and birth,—
To see what day or night can be,   25
The sun and the frost, the land and the sea,
Summer, Autumn, Winter, Spring,—
With a poor man of any sort, down to a king,
Standing upright out in the air
Wondering where he shall journey, O where?'   30

Compare these poems.

14

A   Thou hast made me, and shall thy worke decay?
Repaire me now, for now mine end doth haste,
I runne to death, and death meets me as fast,
And all my pleasures are like yesterday;
I dare not move my dimme eyes any way,   5
Despaire behind, and death before doth cast
Such terrour, and my feeble flesh doth waste
By sinne in it, which it t'wards hell doth weigh;
Only thou art above, and when towards thee
By thy leave I can looke, I rise againe;   10
But our old subtle foe so tempteth me,
That not one houre my selfe I can sustaine;
Thy Grace may wing me to prevent his art,
And thou like Adamant draw mine iron heart.

14) *Adamant*, a loadstone or magnet

173

B TO HEAVEN

Good, and great GOD, can I not thinke of thee,
   But it must, straight, my melancholy bee?
Is it interpreted in me disease,
   That, laden with my sinnes, I seeke for ease?
O, be thou witnesse, that the reines dost know,   5
   And hearts of all, if I be sad for show,
And judge me after: if I dare pretend
   To ought but grace, or ayme at other end.
As thou art all, so be thou all to mee,
   First, midst, and last, converted one, and three;   10
My faith, my hope, my love: and in this state,
   My judge, my witnesse, and my advocate.
Where have I beene this while exil'd from thee?
   And whither rap'd, now thou but stoop'st to mee?
Dwell, dwell here still: O, being every-where,   15
   How can I doubt to finde thee ever, here?
I know my state, both full of shame, and scorne,
   Conceiv'd in sinne, and unto labour borne,
Standing with feare, and must with horror fall,
   And destin'd unto judgement, after all.   20
I feele my griefs too, and there scarce is ground,
   Upon my flesh t'inflict another wound.
Yet dare I not complaine, or wish for death
   With holy PAUL, lest it be thought the breath
Of discontent; or that these prayers bee   25
   For wearinesse of life, not love of thee.

Compare these poems.

15

SONNET

Bright star! would I were steadfast as thou art—
   Not in lone splendour hung aloft the night,
And watching, with eternal lids apart,
   Like Nature's patient, sleepless Eremite,
The moving waters at their priestlike task   5
   Of pure ablution round earth's human shores,
Or gazing on the new soft fallen mask
   Of snow upon the mountains and the moors—
No—yet still steadfast, still unchangeable,
   Pillow'd upon my fair love's ripening breast,   10

        4) *Eremite*, hermit

To feel for ever its soft fall and swell,
    Awake for ever in a sweet unrest,
Still, still to hear her tender-taken breath,
And so live ever—or else swoon to death.

Write an appreciation of this sonnet.

16

A   ON FINDING A FAN

    In one who felt as once he felt,
      This might, perhaps, have fann'd the flame;
    But now his heart no more will melt,
      Because that heart is not the same.

    As when the ebbing flames are low,   5
      The aid which once improved their light,
    And bade them burn with fiercer glow,
      Now quenches all their blaze in night.

    Thus has it been with passion's fires—
      As many a boy and girl remembers—   10
    While every hope of love expires,
      Extinguish'd with the dying embers.

    The *first*, though not a spark survive,
      Some careful hand may teach to burn;
    The *last*, alas! can ne'er survive;   15
      No touch can bid its warmth return

    Or, if it chance to wake again,
      Not always doom'd its heat to smother,
    It sheds (so wayward fates ordain)
      Its former warmth around another.   20

B   SO WE'LL GO NO MORE A-ROVING

    So we'll go no more a roving
      So late into the night,
    Though the heart be still as loving,
      And the moon be still as bright.

    For the sword outwears its sheath,   5
      And the soul wears out the breast,
    And the heart must pause to breathe,
      And love itself have rest.

Though the night was made for loving,
And the day returns too soon,   10
Yet we'll go no more a roving
By the light of the moon.

Compare these poems, which are by the same poet.

17

A   Thy peace is made; and, when man's state is well,
'Tis better, if he there can dwell.
God wisheth, none should wracke on a strange shelf:
To him, man's dearer, then t' himself.
And, howsoever we may think things sweet,   5
He always gives what he knows meet;
Which who can use is happy: Such be thou.
Thy morning's, and thy evening's vow
Be thanks to him, and earnest prayer, to find
A body sound, with sounder mind;   10
To do thy country service, thy self right;
That neither want do thee affright,
Nor death; but when thy latest sand is spent,
Thou mayest think life, a thing but lent.

       3) *wracke*, i.e. be shipwrecked

B   Enquirer, cease, Petitions yet remain,
Which Heav'n may hear, nor deem Religion vain.
Still raise for Good the supplicating Voice,
But leave to Heav'n the Measure and the Choice:
Safe in his Pow'r, whose Eyes discern afar   5
The secret Ambush of a specious Pray'r.
Implore his Aid, in his Decisions rest,
Secure, whate'er he gives, he gives the best.
Yet when the Sense of sacred Presence fires,
And strong Devotion to the Skies aspires,   10
Pour forth thy Fervours for a healthful Mind,
Obedient Passions, and a Will resign'd;
For Love, which scarce collective Man can fill;
For Patience, Sov'reign o'er transmuted ill;
For Faith, that panting for a happier Seat,   15
Counts Death kind Nature's Signal of Retreat.
These Goods for Man the Laws of Heav'n ordain,

These Goods he grants, who grants the Pow'r to gain;
With these celestial Wisdom calms the mind,
And makes the Happiness she does not find.   20

Compare these extracts. They are both free renderings of a passage
from a Latin poem and can be considered as self-sufficient poetry.

18

A TUTORIAL

                    Like a propped skull
                    His humour is medieval.

                    What are those tilted tomes? Boards
                    Pressing the drying remains of men.
                    He brings some out. We stew up words to a dark   5
                              amber and sit sipping.

                    He is gone at the seams, this burst bearskin,
                              but his mind is an electric mantis,
                    Plucking the heads and legs off words,
                                        the homunculi.   10
                    I am thin but I can hardly move my bulk. I
                              go round and round numbly under the
                              ice of the North Pole.

                    This scholar dribbling tea
                    Onto his tie, draining pipe gargle   15
                    Through the wharf-weed that ennobles

                    The mask of his enquiry, advancing into
                                        the depths like a harbour,
                    Like a sphynx cliff,
                    Like the papery skull of a fish   20

                    Lodged in dune sand, with a few straws,
                    Rifled by dry cold.
                    His words

                    Twitch and rustle, twitch
                    And rustle.   25
                    The scarred world looks through their gaps.

                    I listen
                    With bleak eyeholes.

                         10) *homunculi*, little men

B   THE SCHOLARS

Bald heads forgetful of their sins,
Old, learned, respectable bald heads
Edit and annotate the lines
That young men, tossing on their beds,
Rhymed out in love's despair   5
To flatter beauty's ignorant ear.

All shuffle there; all cough in ink;
All wear the carpet with their shoes;
All think what other people think;
All know the man their neighbour knows.   10
Lord, what would they say
Did their Catullus walk that way?

Compare the different kinds of success achieved (or not achieved) by
these poems.

19

A   VICTORIOUS MEN OF EARTH

Victorious men of Earth, no more
Proclaime how wide your Empires are;
Though you bind in every shore,
    And your triumphs reach as far
        As Night or Day,   5
    Yet you proud Monarchs must obey,
And mingle with forgotten ashes, when
Death calls ye to the crowd of common men.

Devouring Famine, Plague, and War,
    Each able to undo Man-kind,   10
Death's servile Emissaries are,
    Nor to these alone confin'd,
        He hath at will
    More quaint and subtle waies to kill.
A smile or kiss, as he will use the art,   15
Shall have the cunning skill to break a heart.

B   THE GLORIES OF OUR BLOOD AND STATE

The glories of our blood and state,
    Are shadows, not substantial things,
There is no armour against fate,
    Death lays his icy hand on Kings,

178

Scepter and Crown,   5
Must tumble down,
And in the dust be equal made,
With the poor crooked sithe and spade.

Some men with swords may reap the field,
    And plant fresh laurels where they kill,   10
But their strong nerves at last must yield,
    They tame but one another still;
       Early or late,
       They stoop to fate,
And must give up the murmuring breath,   15
When they pale captives creep to death.

The Garlands wither on your brow,
    Then boast no more your mighty deeds,
Upon Deaths purple Altar now,
    See where the Victor-victim bleeds,   20
       Your heads must come,
       To the cold Tomb;
Onely the actions of the just
Smell sweet, and blossom in their dust.

Compare these poems, which are by the same poet.

20

A SONNET

Let dainty wits cry on the Sisters nine,
    That, bravely masked, their fancies may be told;
Or Pindar's apes flaunt they in phrases fine,
    Enamelling with pied flowers their thoughts of gold;
Or else let them in statelier glory shine,   5
    Ennobling new-found tropes with problems old;
Or with strange similes enrich each line,
    Of herbs or beasts which Ind or Afric hold.
For me, in sooth, no Muse but one I know;
Phrases and problems from my reach do grow,   10
    And strange things cost too dear for my poor sprites.
How then? even thus—in Stella's face I read
What love and beauty be; then all my deed
    But copying is, what in her Nature writes.

1) *Sisters nine*, the muses   3) *Pindar's apes*, abjectly imitating Pindar, the Greek poet   6) *tropes*, figurative language

B JORDAN

> Who sayes that fictions onely and false hair
> > Become a verse? Is there in truth no beautie?
> Is all good structure in a winding stair?
> May no lines passe, except they do their dutie
> > Not to a true, but painted chair?　　　　　5
>
> Is it no verse, except enchanted groves
> And sudden arbours shadow course-spunne lines?
> Must purling streams refresh a lovers loves?
> Must all be vail'd, while he that reades, divines,
> > Catching the sense at two removes?　　　　10
>
> Shepherds are honest people; let them sing:
> Riddle who list, for me, and pull for Prime:
> I envie no mans nightingale or spring;
> Nor let them punish me with losse of ryme,
> > Who plainly say, *My God, My King.*　　　　15

6) *enchanted groves*, etc., i.e. the furniture of pastoral poetry　　12) *pull for Prime*, draw for a winning hand at cards, i.e. play a game to decide who is the best poet.

Which poem makes the more effective criticism of artificiality in poetry?

21

A THE THREE RAVENS

> There were three ravens sat on a tree,
> They were as black as they might be.
>
> The one of them said to his make,
> 'Where shall we our breakfast take?'
>
> 'Down in yonder greene field　　　　　5
> There lies a knight slain under his shield;
>
> 'His hounds they lie down at his feet,
> So well do they their master keep;
>
> 'His hawks they flie so eagerly,
> There's no fowl dare come him nigh.　　　　10
>
> 'Down there comes a fallow doe
> As great with young as she might goe.
>
> 'She lift up his bloudy head
> And kist his wounds that were so red.

'She gat him up upon her back   15
And carried him to earthen lake.

'She buried him before the prime,
She was dead herself ere evensong time.

'God send every gentleman
Such hounds, such hawks, and such a leman!'   20

3) *make*, mate   16) *lake*, pit   20) *leman*, lover

B   THE TWA CORBIES

(Scottish Version)

As I was walking all alane,
I heard twa corbies making a mane:
The tane unto the thither did say,
'Whar sall we gang and dine the day?'

'—In behint yon auld fail dyke   5
I wot there lies a new-slain knight;
And naebody kens that he lies there
But his hawk, his hound, and his lady fair.

'His hound is to the hunting gane,
His hawk to fetch the wild-fowl hame,   10
His lady's ta'en anither mate,
So we may mak' our dinner sweet.

'Ye'll sit on his white hause-bane,
And I'll pike out his bonny blue e'en:
Wi'a ae lock o' his gowden hair   15
We'll theek our nest when it grows bare.

'Mony a one for him maks mane,
But nane sall ken whar he is gane:
O'er his white banes, when they are bare,
The wind sall blaw for evermair.'   20

2) *corbies*, ravens   5) *fail*, turf   7) *kens*, knows   13) *hause*, neck
16) *theek*, thatch   19) *banes*, bones

These are different versions of a ballad, i.e. a poem of the late middle ages which was handed down orally. In A, which celebrates faithfulness, the doe stands for the slain knight's lover. B is a Scottish version. Write an appreciation of the poems.

22

A   TO THE WORLD

False world, thou ly'st: Thou canst not lend
    The least delight:
Thy favours cannot gain a Friend,
    They are so slight:
Thy morning pleasures make an end   5
    To please at night:
Poore are the wants that thou supply'st:
And yet thou vaunt'st, and yet thou vy'st
With heav'n; Fond earth, thou boasts; false world, thou ly'st.

Thy babbling tongue tells gold tales   10
    Of endless treasure;
Thy bountie offers easie sales
    Of lasting pleasure;
Thou ask'st the Conscience what she ails,
    And swear'st to ease her;   15
There's none can want where thou supply'st:
There's none can give where thou deny'st.
Alas, fond world, thou boasts; false world, thou ly'st.

What well-advised ear regards
    What earth can say?   20
Thy words are gold, but thy rewards
    Are painted clay;
Thy cunning can but pack the cards;
    Thou canst not play:
Thy game at weakest, still thou vy'st;   25
If seen, and then revy'd, deny'st;
Thou art not what thou seem'st: false world, thou ly'st.

Thy tinsel bosome seems a mint
    Of new-coin'd treasure,
A Paradise, that has no stint,   30
    No change, no measure;
A painted cask, but nothing in't,
    Nor wealth, nor pleasure:
Vain earth! that falsly thus comply'st
With man: Vain man! that thus rely'st   35
On earth: Vain man, thou dot'st: Vain earth, thou ly'st.

What mean dull souls, in this high measure
    To haberdash

In earth's base wares; whose greatest treasure
    Is dross and trash?   40
The height of whose inchanting pleasure
    Is but a flash?
Are these the goods that thou supply'st
Us mortalls with? Are these the high'st?
Can these bring cordial peace? False world, thou ly'st.   45

      26) *revy'd*, challenged

B   TO THE WORLD: A FAREWELL FOR A GENTLE-WOMAN,
VERTUOUS AND NOBLE

    False world, good-night: since thou hast brought
        That houre upon my morne of age,
    Hence-forth I quit thee from my thought,
        My part is ended on thy stage.
    Doe not once hope, that thou canst tempt   5
        A spirit so resolv'd to tread
    Upon thy throate, and live exempt
        From all the nets that thou canst spread.
    I know thy formes are studyed arts,
        Thy subtle wayes, be narrow straits;   10
    Thy curtesie but sodaine starts,
        And what thou call'st thy gifts are baits.
    I know too, though thou strut, and paint,
        Yet art thou both shrunke up, and old,
    That onely fooles make thee a saint,   15
        And all thy good is to be sold.
    I know thou whole art but a shop
        Of toyes, and trifles, traps, and snares,
    To take the weake, or make them stop:
        Yet art thou falser then thy wares.   20
    And, knowing this, should I yet stay,
        Like such as blow away their lives,
    And never will redeeme a day,
        Enamor'd of their golden gyves?
    Or, having scap'd, shall I returne,   25
        And thrust my necke into the noose,
    From whence, so lately, I did burne,
        With all my powers, my selfe to loose?
    What bird, or beast, is knowne so dull,
        That fled his cage, or broke his chaine,   30
    And tasting ayre, and freedome, wull
        Render his head in there againe?

If these, who have but sense, can shun
    The engines, that have them annoy'd;
Little, for me, had reason done,   35
    If I could not thy ginnes avoyd.
Yes, threaten, doe. Alas I feare
    As little, as I hope from thee:
I know thou canst nor shew, nor beare
    More hatred, then thou hast to mee.   40
My tender, first, and simple yeeres
    Thou did'st abuse, and then betray;
Since stird'st up jealousies and feares,
    When all the causes were away.
Then, in a soile hast planted me,   45
    Where breathe the basest of thy fooles;
Where envious arts professed be,
    And pride, and ignorance the schooles,
Where nothing is examin'd, weigh'd,
    But, as 'tis rumor'd, so beleev'd: 50
Where every freedome is betray'd,
    And every goodnesse tax'd, or griev'd.
But, what we' are borne for, we must beare:
    Our fraile condition it is such,
That, what to all may happen here,   55
    If't chance to me, I must not grutch.
Else, I my state should much mistake,
    To harbour a divided thought
From all my kinde: that, for my sake,
    There should a miracle be wrought.   60
No, I doe know, that I was borne
    To age, misfortune, sicknesse, griefe:
But I will beare these, with that scorne,
    As shall not need thy false reliefe.
Nor for my peace will I goe farre,   65
    As wandrers doe, that still doe rome,
But make my strengths, such as they are,
    Here in my bosome, and at home.

    24) *gyves*, fetters   36) *ginnes*, traps   56) *grutch*, complain
Compare these poems.

23

A SHADOWS

And if to-night my soul may find her peace
in sleep, and sink in good oblivion,
and in the morning wake like a new-opened flower
then I have been dipped again in God, and new-created.

And if, as weeks go round, in the dark of the moon   5
my spirit darkens and goes out, and soft strange gloom
pervades my movements and my thoughts and words,
then I shall know that I am walking still
with God, we are close together now the moon's in shadow.

And if, as autumn deepens and darkens,   10
I feel the pain of falling leaves, and stems that break in storms
and trouble and dissolution and distress
and then the softness of deep shadows folding, folding
around my soul and spirit, around my lips
so sweet, like a swoon, or more like the drowse of a low, sad song   15
singing darker than the nightingale, on, on to the solstice
and the silence of short days, the silence of the year, the shadow,
then I shall know that my life is moving still
with the dark earth, and drenched
with the deep oblivion of earth's lapse and renewal.   20

And if, in the changing phases of man's life,
I fall in sickness and in misery,
my wrists seem broken and my heart seems dead
and strength is gone, and my life
is only the leavings of a life: 25

and still, among it all, snatches of lovely oblivion, and snatches of
        renewal,
odd, wintry flowers upon the withered stem, yet new, strange flowers
such as my life has not brought forth before, new blossoms of me.
Then I must know that still
I am in the hands of the unknown God,   30
he is breaking me down to his own oblivion
to send me forth on a new morning, a new man.

16) *solstice*, the mid-point

B BRETON AFTERNOON

Here, where the breath of the scented-gorse floats through the sun-
    stained air,
On a steep hill-side, on a grassy ledge, I have lain hours long and
    heard
Only the faint breeze pass in a whisper like a prayer,
And the river ripple by and the distant call of a bird.

On the lone hill-side, in the gold sunshine, I will hush me and repose,   5
And the world fades into a dream and a spell is cast on me;
And what was all the strife about, for the myrtle or the rose,
And why have I wept for white girl's paleness passing ivory!

Out of the tumult of angry tongues, in a land alone, apart,
In a perfumed dream-land set betwixt the bounds of life and death,   10
Here will I lie while the clouds fly by and delve an hole where my
    heart
May sleep deep down with the gorse above and red, red earth be-
    neath.

Sleep and be quiet for an afternoon, till the rose-white angelus
Softly steals my way from the village under the hill:
Mother of God, O Misericord, look down in pity on us,   15
The weak and blind who stand in our light and wreak ouselves such ill.

Consider the intentions of the poets in the above poems. How far is
each successful?

13) *angelus*, bell for evening service   15) *Misericord*, pity

24

A THE DEFINITION OF LOVE

My love is of a birth as rare
As 'tis for object strange and high:
It was begotten by Despair
Upon Impossibility.

Magnanimous Despair alone   5
Could show me so divine a thing,
Where feeble Hope could ne'er have flown
But vainly flap its Tinsel Wing.

And yet I quickly might arrive
Where my extended Soul is fixt,   10
But Fate does Iron wedges drive,
And alwaies crowds it self betwixt.

For Fate with jealous Eye does see
Two perfect Loves; nor lets them close:
Their union would her ruine be,   15
And her Tyrannick pow'r depose.

And therefore her Decrees of Steel
Us as the distant Poles have plac'd,
(Though Loves whole World on us doth wheel)
Not by themselves to be embrac'd.   20

Unless the giddy Heaven fall,
And Earth some new Convulsion tear;
And, us to joyn, the World should all
Be cramp'd into a *Planisphere*.

As Lines so Loves oblique may well   25
Themselves in every Angle greet:
But ours so truly *Parallel*,
Though infinite can never meet.

Therefore the Love which us doth bind,
But Fate so enviously debars,   30
Is the Conjunction of the Mind,
And Opposition of the Stars.

24) *Planisphere*, a map made by a projection of a sphere on a plane

B   A VALEDICTION: FORBIDDING MOURNING
          As virtuous men passe mildly away,
                And whisper to their soules, to goe,
          Whilst some of their sad friends doe say,
                The breath goes now, and some say, no:

          So let us melt, and make no noise,   5
                No teare-floods, nor sigh-tempests move,
          T'were prophanation of our joyes
                To tell the layetie our love.

          Moving of th'earth brings harmes and feares,
                Men reckon what it did and meant,   10
          But trepidation of the spheares,
                Though greater farre, is innocent.

11) *trepidation*, trembling; *the spheres*, the hollow, concentric, invisible spheres which were imagined to surround the globe carrying with them the heavenly bodies

Dull sublunary lovers love
    (Whose soule is sense) cannot admit
Absence, because it doth remove   15
    Those things which elemented it.

But we by a love, so much refin'd,
    That our selves know not what it is,
Inter-assured of the mind,
    Care lesse, eyes, lips, and hands to misse.   20

Our two soules therefore, which are one,
    Though I must goe, endure not yet
A breach, but an expansion,
    Like gold to aiery thinnesse beate.

If they be two, they are two so   25
    As stiffe twin compasses are two,
Thy soule the fixt foot, makes no show
    To move, but doth, if the'other doe.

And though it in the center sit,
    Yet when the other far doth rome,   30
It leanes, and hearkens after it,
    And growes erect, as that comes home.

Such wilt thou be to mee, who must
    Like th'other foot, obliquely runne;
Thy firmness makes my circle just,   35
    And makes me end, where I begunne.

Compare these poems.

25

ELEGY FOR ALFRED HUBBARD

Hubbard is dead, the old plumber;
who will mend our burst pipes now,
the tap has dripped all summer,
testing the sink's overflow?

No other like him. Young men with knowledge   5
of new techniques, theories from books,
may better his work straight from college,
but who will challenge his squint-eyed looks

in kitchen, bathroom, under floorboards,
rules of thumb which were often wrong;   10

seek as erringly stopcocks in cupboards,
or make a job last half as long?

He was a man who knew the ginnels,
alleyways, streets—the whole district,
family secrets, minor annals,   15
time-honoured fictions fused to fact.

Seventy years of gossip muttered
under his cap, his tufty thatch,
so that his talk was slow and clotted,
hard to follow, and too much.   20

As though nothing fell, none vanished,
and time were the maze of Cheetham Hill,
in which the dead—with jobs unfinished—
waited to hear him ring the bell.

For much he never got round to doing,   25
but meant to, when weather bucked up,
or worsened, or when his pipe was drawing,
or when he'd finished this cup.

I thought time, he forget so often,
had forgotten him, but here's Death's pomp   30
over his house, and by the coffin
the son who will inherit his blowlamp,

tools, workshop, cart and cornet
(pride of Cheetham Prize Band),
and there's his mourning widow, Janet,   35
stood at the gate he'd promised to mend.

Soon he will make his final journey;
shaved and silent, strangely trim,
with never a pause to talk to any-
body: how arrow-like, for him!   40

In St Mark's Church, whose dismal tower
he pointed and painted when a lad,
they will sing his praises amidst flowers
while, somewhere, a cellar starts to flood,

And the housewife banging his front-door knocker 45
is not surprised to find him gone,
and runs for Thwaite, who's a better worker,
and sticks at a job until it's done.

13) *ginnels*, narrow passageways

Is this a successful poem?

26

A   PIAZZA PIECE

             —I am a gentleman in a dustcoat trying
             To make you hear. Your ears are soft and small
             And listen to an old man not at all,
             They want the young men's whispering and sighing.
             But see the roses on your trellis dying   5
             And hear the spectral singing of the moon;
             For I must have my lovely lady soon,
             I am a gentleman in a dustcoat trying.

             —I am a lady young in beauty waiting
             Until my true love comes, and then we kiss.   10
             But what grey man among the vines is this
             Whose words are dry and faint as in a dream?
             Back from my trellis, Sir, before I scream!
             I am a lady young in beauty waiting.

           title) *Piazza*, the verandah of a house

B   I COULD NOT STOP FOR DEATH

             Because I could not stop for Death,
             He kindly stopped for me;
             The carriage held but just ourselves
             And Immortality.

             We slowly drove, he knew no haste,   5
             And I had put away
             My labour, and my leisure too,
             For his civility.

             We passed the school where children played
             At wrestling in a ring;   10
             We passed the fields of gazing grain,
             We passed the setting sun.

             We paused before house that seemed
             A swelling of the ground;
             The roof was scarcely visible,   15
             The cornice but a mound.

             Since then 'tis centuries; but each
             Feels shorter than the day
             I first surmised the horses' heads
             Were toward eternity.   20

Compare these poems.

27

A   With that low Cunning, which in fools supplies,
And amply too, the place of being wise,
Which Nature, kind indulgent parent, gave
To qualify the Blockhead for a Knave;
With that smooth Falshood, whose appearance charms,   5
And reason of each wholesome doubt disarms,
Which to the lowest depths of guile descends,
By vilest means pursues the vilest ends,
Wears Friendship's mask for purposes of spite,
Fawns in the day, and Butchers in the night;   10
With that malignant Envy, which turns pale,
And sickens, even if a friend prevail,
Which merit and success pursues with hate,
And damns the worth it cannot imitate;
With the cold Caution of a coward's spleen,   15
Which fears not guilt, but always seeks a screen,
Which keeps this maxim ever in her view—
What's basely done, should be done safely too;
With that dull, rooted, callous Impudence,
Which, dead to shame, and ev'ry nicer sense,   20
Ne'er blush'd, unless, in spreading Vice's snares,
She blunder'd on some Virtue unawares;
With all these bessings, which we seldom find
Lavish'd by Nature on one happy mind,
A Motley Figure, of the Fribble Tribe,   25
Which Heart can scarce conceive, or pen describe,
Came simp'ring on; to ascertain whose sex
Twelve sage, impanell'd Matrons would perplex.
Nor Male, nor Female; Neither, and yet both;
Of Neuter Gender, tho' of Irish growth;   30
A six-foot suckling, mincing in Its gait;
Affected, peevish, prim, and delicate;
Fearful It seem'd, tho' of Atheletic make,
Lest brutal breezes should too roughly shake
Its tender form, and savage motion spread,   35
O'er Its pale cheeks, the horrid manly red.
    Much did It talk, in Its own pretty phrase,
Of Genius and of Taste, of Play'rs and Plays;
Much too of writings, which Itself had wrote,
Of special merit, tho' of little note;   40

25) *fribble*, trifling

For Fate, in a strange humour, had decreed
That what It wrote, none but Itself should read;
Much too It chatter'd of Dramatic Laws,
Misjudging Critics, and misplac'd applause,
Then, with a self-complacent jutting air,   45
It smil'd, It smirk'd, It wriggled to the chair;
And, with an awkward briskness not its own,
Looking around, and perking on the throne,
Triumphant seem'd, when that strange savage Dame,
Known but to few, or only known by name,   50
Plain Common Sense appear'd, by Nature there
Appointed, with plain Truth, to guard the Chair.
The Pageant saw, and blasted with her frown,
To Its first state of Nothing melted down.

  Nor shall the Muse (for even there the pride   55
Of this vain Nothing shall be mortified)
Nor shall the Muse (should Fate ordain her rhimes,
Fond, pleasing thought! to live in after-times)
With such a Trifler's name her pages blot;
Known be the Character, the Thing forgot;   60
Let It, to disappoint each future aim,
Live without Sex, and die without a name!

  Cold-blooded critics, by enervate sires
Scarce hammer'd out, when Nature's feeble fires
Glimmer'd their last; whose sluggish blood, half froze,   65
Creeps lab'ring thro' the veins; whose heart ne'er glows
With fancy-kindled heat:—A servile race,
Who, in mere want of fault, all merit place;
Who blind obedience pay to ancient schools,
Bigots to Greece, and slaves to musty rules;   70
With solemn consequence declar'd that none
Could judge that cause but Sophocles alone.
Dupes to their fancied excellence, the crowd,
Obsequious to the sacred dictate, bow'd.

B   Prompt at the call, around the goddess roll
Broad hats, and hoods, and caps, a sable shoal:
Thick and more thick the black blockade extends,
A hundred head of Aristotle's friends.
Nor wert thou, Isis! wanting to the day,   5
[Though Christchurch long kept prudishly away].

               *   *   *   *   *

As many quit the streams that murmuring fall
To lull the sons of Margaret and Clare Hall,
Where Bentley late tempestuous wont to sport
In troubled waters, but now sleeps in port.   10
Before them marched that awful Aristarch;
Ploughed was his front with many a deep remark:
His hat, which never vailed to human pride,
Walker with reverence took and laid aside.
Low bowed the rest: he, kingly, did but nod;   15
So upright Quakers please both man and God.
'Mistress! dismiss that rabble from your throne:
Avaunt—is Aristarchus yet unknown?
Thy mighty scholiast, whose unwearied pains
Made Horace dull, and humbled Milton's strains.   20
Turn what they will to verse, their toil is vain,
Critics like me shall make it prose again.

    *   *   *   *   *

In ancient sense if any needs will deal,
Be sure I give them fragments, not a meal;
What Gellius or Stobaeus hashed before,   25
Or chewed by blind old scholiasts o'er and o'er.
The critic eye, that microscope of wit,
Sees hairs and pores, examines bit by bit:
How parts relate to parts, or they to whole,
The body's harmony, the beaming soul,   30
Are things which Kuster, Burman, Wasse shall see
When man's whole frame is obvious to a flea.
  'Ah, think not, Mistress! more true dulness lies
In folly's cap, than wisdom's grave disguise.
Like buoys that never sink into the flood,   35
On learning's surface we but lie and nod.

    *   *   *   *   *

For thee we dim the eyes and stuff the head
With all such reading as was never read:
For thee explain a thing till all men doubt it,
And write about it, goddess, and about it: 40
So spins the silk-worm small its slender store,
And labours till it clouds itself all o'er.
  'What though we let some better sort of fool
Thrid ev'ry science, run through ev'ry school?
Never by tumbler through the hoops was shown   45
Such skill in passing all, and touching none;

He may indeed (if sober all this time)
Plague with dispute, be persecute with rhyme.
We only furnish what he cannot use,
Or wed to what he must divorce, a Muse: 50
Full in the midst of Euclid dip at once,
And petrify a genius to a dunce;
Or set on metaphysic ground to prance
Show all his paces, not a step advance.
With the same cement, ever sure to bind,   55
We bring to one dead level ev'ry mind.
Then take him to develop, if you can,
And hew the block off, and get out the man.
But wherefore waste I words? I see advance
W——, pupil, and laced governor from France.   60
Walker! our hat—' nor more he deigned to say,
But, stern as Ajax' spectre, strode away.

2) *broad hats*, etc., academic dress   5) *Isis*, a river at Oxford   8) *Margaret and Clare Hall*, Colleges at Cambridge   9) *Bentley*, a redoubtable but pedantic critic   11) *Aristarchus*, an ancient commentator on Homer. The poet uses the name because Bentley (here called Aristarchus) had attacked his translation of Homer   22) *make it prose again*, Bentley had much injured Milton by his fancied improvements (author's note)   25) and 31) *Gellius, Stobaeus, Kuster, Burman, Wasse*, pedantic critics   58) *hew the block off*, a notion of Aristotle that there was originally in every block of marble a statue which would appear on the removal of the superfluous parts (author's note)   61) *Walker*, master at Trinity College, Cambridge, where Bentley was master

The above extracts are taken from eighteenth-century mock-heroic satires. In the first, a playwright and critic is satirised, in the second, a literary critic and scholar. Comment on the relative effectiveness of the passages.

28

MR NIXON

In the cream gilded cabin of his steam yacht
Mr Nixon advised me kindly, to advance with fewer
Dangers of delay. 'Consider
　　　Carefully the reviewer.

'I was as poor as you are;   5
When I began I got, of course,
Advance on royalties, fifty at first,' said Mr Nixon,
'Follow me, and take a column,
Even if you have to work free.

'Butter reviewers. From fifty to three hundred   10
I rose in eighteen months;
The hardest nut I had to crack
Was Dr Dundas.

'I never mentioned a man but with the view
Of selling my own works.   15
The tip's a good one, as for literature
It gives no man a sinecure.

'And no one knows, at sight, a masterpiece.
And give up verse, my boy,
There's nothing in it.'   20

*   *   *   *   *

Likewise a friend of Blougram's once advised me:
Don't kick against the pricks,
Accept opinion. The 'Nineties' tried your game
And died, there's nothing in it.

B   MR APOLLINAX

When Mr Apollinax visited the United States
His laughter tinkled among the teacups.
I thought of Fragilion, that shy figure among the birch-trees,
And of Priapus in the shrubbery
Gaping at the lady in the swing.   5
In the palace of Mrs Phlaccus, at Professor Channing-Cheetah's
He laughed like an irresponsible foetus.
His laughter was submarine and profound
Like the old man of the sea's
Hidden under coral islands   10
Where worried bodies of drowned men drift down in the green
      silence,
Dropping from fingers of surf.
I looked for the head of Mr Apollinax rolling under a chair

Or grinning over a screen
With seaweed in its hair.   15
I heard the beat of centaur's hoofs over the hard turf
As his dry and passionate talk devoured the afternoon.
'He is a charming man'—'But after all what did he mean?'—
'His pointed ears...He must be unbalanced,'—
'There was something he said that I might have challenged.' 20

3) *Fragilion*, a fanciful name   4) *Priapus*, a god of gardens, also of sexual
fertility

Of dowager Mrs Phlaccus, and Professor and Mrs Cheetah
I remember a slice of lemon, and a bitten macaroon.

> Discuss the intentions of the poets and the means they use to achieve
> their ends. You are not required to state a preference unless you want
> to.

29

A SON

> My son was killed while laughing at some jest. I would I knew
> What it was, and it might serve me in a time when jests are few.

SHOCK

> My name, my speech, my self I had forgot.
> My wife and children came—I knew them not.
> I died. My mother followed. At her call
> And on her bosom I remembered all.

THE BEGINNER

> On the first hour of my first day
>   In the front trench I fell.
> (Children in boxes at a play
>   Stand up to watch it well).

THE REFINED MAN

> I was of delicate mind. I stepped aside for my needs,
>   Disdaining the common office. I was seen from afar and killed.
> How is this matter for mirth? Let each man be judged by his deeds.
>   *I have paid my price to live with myself on the terms that I willed.*

UNKNOWN FEMALE CORPSE

> Headless, lacking foot and hand,
> Horrible I come to land.
> I beseech all women's sons
> Know I was a mother once.

A DEAD STATESMAN

> I could not dig: I dared not rob:
> Therefore I lied to please the mob.
> Now all my lies are proved untrue
> And I must face the men I slew.
> What tale shall serve me here among
> Mine angry and defrauded young?

> Comment on the effectiveness of these epigrammatic verses taken
> from a collection called 'Epitaphs of the War'.

Exercises: Prose

30

A Upon one of these excursions, while Reuben was otherwise employed, David alone acted as Lady Staunton's guide, and promised to show her a cascade in the hills, grander and higher than any they had yet visited. It was a walk of five long miles, and over rough ground, varied, however, and cheered, by mountain views, and peeps now of the firth and its islands, now of distant lakes, now of rocks and precipices. The scene itself, too, when they reached it, amply rewarded the labour of the walk. A single shoot carried a considerable stream over the face of a black rock, which contrasted stongly in colour with the white foam of the cascade, and, at the depth of about twenty feet, another rock intercepted the view of the bottom of the fall. The water, wheeling out far beneath, swept round the crag, which thus bounded their view, and tumbled down the rocky glen in a torrent of foam. Those who love nature always desire to penetrate into its utmost recesses, and Lady Staunton asked David whether there was not some mode of gaining a view of the abyss at the foot of the fall. He said that he knew a station on a shelf on the further side of the intercepting rock, from which the whole waterfall was visible, but that the road to it was steep and slippery and dangerous. Bent, however, on gratifying her curiosity, she desired him to lead the way; and accordingly he did so over crag and stone, anxiously pointing out to her the resting-places where she ought to step, for their mode of advancing soon ceased to be walking, and became scrambling.

In this manner, clinging like sea-birds to the face of the rock, they were enabled at length to turn round it, and came full in front of the fall, which here had a most tremendous aspect, boiling, roaring, and thundering with unceasing din into a black cauldron, a hundred feet at least below them, which resembled the crater of a volcano. The noise, the dashing of the waters, which gave an unsteady appearance to all around them, the trembling even of the huge crag on which they stood, the precariousness of their footing, for there was scarce room for them to stand on the shelf of rock which they had thus attained, had so powerful an effect on the senses and imagination of Lady Staunton, that she called out to David she was falling, and would in fact have dropped from the crag had he not caught hold of her. The boy was bold and stout of his age; still he was but fourteen years old, and as his assistance gave no confidence to Lady Staunton, she felt her situation become really perilous. The chance was that, in the appalling novelty of the circumstances, he might have caught the infection of her panic, in which case it is likely that both must have perished. She now screamed with terror, though without hope of calling any one to her assistance. To her amazement, the scream was answered by a whistle from above, of a tone so clear and shrill that it was heard even amid the noise of the waterfall.

B The *Nan-Shan* was being looted by the storm with a senseless, destructive fury: trysails torn out of the extra gaskets, double-lashed awnings blown away, bridge swept clean, weather-cloths burst, rails twisted, light-screens smashed—and two of the boats had gone already. They had gone unheard and unseen, melting, as it were, in the shock and smother of the wave. It was only later, when upon the white flash of another high sea hurling itself amid-ships, Jukes had a vision of two pairs of davits leaping black and empty out of the solid blackness, with one overhauled fall flying and an iron-bound block capering in the air, that he became aware of what had happened within about three yards of his back.

. . . .

They held hard. An outburst of unchained fury, a vicious rush of the wind absolutely steadied the ship; she rocked only, quick and light like a child's cradle, for a terrific moment of suspense, while the whole atmosphere, as it seemed, streamed furiously past her, roaring away from the tenebrous earth.

It suffocated them, and with eyes shut they tightened their grasp. What from the magnitude of the shock might have been a column of water running upright in the dark, butted against the ship, broke short, and fell on her bridge, crushingly, from on high, with a dead burying weight.

A flying fragment of that collapse, a mere splash, enveloped them in one swirl from their feet over their heads, filling violently their ears, mouths and nostrils with salt water. It knocked out their legs, wrenched in haste at their arms, seethed away swiftly under their chins; and opening their eyes, they saw the piled-up masses of foam dashing to and fro amongst what looked like the fragments of a ship. She had given way as if driven straight in. Their panting hearts yielded, too, before the tremendous blow; and all at once she sprang up again to her desperate plunging, as if trying to scramble out from under the ruins.

The seas in the dark seemed to rush from all sides to keep her back where she might perish. There was hate in the way she was handled, and a ferocity in the blows that fell. She was like a living creature thrown to the rage of a mob: hustled terribly, struck at, borne up, flung down, leaped upon. Captain MacWhirr and Jukes kept hold of each other, deafened by the noise, gagged by the wind; and the great physical tumult beating about their bodies brought, like an unbridled display of passion, a profound trouble to their souls. One of those wild and appalling shrieks

that are heard at times passing mysteriously overhead in the steady roar
of a hurricane, swooped, as if borne on wings, upon the ship, and Jukes
tried to outscream it.

'Will she live through this?'

The cry was wrenched out of his breast. It was as unintentional as the
birth of a thought in the head, and he heard nothing of it himself. It all
became extinct at once—thought, intention, effort—and of his cry the
inaudible vibration added to the tempest waves of the air.

He expected nothing from it. Nothing at all. For indeed what answer
could be made? But after a while he heard with amazement the frail and
resisting voice in his ear, the dwarf sound, unconquered in the giant
tumult.

'She may!'

Compare these extracts from novels.

31

Meanwhile enters the expectant peer, Mr Bult, an esteemed party man who,
rather neutral in private life, had strong opinions concerning the districts
of the Niger, was much at home also in the Brazils, spoke with decision
of affairs in the South Seas, was studious of his parliamentary and itinerant
speeches, and had the general solidity and suffusive pinkness of a healthy
Briton on the central table-land of life. Catherine, aware of a tacit understanding that he was an undeniable husband for an heiress, had nothing
to say against him but that he was thoroughly tiresome to her. Mr Bult
was amiably confident, and had no idea that his insensibility to counter-
point[1] could ever be reckoned against him. Klesmer he hardly regarded
in the light of a serious human being who ought to have a vote; and he
did not mind Miss Arrowpoint's addiction to music any more than her
probable expenses in antique lace. He was consequently a little amazed
at an after-dinner outburst of Klesmer's on the lack of idealism in English
politics, which left all mutuality between distant races to be determined
simply by the need of a market; the crusades, to his mind, had at least
this excuse, that they had a banner of sentiment round which generous
feelings could rally: of course, the scoundrels rallied too, but what then?
—they rally in equal force round your advertisement van of 'Buy cheap,
sell dear'. On this theme Klesmer's eloquence, gesticulatory and other,
went on for a little while like stray fireworks accidentally ignited, and
then sank into immovable silence. Mr Bult was not surprised that Klesmer's
opinions should be flighty, but was astonished at his command of English
idiom and his ability to put a point in a way that would have told at a

---

[1] A musical term.

constituents' dinner—to be accounted for probably by his being a Pole, or a Czech, or something of that fermenting sort, in a state of political refugeeism which had obliged him to make a profession of his music; and that evening in the drawing-room he for the first time went up to Klesmer at the piano, Miss Arrowpoint being near, and said—

'I had no idea before that you were a political man.'

Klesmer's only answer was to fold his arms, put out his nether lip, and stare at Mr Bult.

'You must have been used to public speaking. You speak uncommonly well, though I don't agree with you. From what you said about sentiment, I fancy you are a Panslavist.'

'No; my name is Elijah. I am the Wandering Jew,' said Klesmer, flashing a smile at Miss Arrowpoint, and suddenly making a mysterious wind-like rush backwards and forwards on the piano. Mr Bult felt this buffoonery rather offensive and Polish, but—Miss Arrowpoint being there—did not like to move away.

'Herr Klesmer has cosmopolitan ideas,' said Miss Arrowpoint, trying to make the best of the situation. 'He looks forward to a fusion of races.'

'With all my heart,' said Mr Bult, willing to be gracious. 'I was sure he had too much talent to be a mere musician.'

'Ah sir, you are under some mistake there,' said Klesmer, firing up. 'No man has too much talent to be a musician. Most men have too little. A creative artist is no more a mere musician than a great statesman is a mere politician. We are not ingenious puppets, sir, who live in a box and look out on the world only when it is gaping for amusement. We help to rule the nations and make the age as much as any other public men. We count ourselves on level benches with legislators. And a man who speaks effectively through music is compelled to something more difficult than parliamentary eloquence.'

With the last word Klesmer wheeled from the piano and walked away.

Miss Arrowpoint coloured, and Mr Bult observed with his usual phlegmatic solidity, 'Your pianist does not think small beer of himself.'

> Discuss this passage from George Eliot's *Daniel Deronda*. What is the writer attempting to do? What is her attitude towards Mr Bult, Miss Arrowpoint and Herr Klesmer respectively?

32

A   He took out his door-key and let himself into the house. He could hear laughter in the upper rooms. He was in the ball-dress in which he had been captured the night before. He went silently up the stairs; leaning against the banisters at the stair-head.—Nobody was stirring in the house besides—all the servants had been sent away. Rawdon heard laughter within—laughter and singing. Becky was singing a snatch of the song of the night before; a hoarse voice shouted, 'Brava! Brava!'—it was Lord Steyne's.

Rawdon opened the door and went in. A little table with a dinner was laid out—and wine and plate. Steyne was hanging over the sofa on which Becky sat. The wretched woman was in a brilliant full toilette, her arms and all her fingers sparkling with bracelets and rings; and the brilliants on her breast which Steyne had given her. He had her hand in his, and was bowing over it to kiss it, when Becky started up with a faint scream as she caught sight of Rawdon's white face. At the next instant she tried a smile, a horrid smile, as if to welcome her husband: and Steyne rose up, grinding his teeth, pale, and with fury in his looks.

He, too, attempted a laugh—and came forward holding out his hand. 'What, come back! How d'ye do, Crawley?' he said, the nerves of his mouth twitching as he tried to grin at the intruder.

There was that in Rawdon's face which caused Becky to fling herself before him. 'I am innocent, Rawdon,' she said; 'before God, I am innocent.' She clung hold of his coat, of his hands; her own were all covered with serpents, and rings, and baubles. 'I am innocent.—Say I am innocent,' she said to Lord Steyne.

He thought a trap had been laid for him, and was as furious with the wife as with the husband. 'You innocent! Damn you,' he screamed out. 'You innocent! Why, every trinket you have on your body is paid for by me. I have given you thousands of pounds which this fellow has spent, and for which he has sold you. Innocent, by—! You're as innocent as your mother, the ballet-girl, and your husband the bully. Don't think to frighten me as you have done others. Make way, sir, and let me pass;' and Lord Steyne seized up his hat, and, with flame in his eyes, and looking his enemy fiercely in the face, marched upon him, never for a moment doubting that the other would give way.

But Rawdon Crawley springing out, seized him by the neckcloth, until Steyne, almost strangled, writhed, and bent under his arm. 'You lie, you dog!' said Rawdon. 'You lie, you coward and villain!' And he struck the peer twice over the face with his open hand, and flung him bleeding to the ground. It was all done before Rebecca could interpose. She stood there trembling before him. She admired her husband, strong, brave, and victorious.

'Come here,' he said.—She came up at once.

'Take off those things.'—She began, trembling, pulling the jewels from her arms, and the rings from her shaking fingers, and held them all in a heap, quivering and looking up at him. 'Throw them down,' he said, and she dropped them. He tore the diamond ornament out of her breast, and flung it at Lord Steyne. It cut him on his bald forehead. Steyne wore the scar to his dying day.

'Come upstairs,' Rawdon said to his wife. 'Don't kill me, Rawdon,' she said. He laughed savagely.—'I want to see if that man lies about the money as he has about me. Has he given you any?'

'No,' said Rebecca, 'that is—'

'Give me your keys,' Rawdon answered, and they went out together. Rebecca gave him all the keys but one: and she was in hopes that he would not have remarked the absence of that. It belonged to the little desk which Amelia had given her in early days, and which she kept in a secret place. But Rawdon flung open boxes and wardrobes, throwing the multi-farious trumpery of their contents here and there, and at last he found the desk. The woman was forced to open it. It contained papers, love-letters many years old—all sorts of small trinkets and woman's memoranda. And it contained a pocket-book with banknotes. Some of these were dated ten years back, too, and one was quite a fresh one—a note for a thousand pounds which Lord Steyne had given her.

'Did he give you this?' Rawdon said.

'Yes,' Rebecca answered.

'I'll send it to him to-day,' Rawdon said (for day had dawned again, and many hours had passed in this search), 'and I will pay Briggs, who was kind to the boy, and some of the debts. You will let me know where I shall send the rest to you. You might have spared me a hundred pounds, Becky, out of all this—I have always shared with you.'

'I am innocent,' said Becky. And he left her without another word.

B   There was a pause. He watched her with eyes glittering to a point.

'Have you been havin' owt to do with him?' he asked.

'I've just spoken to him when I've seen him,' she said. 'He's not as bad as you would make out.'

'Isn't he?' he cried, a certain wakefulness in his voce. 'Them who has anything to do wi' him is too bad for me, I tell you.'

'Why, what are you frightened of him for?' she mocked.

She was rousing all his uncontrollable anger. He sat glowering. Every one of her sentences stirred him up like a red-hot iron. Soon it would be too much. And she was afraid herself; but she was neither conquered nor convinced.

A curious little grin of hate came on his face. He had a long score against her.

'What am I frightened of him for?' he repeated automatically. 'What am I frightened of him for? Why, for you, you stray-running little bitch.'

She flushed. The insult went deep into her, right home.

'Well, if you're so dull—' she said, lowering her eyelids, and speaking coldly, haughtily.

'If I'm so dull I'll break your neck the first word you speak to him,' he said, tense.

'Pf!' she sneered. 'Do you think I'm frightened of you?' She spoke coldly, detached.

She was frightened, for all that, white round the mouth.

His heart was getting hotter.

'You will be frightened of me, the next time you have anything to do with him,' he said.

'Do you think you'd ever be told—ha!'

Her jeering scorn made him go white-hot, molten. He knew he was incoherent, scarcely responsible for what he might do. Slowly, unseeing, he rose and went out of doors, stifled, moved to kill her.

He stood leaning against the garden fence, unable either to see or hear. Below him, far off, fumed the lights of the town. He stood still, unconscious with a black storm of rage, his face lifted to the night.

Presently, still unconscious of what he was doing, he went indoors again. She stood, a small, stubborn figure with tight-pressed lips and big, sullen, childish eyes, watching him, white with fear. He went heavily across the floor and dropped into his chair.

There was a silence.

'You're not going to tell me everything I shall do, and everything I shan't,' she broke out at last.

He lifted his head.

'I tell you this,' he said, low and intense. 'Have anything to do with Sam Adams, and I'll break your neck.'

She laughed, shrill and false.

'How I hate your word "break your neck",' she said, with a grimace of the mouth. 'It sounds so common and beastly. Can't you say something else—'

There was a dead silence.

'And besides,' she said, with a queer chirrup of mocking laughter, 'what do you know about anything? He sent me an amethyst brooch and a pair of pearl ear-rings.'

'He what?' said Whiston, in a suddenly normal voice. His eyes were fixed on her.

'Sent me a pair of pearl ear-rings, and an amethyst brooch,' she repeated, mechanically, pale to the lips.

And her big, black, childish eyes watched him, fascinated, held in her spell.

He seemed to thrust his face and his eyes forward at her, as he rose slowly and came to her. She watched transfixed in terror. Her throat made a small sound, as she tried to scream.

Then, quick as lightning, the back of his hand struck her with a crash across the mouth, and she was flung back blinded against the wall. The shock shook a queer sound out of her. And then she saw him still coming on, his eyes holding her, his fist drawn back, advancing slowly. At any instant the blow might crash into her.

Mad with terror, she raised her hands with a queer clawing movement to cover her eyes and her temples, opening her mouth in a dumb shriek. There was no sound. But the sight of her slowly arrested him. He hung before her, looking at her fixedly, as she stood crouched against the wall with open, bleeding mouth, and wide-staring eyes, and two hands clawing over her temples. And his lust to see her bleed, to break her and destroy her, rose from an old source against her. It carried him. He wanted satisfaction.

But he had seen her standing there, a piteous, horrified thing, and he turned his face aside in shame and nausea. He went and sat heavily in his chair, and a curious ease, almost like sleep, came over his brain.

She walked away from the wall towards the fire, dizzy, white to the lips, mechanically wiping her small, bleeding mouth. He sat motionless. Then, gradually, her breath began to hiss, she shook, and was sobbing silently, in grief for herself. Without looking, he saw. It made his mad desire to destroy her come back.

At length he lifted his head. His eyes were glowing again, fixed on her.

'And what did he give them you for?' he asked, in a steady, unyielding voice.

Her crying dried up in a second. She also was tense.

'They came as valentines,' she replied, still not subjugated even if beaten.

'When, to-day?'

'The pearl ear-rings to-day—the amethyst brooch last year.'

'You've had it a year?'

'Yes.'

She felt that now nothing would prevent him if he rose to kill her. She could not prevent him any more. She was yielded up to him. They both trembled in the balance, unconscious.

'What have you had to do with him?' he asked, in a barren voice.

'I've not had anything to do with him,' she quavered.

'You just kept 'em because they were jewellery?' he said.

A weariness came over him. What was the worth of speaking any more of it? He did not care any more. He was dreary and sick.

She began to cry again, but he took no notice. She kept wiping her mouth on her handkerchief. He could see it, the blood-mark. It made him only more sick and tired of the responsibility of it, the violence, the shame.

When she began to move about again, he raised his head once more from his dead, motionless position.

'Where are the things?' he said.

'They are upstairs,' she quavered. She knew the passion had gone down in him.

'Bring them down,' he said.

'I won't,' she wept, with rage. 'You're not going to bully me and hit me like that on the mouth.'

And she sobbed again. He looked at her in contempt and compassion and in rising anger.

'Where are they?' he said.

'They're in the little drawer under the looking-glass,' she sobbed.

He went slowly upstairs, struck a match, and found the trinkets. He brought them downstairs in his hand.

'These?' he said, looking at them as they lay in his palm.

She looked at them without answering. She was not interested in them any more.

He looked at the little jewels. They were pretty.

'It's none of their fault,' he said to himself.

And he searched round slowly, persistently, for a box. He tied the things up and addressed them to Sam Adams. Then he went out in his slippers to post the little package.

When he came back she was still sitting crying.

'You'd better go to bed,' he said.

She paid no attention. He sat by the fire. She still cried.

'I'm sleeping down here,' he said. 'Go you to bed.'

In a few moments she lifted her tear-stained, swollen face and looked at him with eyes all forlorn and pathetic. A great flash of anguish went over his body. He went over slowly, and very gently took her in his hands. She let herself be taken. Then as she lay against his shoulder, she sobbed aloud:

'I never meant——'

'My love—my little love——' he cried, in anguish of spirit, holding her in his arms.

Compare these extracts from novels.

33

A   This centre to which humanism refers everything, this centripetal energy which counteracts the multifarious centrifugal impulses, this magnetic will which draws the flux of our sensations toward it while itself remaining at rest, is the reality which gives rise to religion. Pure humanism is content to describe it thus in physical terms, as an observed fact or experience; it hesitates to pass beyond its experimental knowledge to the dogmatic affirmations of any of the great religions. It cannot bring itself to accept a formal theology (any more than it can accept a romantic idealism) that has been set up in defiance of reason, for it holds that the value of supernatural intuition must be tested by the intellect. Again, it fears the asceticism to which religion tends in consequence of a too harsh dualism of the flesh and the spirit, for, as we have said, humanism calls for completeness, wishing to use and not annihilate dangerous forces. Unlike religion, it assigns an important place to the instruments of both science and art. Nevertheless it agrees with religion in its perception of the ethical will as a power above the ordinary self, an impersonal reality in which all men may share despite the diversity of personal temperament and towards which their attitude must be one of subjection.

B   I do not believe in Belief. But this is an age of faith, and there are so many militant creeds that, in self-defence, one has to formulate a creed of one's own. Tolerance, good temper and sympathy are no longer enough in a world which is rent by religious and racial persecution, in a world where ignorance rules, and science, who ought to have ruled, plays the subservient pimp. Tolerance, good temper and sympathy—they are what matter really, and if the human race is not to collapse they must come to the front before long. But for the moment they are not enough, their action is no stronger than a flower, battered beneath a military jack-boot. They want stiffening, even if the process coarsens them. Faith, to my mind, is a stiffening process, a sort of mental starch, which ought to be applied as sparingly as possible. I dislike the stuff. I do not believe in it, for its own sake, at all. Herein I probably differ from most people, who believe in Belief, and are only sorry they cannot swallow even more than they do.

Compare these passages. Which seems to you the more effective prose?

34

Writer A produced a list of virtues with which he used to test his conduct at the end of each day. Writer B was annoyed by this list, and felt the best way of criticising writer A was to produce a list of his own. Underneath are printed the two lists. What differences in outlook do they reveal, and which seems to you to offer better advice?

TEMPERANCE: A   Eat not to fulness; drink not to elevation.
               B   Eat and carouse with Bacchus, or munch dry bread with Jesus, but don't sit down without one of the gods.
SILENCE: A   Speak not but what may benefit others or yourself; avoid trifling conversation.

B Be still when you have nothing to say; when genuine passion moves you, say what you've got to say, and say it hot.

ORDER: A Let all your things have their places; let each part of your business have its time.

B Know that you are responsible to the gods inside you and to the men in whom the gods are manifest. Recognise your superiors and your inferiors, according to the gods. This is the root of all order.

RESOLUTION: A Resolve to perform what you ought; perform without fail what you resolve.

B Resolve to abide by your own deepest promptings, and to sacrifice the smaller thing to the greater. Kill when you must, and be killed the same: the *must* coming from the gods inside you, or from the men in whom you recognise the Holy Ghost.

FRUGALITY: A Make no expense but to do good to others or yourself—i.e., waste nothing.

B Demand nothing; accept what you see fit. Don't waste your pride or squander your emotion.

INDUSTRY: A Lose no time, be always employed in something useful; cut off all unnecessary action.

B Lose no time with ideals; serve the Holy Ghost; never serve mankind.

SINCERITY: A Use no hurtful deceit; think innocently and justly, and, if you speak, speak accordingly.

B To be sincere is to remember that I am I, and that the other man is not me.

JUSTICE: A Wrong none by doing injuries, or omitting the benefits that are your duty.

B The only justice is to follow the sincere intuition of the soul, angry or gentle. Anger is just, pity is just, but judgment is never just.

MODERATION: A Avoid extremes, forbear resenting injuries as much as you think they deserve.

B Beware of absolutes. There are many gods.

CLEANLINESS: A Tolerate no uncleanliness in body, clothes, or habitation.

B Don't be too clean. It impoverishes the blood.

TRANQUILLITY: A Be not disturbed at trifles, or at accidents common or unavoidable.

B The soul has many motions, many gods come and go. Try and find your deepest issue, in every confusion, and abide by that. Obey the man in whom you recognise the Holy Ghost; command when your honour comes to command.

CHASTITY:

A Rarely use venery but for health and offspring, never to dullness, weakness, or the injury of your own or another's peace or reputation.

B Never 'use' venery at all. Follow your passional impulse, if it be answered in the other being; but never have any motive in mind, neither offspring nor health nor even pleasure, nor even service. Only know that 'venery' is of the great gods. An offering-up of yourself to the very great gods, the dark ones, and nothing else.

HUMILITY:

A Imitate Jesus and Socrates.

B See all men and women according to the Holy Ghost that is within them. Never yield before the barren.

35

A ...If would-be critics to-day genuinely want to acquire a classical point of view, they should study Desmond MacCarthy.

They would learn how to express it too. For Desmond MacCarthy was himself an artist. His writing is a model of what critical prose should be. For he was without the conceit that inspires some critics to expect to find readers, when they have taken no trouble to make their books readable. Desmond MacCarthy was a famous talker, and his style is a talker's style; easy, casual, parenthetical, its unit the sentence rather than the paragraph. But it is conversation glorified and transfigured and purged of its characteristic vagueness and diffuseness. Every sentence is firm and lucid; it gleams at every turn with some picked felicitous phrase—'Swinburne's strong, monotonous melodies', 'Hawthorne's pensive, delicate, collected prose', 'the passion which smoulders in the dark impersonal eyes' of Rembrandt's Jewish portraits. How delightful too it is when the steady, substantial good sense of Desmond MacCarthy's discourse is lit up by the flicker of his playfulness. 'I myself enjoy Swinburne's prose very much, but this is so exceptional a taste that I have been tempted to insert an Agony Column advertisement, "Lonely literary man of moderate means wishes to meet friend; must appreciate Swinburne's prose".'

B 'What I have here not dogmatically but deliberately written' (to invoke again the apt Johnsonian phrase) illustrates a conception of the business of criticism and an associated conception of the importance of poetry. I think it the business of the critic to perceive for himself, to make the finest and sharpest relevant discriminations, and to state his findings as responsibly, clearly and forcibly as possible. Then even if he is wrong he has forwarded the business of criticism—he has exposed himself as openly as possible to correction; for what criticism undertakes is the profitable discussion of literature. Any one who works strenuously in the spirit of this conception must expect to be accused of being both dogmatic and narrow, though, naturally, where my own criticism is concerned I think the accusations unfair.

Compare these passages and the notions of literary criticism which lie behind them.

36

A   It is to the Strength of this amazing Invention we are to attribute that Unequal'd Fire and Rapture, which is so forcible in *Homer*, that no Man of a true Poetical Spirit is Master of himself while he reads him. What he writes is of the most animated Nature imaginable; every thing moves, every thing lives, and is put into Action. If a Council be call'd, or a Battle fought, you are not coldly inform'd of what was said or done as from a third Person; the Reader is hurry'd out of himself by the Force of the Poet's Imagination, and turns in one place into a Hearer, in another to a Spectator. The Course of his Verses resembles that of the Army he describes... 'They pour along like a Fire that sweeps the whole Earth before it'. 'Tis however remarkable that his Fancy, which is every where vigorous, is not discover'd immediately at the beginning of his Poem in its fullest Splendour: It grows in the Progress both upon himself and others, and becomes on Fire like a Chariot-Wheel, by its own Rapidity. Exact Disposition, just Thought, correct Elocution, polish'd Numbers may have been found in a thousand; but this Poetical *Fire*, this *Vivida vis animi*[1] in a very few. Even in Works where all those are imperfect or neglected, this can over-power Criticism, and make us admire even while we disapprove... This *Fire* is discern'd in *Virgil*, but discern'd as through a Glass, reflected, and more shining than warm, but every where equal and constant...

    ...As there is more variety of Characters in the *Iliad*, so there is of Speeches, than in any other Poem. *Every thing in it has manners* (as *Aristotle* expresses it) that is, every thing is acted or spoken. It is hardly credible in a Work of such length, how small a Number of Lines are employ'd in Narration. In *Virgil* the Dramatic Part is less in proportion to the Narrative; and the speeches often consist of general Reflections or Thoughts, which might be equally just in any Person's Mouth upon the

---

[1] A vivid force of spirit.

same Occasion. As many of his Persons have no apparent Characters, so many of his Speeches escape being apply'd and judg'd by the Rule of Propriety. We oftner think of the Author himself when we read *Virgil*, than when we are engag'd in *Homer:* All which are the Effects of a colder Invention, that interests us less in the Action describ'd: *Homer* makes us Hearers, and *Virgil* leaves us Readers.

B Among great Genius's, those few draw the Admiration of all the World upon them, and stand up as the Prodigies of Mankind, who by the mere Strength of natural Parts, and without any Assistance of Art or Learning, have produced Works that were the Delight of their own Times and the Wonder of Posterity. There appears something nobly wild and extravagant in these great natural Genius's, that is infinitely more beautiful than all the Turn and Polishing of what the *French* call a *Bel Esprit*,[1] by which they would express a Genius refined by Conversation, Reflection, and the Reading of the most polite Authors. The greatest Genius which runs through the Arts and Sciences, takes a kind of Tincture from them, and falls unavoidably into Imitation.

Many of these great natural Genius's that were never disciplined and broken by Rules of Art, are to be found among the Ancients, and in particular among those of the more Eastern Parts of the World. *Homer* has innumerable Flights that *Virgil* was not able to reach, and in the Old Testament we find several Passages more elevated and sublime than any in *Homer*. At the same Time that we allow a greater and more daring Genius to the Ancients, we must own that the greatest of them very much failed in, or, if you will, that they were much above the Nicety and Correctness of the Moderns. In their Similitudes and Allusions, provided there was a Likeness, they did not much trouble themselves about the Decency of the Comparison... *Homer* illustrates one of his Heroes encompassed with the Enemy, by an Ass in a Field of Corn that has his Sides belaboured by all the Boys of the Village without stirring a Foot for it; and another of them tossing to and fro in his Bed and burning with Resentment, to a Piece of Flesh broiled on the Coals. This particular Failure in the Ancients, opens a large Field of Raillerie to the little Wits, who can laugh at an Indecency but not relish the Sublime in these Sorts of Writings. The present Emperor of *Persia*, conformable to this Eastern way of Thinking, amidst a great many pompous Titles, denominates himself the Sun of Glory, and the *Nutmeg of Delight*. In short, to cut off all Cavelling against the Ancients, and particularly those of the warmer Climates, who had most Heat and Life in their Imaginations, we are to consider that the Rule of observing what the *French* call the *Bienseance*[2] in an Allusion, has been found out of latter Years and in the colder

[1] Wit.   [2] Literary tact.

Regions of the World; where we would make some Amends for our want
of Force and Spirit, by a scrupulous Nicety and Exactness in our Compositions...

Compare these two passages. Which is the better piece of criticism?

37

Our young friend had to think a minute. 'I see, I see. Nothing is more
probable than that I've said something nasty; but which of my particular
horrors—?'

'Well, then, your conveying that she makes her daughter out
younger—.'

'To make herself out the same?'—Vanderbank took him straight up.
'It was nasty my doing that? I see, I see. Yes, yes: I rather gave her away,
and you're struck by it—as is most delightful you *should* be—because
you're, in every way, of a better tradition and, knowing Mrs Brookenham's
my friend, can't conceive of one's playing on a friend a trick so vulgar
and odious. It strikes you also probably as the kind of thing we must be
constantly doing; it strikes you that, right and left, probably, we keep
giving each other away. Well, I dare say we do. Yes, "come to think of
it" as they say in America, we do. But what shall I tell you? Practically
we all know it and allow for it, and it's as broad as it's long. What's London
life after all? It's tit for tat!'

'Ah, but what becomes of friendship?' Mr Longdon earnestly and
pleadingly asked.

The young man met his eyes only the more sociably. 'Friendship?'

'Friendship.' Mr Longdon maintained the full value of the word.

'Well,' his companion risked, 'I dare say it isn't in London by any
means what it is at Beccles. I quite literally mean that,' Vanderbank re-
assuringly added; 'I never really have believed in the existence of friendship in big societies—in great towns and great crowds. It's a plant that
takes time and space and air; and London society is a huge "squash,"
as we elegantly call it—an elbowing, pushing, perspiring, chattering mob.'

'Ah, I don't say *that* of you!' Mr Longdon murmured, with a with-
drawal of his hand and visible scruple for the sweeping concession he had
evoked.

'Do say it, then—for God's sake; let some one say it, so that something
or other, whatever it may be, may come of it! It's impossible to say too
much—it's impossible to say enough. There isn't anything any one can
say that I won't agree to.'

'That shows you really don't care,' the old man returned with acuteness.

'Oh, we're past saving, if that's what you mean!' Vanderbank laughed.

Do you consider that 'all the resources of the novelist's technique are entirely at the service of a perceptive and profound intelligence' in the above passage?

38

A   And do you know what I thought? I thought I would part company as soon as I could. I wanted to have my first command all to myself. I wasn't going to sail in a squadron if there was a chance for independent cruising. I would make land by myself. I would beat the other boats. Youth! All youth! The silly, charming, beautiful youth...

I need not tell you what it is to be knocking about in an open boat. I remember nights and days of calm, when we pulled, we pulled, and the boat seemed to stand still, as if bewitched within the circle of the sea horizon. I remember the heat, the deluge of rain-squalls that kept us baling for dear life (but filled our water-cask), and I remember sixteen hours on end with a mouth dry as a cinder and a steering-oar over the stern to keep my first command head on to a breaking sea. I did not know how good a man I was till then. I remember the drawn faces, the dejected figures of my two men, and I remember my youth and the feeling that will never come back any more—the feeling that I could last for ever, outlast the sea, the earth, and all men; the deceitful feeling that lures us on to joys, to perils, to love, to vain effort—to death; the triumphant conviction of strength, the heat of life in the handful of dust, the glow in the heart that with every year grows dim, grows cold, grows small and expires—and expires too soon, too soon—before life itself.

And this is how I see the East. I have seen its secret places and have looked into its very soul; but now I see it always from a small boat, a high outline of mountains, blue and afar in the morning; like faint mist at noon; a jagged wall of purple at sunset. I have the feel of the oar in my hand, the vision of a scorching blue sea in my eyes. And I see a bay, a wide bay, smooth as glass and polished like ice, shimmering in the dark. A red light burns far off upon the gloom of the land, and the night is soft and warm. We drag at the oars with aching arms, and suddenly a puff of wind, a puff faint and tepid and laden with strange odours of blossoms, of aromatic wood, comes out of the still night—the first sigh of the East on my face. That I can never forget. It was impalpable and enslaving, like a charm, like a whispered promise of mysterious delight...
The mysterious East faced me, perfumed like a flower, silent like death, dark like a grave.

And I sat weary beyond expression, exulting like a conqueror, sleepless and entranced as if before a profound, a fateful enigma.

B But directly my eyes had rested on my ship all my fear vanished. It went off swiftly, like a bad dream. Only that a dream leaves no shame behind it, and that I felt a momentary shame at my unworthy suspicions.

Yes, there she was. Her hull, her rigging filled my eye with a great content. That feeling of life-emptiness which had made me so restless for the last few months lost its bitter plausibility, its evil influence, dissolved in a flow of joyous emotion.

At the first glance I saw that she was a high-class vessel, a harmonious creature in the lines of her fine body, in the proportioned tallness of her spars. Whatever her age and her history, she had preserved the stamp of her origin. She was one of those craft that in virtue of their design and complete finish will never look old. Amongst her companions moored to the bank, and all bigger than herself, she looked like a creature of high breed—an Arab steed in a string of cart-horses.

A voice behind me said in a nasty equivocal tone: 'I hope you are satisfied with her, Captain.' I did not even turn my head. It was the master of the steamer, and whatever he meant, whatever he thought of her, I knew that, like some rare women, she was one of those creatures whose mere existence is enough to awaken an unselfish delight. One feels that it is good to be in the world in which she has her being.

That illusion of life and character which charms one in men's finest handiwork radiated from her. An enormous baulk of teak-wood timber swung over her hatchway; lifeless matter, looking heavier and bigger than anything aboard of her. When they started lowering it the surge of the tackle sent a quiver through her from water-line to the trucks up the fine nerves of her rigging, as though she had shuddered at the weight. It seemed cruel to load her so...

Half-an-hour later, putting my foot on her deck for the first time, I received the feeling of deep physical satisfaction. Nothing could equal the fullness of that moment, the ideal completeness of that emotional experience which had come to me without the preliminary toil and disenchantments of an obscure career.

My rapid glance ran over her, enveloped, appropriated the form concreting the abstract sentiment of my command. A lot of details perceptible to a seaman struck my eye vividly in that instant. For the rest, I saw her disengaged from the material conditions of her being. The shore to which she was moored was as if it did not exist. What were to me all the countries of the globe? In all the parts of the world washed by navigable waters our relation to each other would be the same—and more intimate than there are words to express in the language.

Compare these passages from novels, which are by the same author. In A, a seaman recalls his adventures in his first command (of a ship's lifeboat after a disaster at sea); B describes a young captain's first glimpse of his first command.

39

A   First, about the scientists' optimism. This is an accusation which has been made so often that it has become a platitude. It has been made by some of the acutest non-scientific minds of the day. But it depends upon a confusion between the individual experience and the social experience, between the individual condition of man and his social condition. Most of the scientists I have known well have felt—just as deeply as the non-scientists I have known well—that the individual condition of each of us is tragic. Each of us is alone: sometimes we escape from solitariness, through love or affection or perhaps creative moments, but those triumphs of life are pools of light we make for ourselves while the edge of the road is black: each of us dies alone. Some scientists I have known have had faith in revealed religion. Perhaps with them the sense of the tragic condition is not so strong. I don't know. With most people of deep feeling, however high-spirited and happy they are, sometimes most with those who are happiest and most high-spirited, it seems to be right in the fibres, part of the weight of life. That is as true of the scientists I have known best as of anyone at all.

But nearly all of them—and this is where the colour of hope genuinely comes in—would see no reason why, just because the individual condition is tragic, so must the social condition be. Each of us is solitary: each of us dies alone: all right, that's a fate against which we can't struggle—but there is plenty in our condition which is not fate, and against which we are less than human unless we do struggle.

Most of our fellow human beings, for instance, are underfed and die before their time. In the crudest terms, *that* is the social condition. There is a moral trap which comes through the insight into man's loneliness; it tempts one to sit back, complacent in one's unique tragedy, and let the others go without a meal.

As a group, the scientists fall into that trap less than others. They are inclined to be impatient to see if something can be done: and inclined to think that it can be done, until it's proved otherwise. That is their real optimism, and it's an optimism that the rest of us badly need...

Industrialisation is the only hope of the poor. I use the word 'hope' in a crude and prosaic sense. I have not much use for the moral sensibility of anyone who is too refined to use it so. It is all very well for us, sitting pretty, to think that material standards of living don't matter all that much. It is all very well for one, as a personal choice, to reject industrialisation...But I don't respect you in the slightest if, even passively, you try to impose the same choice on others who are not free to choose. In fact, we know what their choice would be. For, with singular unanimity, in

any country where they have had the chance, the poor have walked off
the land into the factories as fast as the factories could take them...

These transformations [i.e. the industrial transformations of the U.S.S.R.
and China] were made with inordinate effort with great suffering. Much
of the suffering was unnecessary; the horror is hard to look at straight,
standing in the same decades. Yet they've proved that common men can
show astonishing fortitude in chasing jam tomorrow. Jam today, and
men aren't at their most exciting: jam tomorrow, and one often sees them
at their noblest. The transformations have also proved something which
only the scientific culture can take in its stride. Yet, when we don't take
it in our stride, it makes us look silly.

B   The sensitive person's hostility to the machine is in one sense un-
realistic, because of the obvious fact that the machine has come to stay.
But as an attitude of mind there is a great deal to be said for it. The machine
has got to be accepted, but it is probably better to accept it rather as one
accepts a drug—that is, grudgingly and suspiciously. Like a drug, the
machine is useful, dangerous, and habit-forming. The oftener one sur-
renders to it the tighter its grip becomes. You have only to look about
you at this moment to realise with what sinister speed the machine is
getting us into its power. To begin with, there is the frightful debauchery
of taste that has already been effected by a century of mechanisation. This
is almost too obvious and too generally admitted to need pointing out.
But as a single instance, take taste in its narrowest sense—the taste for
decent food. In the highly mechanised countries, thanks to tinned food,
cold storage, synthetic flavouring matters, etc., the palate is almost a dead
organ. As you can see by looking at any greengrocer's shop, what the
majority of English people mean by an apple is a lump of highly-coloured
cotton wool from America or Australia; they will devour these things,
apparently with pleasure, and let the English apples rot under the trees.
It is the shiny, standardised, machine-made look of the American apple
that appeals to them; the superior taste of the English apple is something
they simply do not notice...Wherever you look you will see some slick
machine-made article triumphing over the old-fashioned article that still
tastes of something other than sawdust. And what applies to food applies
also to furniture, houses, clothes, books, amusements, and everything
else that makes up our environment. There are now millions of people,
and they are increasing every year, to whom the blaring of a radio is not
only a more acceptable but a more *normal* background to their thoughts
than the lowing of cattle or the song of birds. The mechanisation of the
world could never proceed very far while taste, even the taste-buds of the
tongue, remained uncorrupted, because in that case most of the products
of the machine would be simply unwanted. In a healthy world there would
be no demand for tinned foods, aspirins, gramophones, gaspipe chairs,

machine guns, daily newspapers, telephones, motor-cars, etc., etc.; and on the other hand there would be a constant demand for the things the machine cannot produce. But meanwhile the machine is here, and its corrupting effects are almost irresistible. One inveighs against it, but one goes on using it. Even a bare-arse savage, given the chance, will learn the vices of civilisation within a few months. Mechanisation leads to the decay of taste, the decay of taste leads to the demand for machine-made articles and hence to more mechanisation, and so a vicious circle is established.

Consider the way the writers of these passages use language. Which passage reveals the better quality of mind?

40

All *definite* knowledge—so I should contend—belongs to science; all *dogma* as to what surpasses definite knowledge belongs to theology. But between theology and science there is a *No Man's Land*, exposed to attack from both sides; this No Man's Land is philosophy. Almost all the questions of most interest to speculative minds are such as science cannot answer, and the confident answers of theologians no longer seem so convincing as they did in former centuries. Is the world divided into mind and matter, and, if so, what is mind and what is matter? Is mind subject to matter, or is it possessed of independent powers? Has the universe any unity or purpose? Is it evolving towards some goal? Are there really laws of nature, or do we believe in them only because of our innate love or order? Is man what he seems to the astronomer, a tiny lump of impure carbon and water impotently crawling on a small and unimportant planet? Or is he what he appears to Hamlet? Is he perhaps both at once? Is there a way of living that is noble, in what does it consist, and how shall we achieve it? Must the good be eternal in order to deserve to be valued, or is it worth seeking if the universe is inexorably moving towards death? Is there such a thing as wisdom, or is what seems such merely the ultimate refinement of folly? To such questions no answer can be found in the laboratory. Theologies have professed to give answers, all too definite; but their very definiteness causes modern minds to view them with suspicion. The studying of these questions, if not the answering of them, is the business of philosophy.

Is there evidence of a distinguished intelligence at work in the above passage?

41

A   About this time I fell into his company. His appearance was decent and manly; his knowledge considerable, his views extensive, his conversation elegant, and his disposition cheerful. By degrees I gained his confidence; and one day was admitted to him when he was immured by a bailiff that was prowling in the street. On this occasion recourse was had to the booksellers, who, on the credit of a translation of Aristotle's Poeticks, which he engaged to write with a large commentary, advanced as much money as enabled him to escape into the country. He shewed me the guineas safe in his hand. Soon afterwards his uncle, Mr Martin, a lieutenant-colonel, left him about two thousand pounds; a sum which Collins could scarcely think exhaustible, and which he did not live to exhaust. The guineas were then repaid, and the translation neglected.

But man is not born for happiness. Collins, who, while he *studied to live*, felt no evil but poverty, no sooner *lived to study* than his life was assailed by more dreadful calamities, disease and insanity...

Such was the fate of Collins, with whom I once delighted to converse, and whom I yet remember with tenderness.

B   The culprit was indeed not unworthy of that great presence. He had ruled an extensive and populous country, had made laws and treaties, had sent forth armies, had set up and pulled down princes. And in his high place he had so borne himself, that all had feared him, that most had loved him, and that hatred itself could deny him no title to glory, except virtue. He looked like a great man, and not like a bad man. A person small and emaciated, yet deriving dignity from a carriage which, while it indicated deference to the court, indicated also habitual self-possession and self-respect, a high and intellectual forehead, a brow pensive, but not gloomy, a mouth of inflexible decision, a face pale and worn, but serene, on which was written, as legibly as under the picture in the council-chamber at Calcutta, *Mens aequa in arduis*; such was the aspect with which the great Proconsul presented himself to his judges.

C   One human being, and one alone, felt the full force of what had happened. The Baron, by his fireside at Coburg, suddenly saw the tremendous fabric of his creation crash down into sheer and irremediable ruin. Albert was gone, and he had lived in vain. Even his blackest hypochondria had never envisioned quite so miserable a catastrophe. Victoria wrote to him, visited him, tried to console him by declaring with passionate conviction that she would carry on her husband's work. He smiled a sad smile and looked into the fire. Then he murmured that he was going where Albert was—that he would not be long. He shrank into himself. His children clustered round him and did their best to comfort him, but it was useless: the Baron's heart was broken. He lingered for eighteen months, and then, with his pupil, explored the shadow and the dust.

Compare and contrast the above passages, which are all taken from biographies.

42

A   Mrs Jellyby, whose face reflected none of the uneasiness which we could not help showing in our own faces, as the dear child's head recorded its passage with a bump on every stair—Richard afterwards said he counted seven, besides one for the landing—received us with perfect equanimity. She was a pretty, very diminutive, plump woman, of from forty to fifty, with handsome eyes, though they had a habit of seeming to look a long way off. As if—I am quoting Richard again—they could see nothing nearer than Africa!

We expressed our acknowledgments, and sat down behind the door where there was a lame invalid on a sofa. Mrs Jellyby had very good hair, but was too much occupied with her African duties to brush it. The shawl in which she had been loosely muffled, dropped on to her chair when she advanced to us; and as she turned to resume her seat, we could not help noticing that her dress didn't nearly meet up the back and that the open space was railed across with a lattice-work of stay-lace—like a summer-house...

All through dinner; which was long, in consequence of such accidents as the dish of potatoes being mislaid in the coal scuttle, and the handle of the corkscrew coming off, and striking the young woman in the chin; Mrs Jellyby preserved the evenness of her disposition. She told us a great deal that was interesting about Borrioboola-Gha and the natives; and received so many letters that Richard, who sat by her, saw four envelopes in the gravy at once. Some of the letters were proceedings of ladies' committees, or resolutions of ladies' meetings, which she read to us; others were applications from people excited in various ways about the cultivation of coffee, and natives; others required answers, and these she sent her eldest daughter from the table three or four times to write. She was full of business, and undoubtedly was, as she told us, devoted to the cause.

B   ...She was a copious, handsome woman, in whom angularity had been corrected by the air of success; she had a rustling dress (it was evident what *she* thought about taste), abundant hair of a glossy blackness, a pair of folded arms, the expression of which seemed to say that rest, in such a career as hers, was as sweet as it was brief, and a terrible regularity of feature. I apply that adjective to her fine placid mask because she seemed to face you with a question of which the answer was pre-ordained, to ask you how a countenance could fail to be noble of which the measurements were so correct. You could contest neither the measurements nor the nobleness, and had to feel that Mrs Farrinder imposed herself. There was a lithographic smoothness about her, and a mixture of the American matron and the public character. There was something public in her eye, which was large, cold and quiet; it had acquired a sort of exposed reticence from the habit of looking down from a lecture-desk, over a sea of heads, while its distinguished owner was eulogised by a leading citizen. Mrs Farrinder, at almost any time, had the air of being introduced by a few remarks. She talked with great slowness and distinctness, and evidently a high sense of responsibility; she pronounced every syllable of every word and insisted on being explicit. If, in conversation with her, you attempted to take anything for granted, or to jump two or three steps at a time, she paused, looking at you with a cold patience as if she knew that trick, and then went on at her own measured pace. She lectured on temperance and the rights of women; the ends she laboured for were to give the ballot to every woman in the country and to take the flowing bowl from every man. She was held to have a very fine manner, and to embody the domestic virtues and the graces of the drawing-room; to be a shining proof, in short, that the forum, for ladies, is not necessarily hostile to the fireside. She had a husband, and his name was Amariah.

Compare the above extracts from novels.

43

A   Since Plato turned his eyes, weary with the flux of things, to a celestial city whose aëry burgomasters kept guard over the perfect and unblemished exemplars of the objects of this bungled world, and not long after, Jesus told his fishermen that they could find their peace only in the Kingdom of Heaven, where the mansions were unnumberable, the subtle and the simple mind alike have been haunted by echoes of an unceasing music and dreams of imperishable beauty. Men's hearts have been swayed between a belief that the echoes and the dreams reached them from a distant eternal world more real than ours, and a premonition that the voice they heard was that of their own soul mysteriously calling them to self-perfection. And even those who have spoken with most conviction and persuasiveness, as though seeing face to face, of the perfect world immune from the rust of time have been the foremost to let fall the warning that their words were a parable. The rare spirits which steer the soul of humanity unite within themselves the contrary impulses of men. They live so intimately with their ideals that they are persuaded of their reality; they think so highly of the soul that a truth for it alone becomes a truth. Therefore they can say in the same breath that the Father's house has many mansions and that the Kingdom of Heaven is within us, and no man can tell for certain whether *The Republic* is an allegory.

This dream or desire is one of the eternal themes of poetry, not because it is superficially more 'poetic' than any other, but because it contains one of the persistent realities of the soul. For if the soul lives in its own right, having a core of active being, it lives by an ideal. There is no escaping the fact of the Kingdom of Heaven which is within you, because it is the condition of the soul's vitality. Once begin to make choice between a worse and a better, and you are inevitably bound to recognise its validity; and to live without making the choice, whatever the intellect may tell us, is not life at all. Life, as we know it, cannot bar the gate against the ideal. If it is a dream it is a dream we live by, and a dream we live by is more real than a reality we ignore.

But if this opposition of the ideal and the real is one of the great essential themes of poetry, it is also one which yields most to the impress of the poet's personality. Between the one pole of a complete belief in the existence of a kingdom of eternal beauty and imperishable perfection, and the other of an unfaltering recognition that these beautitudes exist in and for the soul alone, are infinite possibilities of faith and doubt, inexhaustible opportunities for the creative activity of art. For, apart from the precise mixture of certainty and hesitation in the poet's mind, one of the sovereign gestures of art is to make the ideal real, and to project a dim impersonal awareness on to a structure of definite invention. The sense that we are exiled from our own country, that our rightful heritage has been usurped from us, we know not how, may impel one poet to create his kingdom in words and name it with names, people it with fit inhabitants, and another to record the bare fact of his consciousness as a homeless wanderer.

B Many a man dies too soon and some are born in the wrong age or station. Could these persons drink at the fountain of youth at least once more they might do themselves fuller justice and cut a better figure at last in the universe. Most people think they have stuff in them for greater things than time suffers them to perform. To imagine a second career is a pleasing antidote for ill-fortune; the poor soul wants another chance. But how should a future life be constituted if it is to satisfy this demand, and how long need it last? It would evidently have to go on in an environment closely analogous to earth; I could not, for instance, write in another world the epics which the necessity of earning my living may have stifled here, did that other world contain no time, no heroic struggles, or no metrical language. Nor is it clear that my epics, to be perfect, would need to be quite endless. If what is foiled in me is really poetic genius and not simply a tendency toward perpetual motion, it would not help me if in heaven, in lieu of my dreamt-of epics, I were allowed to beget several robust children. In a word, if hereafter I am to be the same man improved I must find myself in the same world corrected. Were I transformed into a cherub or transported into a timeless ecstasy, it is hard to see in what sense I should continue to exist. Those results might be interesting in themselves and might enrich the universe; they would not prolong my life nor retrieve my disasters.

For this reason a future life is after all best represented by those frankly material ideals which most Christians—being Platonists—are wont to despise. It would be genuine happiness for a Jew to rise again in the flesh and live for ever in Ezekiel's New Jerusalem, with its ceremonial glories and civic order. It would be truly agreeable for any man to sit in well-watered gardens with Mohammed, clad in green silks, drinking delicious sherbets, and transfixed by the gazelle-like glance of some young girl, all innocence and fire. Amid such scenes a man might remain himself and might fulfil hopes that he had actually cherished on earth. He might also find his friends again, which in somewhat generous minds is perhaps the thought that chiefly sustains interest in a posthumous existence. But to recognise his friends a man must find them in their bodies, with their familiar habits, voices, and interests; for it is surely an insult to affection to say that he could find them in an eternal formula expressing their idiosyncrasy. When, however, it is clearly seen that another life, to supplement this one, must closely resemble it, does not the magic of immortality altogether vanish? Is such a reduplication of earthly society at all credible? And the prospect of awakening again among houses and trees, among children and dotards, among wars and rumours of wars, still fettered to one personality and one accidental past, still uncertain of the future, is not this prospect wearisome and deeply repulsive? Having passed through these things once and bequeathed them to posterity, is it not time for each soul to rest?

Compare these passages. Which seems to you the more effective piece of writing?

44

A   My earliest memory is a smell of bacon. It has become the memory of a memory, for I can never recall it now with the direct, almost sensual assurance which, vague and dreamy though this memory was, used to distinguish it when it recurred in the long, white forenoon of childhood, as I lay ill or convalescent, wafting up through the muted sounds of traffic, footsteps, voices, or as it came to me, more legendary now but still authentic, at moments between sleeping and waking in adolescence. From very far back too, and with the same sensual magic, there reached me another smell—a stale, sweetish smell, which I dimly associated with breadcrumbs on a side-board in a room that has not yet been aired after the night. The smell of bacon and the smell of breadcrumbs have always been closed memories for me, leading nowhere, bringing nothing but themselves.

My only visual recollection which seemed to possess the same arche-
typal quality—but it may have had its source in a dream or a picture
book—is the recurring image of a white china cup in a green wood: the
leaves and grass are a sullen, emerald green; the whiteness of the cup,
standing alone on the grass, is dazzling: the whole picture, clear yet
elusive, is bathed in a brooding, sub-aqueous light.

B   The June grass, amongst which I stood, was taller than I was, and I
wept. I have never been so close to grass before. It towered above me and
all around me, each blade tattooed with tiger-skins of sunlight. It was
knife-edged, dark and a wicked green, thick as a forest and alive with
grasshoppers that chirped and chattered and leapt through the air like
monkeys.

I was lost and didn't know where to move. A tropic heat oozed up from
the ground, rank with sharp odours of roots and nettles. Snow-clouds of
elder-blossom banked in the sky, showering upon me the fumes and flakes
of their sweet and giddy suffocation. High overhead ran frenzied larks,
screaming as though the sky were tearing apart.

For the first time in my life I was out of the sight of humans. For the
first time in my life I was alone in a world whose behaviour I could neither
predict nor fathom: a world of birds that squealed, of plants that stank,
of insects that sprang about without warning. I was lost and I did not
expect to be found again. I put back my head and howled, and the sun
hit me smartly in the face, like a bully.

C   Here too, was the scrubbing of floors and boots, of arms and necks,
of red and white vegetables. Walk in to the morning disorder of this room
and all the garden was laid out dripping on the table. Chopped carrots
like copper pennies, radishes and chives, potatoes dipped and stripped
clean from their coats of mud, the snapping of tight pea pods, long shells
of green pearls, and the tearing of glutinous beans from their nests of wool.

Grown stealthy, marauding among these preparations, one nibbled
one's way like a rat through roots and leaves. Peas rolled under the tongue,
fresh cold, like solid water; teeth chewed green peel of apples, acid sharp,
and the sweet white starch of swedes. Beaten away by wet hands gloved
with flour, one returned in a morose and speechless lust. Slivers of raw
pastry, moulded, warm, went down in the shapes of men and women—
heads and arms of unsalted flesh seasoned with nothing but a dream of
cannibalism.

Large meals were prepared in this room, cauldrons of stew for the
insatiate hunger of eight.

D   Here is a long passage—what an enormous perspective I make of it!
—leading from Peggotty's kitchen to the front-door. A dark store-room

opens out of it, and that is a place to be run past at night; for I don't know what may be among those tubs and jars and old tea-chests, when there is nobody in there with a dimly-burning light, letting a mouldy air come out at the door, in which there is the smell of soap, pickles, pepper, candles, and coffee, all at one whiff. Then there are the two parlours; the parlour in which we sit of an evening, my mother and I and Peggotty—for Peggotty is quite our companion, when her work is done and we are alone—and the best parlour where we sit on a Sunday; grandly, but not so comfortably. There is something of a doleful air about that room to me, for Peggotty has told me—I don't know when, but apparently ages ago—about my father's funeral, and the company having their black cloaks put on. One Sunday night my mother reads to Peggotty and me in there, how Lazarus was raised up from the dead. And I am so frightened that they are afterwards obliged to take me out of bed, and show me the quiet churchyard out of the bedroom window, with the dead all lying in their graves at rest, below the solemn moon.

> Passages A, B and C are all taken from autobiographies. Do they seem to have any characteristics in common? You can, if you wish, use passage D, which is taken from a novel, in your discussion.

45

A   A soldier attached to our staff as cobbler said to Sister B.: 'I am now forty-six years old, and yet I am taken for military service, although I have paid my exemption-tax regularly every year. I have never done anything against the government, and now they are taking from me my whole family, my seventy-year-old mother, my wife and five children, and I do not know where they are going.' He was especially affected by the thought of his little daughter, a year and half old; 'She is so sweet. She has such pretty eyes'; he wept like a child. The next day he came back; 'I know the truth. They are all dead.' And it was only too true...

B   A shifting carpet woven with the threads of blood-stained destinies. It is always the same. After the first few days on the roads all the young men and the men in the prime of life get separated off from the rest of the convoy. Here, for instance, a man of forty-six, in good clothes, an engineer. It needs many cudgel blows to get him away from his wife and children. His youngest is about one and a half. This man is to be enrolled in a labour battalion, for road-making. He stumbles in the long line of men and shuffles, gibbering like a half-wit: 'I never missed paying my bedel... paying my bedel.' Suddenly he grips hold of his neighbour. 'You've never seen such a lovely baby.' ...A torrent of sentimental agony. 'Why, the girl had eyes as big as plates. If only I could, I'd crawl after them on my belly like a snake.' And he shuffles on, enveloped in his grief, completely isolated. That evening they lie down to rest on a hillside. Long after midnight he shakes the same neighbour out of his sleep. 'They're all dead now.' He is perfectly calm.

> Passage A is taken from an official document relating to the mass deportation and extermination of the Armenian minority in Turkey during the First World War. The document is a 'Statement by two Red Cross Nurses of Danish Nationality'. Passage B is taken from a novel which is based on this and similar documents. Consider the differences in tone, attitude and quality between the two pieces of writing.

46

A   The qualifications of a good critic and a good historian are...very different. The intuitions of the critic emerge from a temperament worlds away from the sober evidence-weighing of the historian. Taste, literary skill, a certain self-confidence, and finally an imperious urge to impose order upon the chaos of contemporary opinion—these are perhaps the *desiderata* of criticism. Literary history, on the other hand, demands the more prosaic virtues only of curiosity, learning, patience and accuracy.

B   ...it is fairly certain that 'interpretation' is only legitimate when it is not interpretation at all, but merely putting the reader in possession of facts which he would otherwise have missed...Any book, any essay, any note in *Notes and Queries*, which produces a fact even of the lowest order about a work of art is a better piece of work than nine-tenths of the most pretentious critical journalism, in journals or in books...*Fact* cannot corrupt taste; it can at worst gratify one taste—a taste for history, let us say, or antiquities or biography—under the illusion that it is assisting another. The real corrupters are those who supply opinion or fancy; and Goethe and Coleridge are not guiltless—for what is Coleridge's *Hamlet*: is it an honest enquiry as far as the data permit, or is it an attempt to present Coleridge in an attractive costume?

> Consider these statements about criticism, indicating your own views on the subjects discussed.

Index of Authors, Titles and Sources

In some cases spelling and punctuation have been modernised.

The Shakespeare passages are drawn from the Arden and New Shakespeare (Cambridge) editions. The Webster passage is drawn from *Six Plays by Contemporaries of Shakespeare*, ed. C. B. Wheeler (World's Classics). London: Oxford University Press, 1962.

POETRY

1 A Keats, 'Ode To Autumn', *The Poems and Verses of John Keats*, ed. Middleton Murry, p. 408. London: Eyre and Spottiswoode, 1949.

  B Hood, 'Ode: Autumn', *Oxford Book of Nineteenth-Century Verse*, ed. J. Hayward, pp. 420–2. London: Oxford University Press, 1964.

2 A Shakespeare, *The Merchant of Venice*, act IV, sc. i.

  B Shakespeare, *Measure for Measure*, act II, sc. ii.

3 A Shakespeare, *Richard III*, act V, sc. iii.

  B Shakespeare, *Macbeth*, act I, sc. vii.

  C Webster, *The Duchess of Malfi*, act IV, sc. ii.

4 A Jonson, 'On My First Daughter', *Works*, vol. VIII, ed. Herford and Simpson, pp. 33–4. London: Oxford University Press, 1947.

  B Jonson, 'On My First Son', *ibid.*, p. 41.

5 A Blake, 'London' [draft version], *Complete Poetry and Prose*, ed. G. Keynes, pp. 92–3. London: The Nonesuch Press, 1961.

  B Blake, 'London', *ibid.*, p. 75.

6 Blake, 'The Human Abstract', *ibid.*, pp. 75–6.

7 A Jonson, 'Song' (from *The Silent Woman*), *Oxford Book of Seventeenth-Century Verse*, ed. Grierson and Bullough, p. 107. London: Oxford University Press, 1934.

  B Herrick, 'Delight in Disorder', *Poems*, p. 29. London: Oxford University Press, 1933.

8 A E. B. Browning, 'Irreparableness', *Poems*, p. 89. London: Routledge and Sons, 1889.

  B G. Herbert, 'Life', *Works*, ed. F. E. Hutchinson, p. 94. London: Oxford University Press, 1941.

9 A G. Herbert, 'Nature', *Works*, p. 45.

  B G. Herbert, 'The Collar', *Works*, pp. 153–4.

10 A Wyatt; B, Heywood; C, Cowley; D, G. Granville, Lord Lansdowne; E, Marvell, quoted in H. A. Mason, *Humanism and Poetry in the Early Tudor Period*, chapter V. London: Routledge and Kegan Paul, 1959.

11 1A *Titus Andronicus*, act II, sc. iii.
  B *Macbeth*, act III, sc. ii.
  2 *Henry IV Part Two*, act III, sc. i.
  3 *Coriolanus*, act II, sc. ii.
  4A *Romeo and Juliet*, act II, sc. ii.
  B *The Winter's Tale*, act IV, sc. iv.
  5 *Hamlet*, act I, sc. v.

12 A Hardy, 'The Shadow on the Stone', *Collected Poems*, p. 498. London: Macmillan, 1952.
  B Hardy, 'The Voice', *ibid.*, pp. 325–6.

13 A Frost, 'The Road Not Taken', *Oxford Book of American Verse*, ed. F. O. Matthiessen, p. 556. New York: Oxford University Press, 1951.
  B E. Thomas, 'The Sign-Post', *Collected Poems*, p. 22. London: Faber and Faber, 1936.

14 A Donne, 'Thou Hast Made Me', *Complete Poetry and Selected Prose*, ed. J. Hayward, pp. 279–80. London: Nonesuch Press, 1929.
  B Jonson, 'To Heaven', *Works*, vol. VIII, p. 122.

15 Keats, 'Sonnet', *The Poems and Verses of John Keats*, p. 455.

16 A Byron, 'On Finding A Fan', *Poetical Works* (Oxford Standard Authors), p. 50. London: Oxford University Press, 1945.
  B Byron, 'So We'll Go No More A-Roving', *ibid.*, p. 101.

17 A Jonson, 'To Sir Robert Wroth', *Works*, vol. VIII, pp. 99–100.
  B Johnson, 'The Vanity of Human Wishes', *Poetry and Prose*, ed. Mona Wilson, p. 170. London: Rupert Hart-Davies, 1950.

18 A Ted Hughes, 'Tutorial', *New Statesman*, vol. LXIV, no. 1651, 2 Nov. 1962, p. 628.
  B Yeats, 'The Scholars', *Collected Poems*, p. 158. London: Macmillan 1955.

19 A Shirley, 'Victorious Men of Earth', *Oxford Book of Seventeenth-Century Verse*, pp. 411–12.
  B Shirley, 'The Glories of Our Blood and State', *ibid.*, pp. 412–13.

20 A Sidney, 'Sonnet III' from *Astrophel and Stella*, *Silver Poets of the Sixteenth Century*, ed. G. Bullett, pp. 173–4. London: J. M. Dent and Sons, 1947.
  B G. Herbert, 'Jordan I', *Works*, pp. 56–7.

21 A Anon., 'The Three Ravens', *Oxford Book of Ballads*, ed. A. Quiller-Couch, p. 294. London: Oxford University Press, 1910.
  B Anon., 'The Twa Corbies', *ibid.*, p. 293.

22 A Quarles, 'To The World' (on Proverbs xxiii, 5), *Oxford Book of Seventeenth-Century Verse*, pp. 344–6.
  B Jonson, 'To The World: A Farewell for a Gentlewoman, vertuous and noble', *Works*, vol. VIII, pp. 100–2.

23 A D. H. Lawrence, 'Shadows', *Stories, Essays and Poems*, sel.
D. Hawkins, pp. 354–5. London: J. M. Dent and Sons, 1939.

   B Dowson, 'Breton Afternoon', *Oxford Book of Nineteenth-Century
Verse*, p. 945.

24 A Marvell, 'The Definition of Love', *Oxford Book of Seventeenth-
Century Verse*, pp. 747–8.

   B Donne, 'A Valediction: forbidding mourning', *ibid.*, pp. 104–5.

25 Tony Connor, 'Elegy for Alfred Hubbard', *With Love Somehow*,
pp. 10–11. London: Oxford University Press, 1962.

26 A John Crowe Ransom, 'Piazza Piece', *Oxford Book of American
Verse*, p. 847.

   B Emily Dickinson, 'Because I Could Not Stop For Death', *ibid.*,
pp. 439–40.

27 A Churchill, 'The Rosciad', *The Poetical Works of Charles Churchill*,
ed. D. Grant, pp. 6–8. London: Oxford University Press, 1956.

   B Pope, 'The Dunciad', Book IV, *Collected Poems*, pp. 167–70.
London: J. M. Dent and Sons, 1924.

28 A Pound, 'Mr Nixon', *Selected Poems*, ed. with an intro. by T. S.
Eliot, pp. 178–9. London: Faber and Faber, 1959.

   B T. S. Eliot, 'Mr Apollinax', *Collected Poems 1909–1935*, p. 31.
London: Faber and Faber, 1936.

29 Kipling, 'Epitaphs of the War', *A Choice of Kipling's Verse* made
by T. S. Eliot, with an essay on R. K., pp. 161–5. London: Faber
and Faber, 1946.

PROSE

30 A Scott, *The Heart of Midlothian*, pp. 506–7. London: A. and C.
Black, 1893.

   B Conrad, *Typhoon* in *The Shadow-Line and Two Other Tales*, ed.
with an intro. by M. D. Zabel, pp. 73–4. New York: Doubleday
Anchor Books, 1959.

31 George Eliot, *Daniel Deronda*, pp. 178–80. New York: Harper
Torchbooks, 1961.

32 A Thackeray, *Vanity Fair*, pp. 536–8. London: J. M. Dent and Sons,
1908.

   B D. H. Lawrence, 'The White Stocking', *The Complete Short
Stories*, vol. I, pp. 262–6. London: Heinemann, 1955.

33 A N. Foerster, *American Criticism: a study in literary theory from
Poe to the present*, p. 244. Boston and New York: Houghton
Mifflin Co., 1928.

   B E. M. Forster, 'What I Believe', *Two Cheers For Democracy*, p. 77.
London: Edwin Arnold 1951.

34 A Franklin, Aphorisms, quoted in D. H. Lawrence, *Studies in Classic*

American Literature, pp. 21–2. New York: Doubleday Anchor Books, 1953.

B D. H. Lawrence, 'Benjamin Franklin', *ibid.*, pp. 26–8.

35 A Lord David Cecil, Preface to *Humanities*, by Desmond MacCarthy, pp. xi–xii. London: MacGibbon and Kee, 1953.

B Leavis, *Revaluation*, pp. 8–9. London: Chatto and Windus, 1962.

36 A Pope, Preface to *The Iliad*, *Prose Works*, vol. I, ed. N. Ault, pp. 230–1. London: Methuen, 1936.

B Addison, *The Spectator*, no. 160, vol. I, pp. 482–3. London: J. M. Dent and Sons, 1954.

37 Henry James, *The Awkward Age*, pp. 12–13. New York: Doubleday Anchor Books, 1958.

38 A Conrad, *Youth*, in *Youth, Heart of Darkness, End of the Tether*, pp. 34, 36–8, London: J. M. Dent and Sons, 1961.

B Conrad, *The Shadow-Line*, in *The Shadow-Line and Two Other Tales*, pp. 205–6.

39 A C. P. Snow, 'The Two Cultures', *Encounter*, no. 69 (June 1959), p. 18, and no. 70 (July 1959), pp. 25–6.

B Orwell, *The Road To Wigan Pier*, pp. 202–4. London: Secker and Warburg, 1965.

40 B. Russell, *A History of Western Philosophy*, pp. 10–11. London: G. Allen and Unwin, 1946.

41 A Johnson, 'Life of Collins', *Lives of the English Poets*, vol. II, pp. 314–15. London: J. M. Dent and Sons, 1961.

B Macaulay, 'Warren Hastings', *The Complete Works*, vol. IX, pp. 527–9. London: Longmans, Green, 1898.

C Lytton Strachey, *Queen Victoria*, pp. 192–3. London: Chatto and Windus, 1946.

42 A Dickens, *Bleak House*, pp. 33–34, 37. London: J. M. Dent and Sons, 1954.

B Henry James, *The Bostonians*, Chiltern Library, pp. 38–9. London: John Lehmann, 1952.

43 A Middleton Murry, 'The Poetry of Walter de la Mare', *John Clare and Other Studies*, pp. 98–9. London and New York: Peter Neville, 1950.

B Santayana, 'The Belief in a Future Life', *The Life of Reason*, 1-vol. edition, pp. 280–2. New York: C. Scribner's Sons, 1955.

44 A B C, from contemporary autobiographies quoted by R. Hoggart in 'A Question of Tone', *The Critical Quarterly*, vol. V, no. 1 (Spring, 1963); A, p. 74; B, pp. 75–6; C, p. 84.

D Dickens, *David Copperfield*, p. 30. London: Collins, 1952.

45 A from 'A Statement by two Red Cross Nurses of Danish Nationality' in *The Treatment of Armenians in the Ottoman Empire*, ed. Arnold

Toynbee, quoted by D. J. Enright in *The Apothecary's Shop*, pp. 149– 50. London: Secker and Warburg, 1957.

B Franz Werfel, *The Forty Days of Musa Dagh*, trans. G. Dunlop, pp. 155–6. New York: The Modern Library, 1934 (also quoted by Enright, *op. cit.*).

46 A F. W. Bateson, *Scrutiny*, vol. IV, no. 2 (Sept. 1935), p. 183.

B T. S. Eliot, 'The Function of Criticism', *Selected Essays*, p. 33. London: Faber and Faber, 1932.